D0387557

PRIVATE
INVESTIGATIONS

PRIVATE
INVESTIGATIONS

—

Mystery Writers on the Secrets,
Riddles, and Wonders of Their Lives

EDITED BY
VICTORIA ZACKHEIM

SEAL
NEW YORK

Copyright © 2020 by Victoria Zackheim
Cover design by Ann Kirchner
Cover images © Michael Squier / EyeEm / Getty Images; © Magnia / Shutterstock.com
Cover copyright © 2020 Hachette Book Group, Inc.

Seal Press
Hachette Book Group
1290 Avenue of the Americas, New York, NY 10104
sealpress.com @sealpress

Printed in the United States of America
First Edition: April 2020

Published by Seal Press, an imprint of Perseus Books, LLC, a subsidiary of Hachette Book Group, Inc. The Seal Press name and logo is a trademark of the Hachette Book Group.

The Hachette Speakers Bureau provides a wide range of authors for speaking events. To find out more, go to www.hachettespeakersbureau.com or call (866) 376-6591.

The publisher is not responsible for websites (or their content) that are not owned by the publisher.

Print book interior design by Linda Mark

Library of Congress Cataloging-in-Publication Data
Names: Zackheim, Victoria, editor.
Title: Private investigations : mystery writers on the secrets, riddles, and wonders in their lives / edited by Victoria Zackheim.
Description: First edition. | New York : Seal Press, 2020. | Summary: "In Private Investigations, twenty fan-favorite mystery writers share their first-person stories of grappling with mysteries they've personally encountered, at home and in the world. Caroline Leavitt regales us with a medical mystery, a time when she lost her voice and doctors couldn't find a cure; Martin Limon travels back to his military stint in Korea to grapple with the chaos of war; Anne Perry ponders the magical powers of stories conjured from writers' imaginations, and more"—Provided by publisher.
Identifiers: LCCN 2019032305 | ISBN 9781580059213 (hardcover) | ISBN 9781580059220 (ebook)
Subjects: LCSH: Novelists, American—20th century—Biography. | Novelists, English—20th century—Biography. | Detective and mystery stories, American—Authorship. | Detective and mystery stories, English—Authorship.
Classification: LCC PS379 .P75 2020 | DDC 813/.087208—dc23
LC record available at https://lccn.loc.gov/2019032305

ISBNs: 978-1-58005-921-3 (hardcover); 978-1-58005-922-0 (ebook)

LSC-C

10 9 8 7 6 5 4 3 2 1

CONTENTS

VICTORIA ZACKHEIM INTRODUCTION:
SOLVING THE MYSTERY 1

HALLIE EPHRON GHOSTED 7

JEFFERY DEAVER PLOT TWISTS: THIS WRITER'S LIFE 21

SULARI GENTILL AN EXTRA CHILD 33

CARA BLACK FIELD NOTES À LA MAIGRET
FROM PARIS 45

CONNIE MAY FOWLER LYDIA AND JACK 57

MARTIN LIMÓN THE LAND OF THE MORNING
CALM (AND OTHER
MILITARY MYSTERIES) 81

WILLIAM KENT KRUEGER THE CLAY THAT WE SHAPE 95

AUSMA ZEHANAT KHAN ORIGINS AND DESTINATIONS 105

Contents

KRISTEN LEPIONKA   A TRICK OF THE LIGHT   119

LYNN CAHOON   THE MYSTERY OF DECEPTION   131

RHYS BOWEN   THE LONG SHADOW OF WAR   143

RACHEL HOWZELL HALL   I DON'T KNOW THIS WORD   155

STEPH CHA   THE BEAMS KEEP FALLING   175

JACQUELINE WINSPEAR   WRITING ABOUT WAR   187

TASHA ALEXANDER   CAN WE LIVE WITHOUT MYSTERY?   207

CAROLE NELSON DOUGLAS   GODFATHERS, NANCY DREW, AND CATS   221

CAROLINE LEAVITT   THE MYSTERY OF MY LOST VOICE   243

CHARLES TODD   REMEMBERING THE PAST   259

ROBERT DUGONI   NUNS, MAGIC, AND STEVEN KING   273

ANNE PERRY   I WANT TO BE A MAGICIAN   287

Loving thanks to CeCe Sloan
for your unceasing encouragement

INTRODUCTION

Solving the Mystery

– Victoria Zackheim –

WHEN IT WAS SUGGESTED THAT I CONSIDER A COLLECTION of essays written by mystery writers revealing the mysteries of their lives, I couldn't help but think of my own. Were the life-changing mysteries that had shaped my life shared by the twenty gifted writers in this collection? I quickly discovered that all of us view *mystery* in very different and personal ways.

The mysteries we discover in the course of everyday living are real, imagined, dreamed, even hoped for, feared, and anticipated. A mystery can present itself as an enigma, a solution, a challenge, a surprise. A thing of despair—or something magical. Falling in love—or out of love. Gaining stature and reputation or losing respect. Being innocent—and then not. Marriage and divorce, illness and death, the rise and fall of friendships. The expected and the serendipitous. Situations that hurt us and thrill us.

In these stories, you are invited into the private lives of gifted writers, most of them on New York Times and international bestseller lists. You may be a fan, or you may be reading their work for the first time. Their stories, all true, cover the breadth of life experiences, from introspective to mystical, from laugh-out-loud funny to noir. Mysteries, when presented from our very personal perspectives—and all of these certainly are—come in all forms.

So what are the secrets, riddles, and wonders of our lives? Do we focus on our joy or grief, highs or lows, something meticulously defined or so amorphous as to seem impossible to fathom? Whatever form these mysteries take, all of us have had our lives shaped by them. They affect who we are and how we live, love, think . . . behave. We can celebrate those riddles, wonders, and secrets, or we can fear them. Perhaps it's because everything we touch, everything that touches us, has the potential to be a mystery. I felt this when I held my children for the first time. And when I accompanied my daughter to a medical examination and heard the twin heartbeats of my first grandchildren, causing my knees to buckle so that I had to grip the bed rail to stop myself from falling. And when I look into the faces of my son's children and imagine their futures, their dreams.

There are so many mysteries around us. I remember with unusual clarity that moment in 1977 when I saw my father only minutes after his death. He was ten years younger than I am today. Gone too soon, yet his body seemed so peaceful, finally pain-free. I muttered, "This is not my father," which caused a bit of alarm for my mother and the nurse. I tried to explain that I was looking at the shell that had housed his beautiful spirit but that his curiosity about the world around him and his quick sense of humor felt very much alive. This was my first close experience with death, and it left me confused, mystified. If a mystery is an enigma that we must unravel, then I was confronting a mystery.

That same sense returned while I was sitting at my mother's bedside. When she took her last breath, I knew that she was finally at peace. Nearly ninety, she had become increasingly angry that her last years were so difficult. An artist who could no longer paint, a political activist whose voice had been stilled, she felt locked within the walls of her home. Again, I struggled with the *Why?* of it. My complicated, brilliant mother. Who she was will aways remain a mystery in my life.

Mysteries are found in the stories of our lives, some of them challenging believability. Hallie Ephron visits a spiritualist in the hope of understanding her friend's claims to have spoken with her murdered brother, while Sulari Gentill discovers an uncle whose existence was kept a secret . . . until she stumbles upon a family photograph.

We are confronted with mysteries when health is in question. I don't exercise nearly enough, and one of my mysteries is how and why I remain upright and relatively healthy! Rachel Howzell Hall was living her life balancing writing, family, and career until a new word joined her lexicon: cancer. Caroline Leavitt lost her voice, found no answers from medical specialists, and set out to solve this mystery on her own.

INTRODUCTION

Many authors pull from their very personal experiences when mapping out the plots of their novels. Connie May Fowler recalls her abuse at the hands of her mother, the social pressures she felt as a childless woman, and a recent illness that was frightening yet reminded her of the kindness of strangers. William Kent Krueger shares how his childhood was defined by the mysteries of his mother's mental illness—the same woman who became the protagonist of one of his novels.

Life teaches us such varied lessons, some of which are cloaked in mystery, such as our quest for truth and how we respond to love and loss. As different as the stories in this collection are, you will discover similarities of the human spirit. For example, similar themes draw us into the varied and always difficult elements of war: survival, challenge, hardship, discovery. How are we affected by war? Do we honor those who fought to defend our rights? Our liberties? Martin Limón reveals the challenges of a young American soldier dropped into the foreign and sometimes mysterious culture of Korea.

There are mysteries that we discover as we write or as we adjust to a new place in the world. Ausma Zehanat Khan, an international human rights attorney, explores the mystery of her own origins, while Cara Black's Paris is so much a part of her being that Inspector Maigret seems to be evident everywhere she goes.

As you read these stories—I resist calling them essays, although that is what they are, because that label suggests something impersonal, perhaps even cold, whereas these narratives are rich with warmth and intimacy, sharing and trust—you will hear each author's voice, share each story, and in many ways feel as if that author is seated beside you and speaking directly to you.

What are your personal mysteries? What have you seen, survived, and experienced that has made you who you are today? When you read the stories, you might find yourself nodding, smiling, perhaps discovering tears in your eyes, certainly identifying with so much that the twenty authors share with you. It is my hope that you find elements of yourself and your life in some of these stories and that what you find, what you discover, leads you to a greater understanding of who you are and how important you are—an essential thread in this mysterious tapestry we call life.

GHOSTED

-- Hallie Ephron --

IT WAS DUSK TWENTY YEARS AGO, AND I WAS DRIVING THE I-93 North through Boston and beyond, looking for the exit marked MYSTIC AVENUE. This seemed prophetic since I was on my way to a meeting of spiritualists. No, I'm not into parapsychology or the occult, and up to that point in my life I'd been secure in the belief that there is no afterlife. You live, you die; end of story. If something in my house goes bump in the night, I set mousetraps. But my struggle to understand what was happening to my friend Laura (not her real name) had drawn me to Medford to mingle with a group who claimed to be able to talk to ghosts.

If it had been anyone but Laura, I'd have written her off as a nutcase. A single mom and successful real estate agent, she was smart, grounded, endowed with a wonderfully wry sense of humor and a healthy distrust of artifice and flimflam. We'd been friends since high school, and I'd never known her to be the slightest bit unhinged. At least not until her brother Josh was murdered.

Laura and Josh had been business partners. They worked together so closely that Laura often felt as if she could communicate telepathically with him across the glass partition that separated their desks. The client who shot Josh arrived at their office first thing that morning, gunning for Laura. He was convinced that she'd cheated him. But Laura got to work late, and by the time she arrived the building was surrounded by police cruisers, its entrance was blocked by crime-scene tape, and an ambulance with its rear doors flung open was backed up to the front door.

Laura was wracked with grief and guilt. Josh had been her best friend as well as her younger brother. The killer had been her client, not Josh's. She tortured herself with what might have happened if she'd gotten to work on time. Maybe she could have placated the killer. Talked him down. At the very least, she would have been the victim, and Josh would still be alive.

Josh's killer escaped, and in the weeks after the murder, Laura grew more and more terrified to leave her house. She felt safe in her car, a big old Cadillac she'd inherited from her mother. It had power windows, power door locks, and a car phone. But simple acts like walking out her front door to pick up the newspaper or crossing a parking lot from her car to a supermarket entrance triggered panic attacks. Even at home, where at least she felt safe, she was in constant, unbearable pain. "Like when you hurt yourself," she told me, "and the hurt is so bad that you have to cry. It's as if [the killer] blew a hole in my body, too, a gaping wound that everything I see, everything I do, causes it to ache. Only sleep numbs the pain."

Laura became a virtual recluse, barely able to get to her appointments with her therapist, who diagnosed post-traumatic stress disorder and prescribed medication for anxiety and depression.

My understanding of what happened next comes from long conversations that Laura and I shared over the months that followed. She'd talk. I'd listen and record her words, transcribing them later and sending her a copy with the idea that her experiences might become the basis for a book we'd write together about what it's like to lose a loved one to homicide.

Here's how Laura described Josh's first visit:

Early one morning, I'm lying in bed, fully awake. I'm looking out the window when something makes me look up at the ceiling. Josh is here, floating right above me. I feel as if my body isn't mine. For a while I just stare up at him, cemented in place, the whole of my being focused on his presence an arm's length away.

I can't communicate with him at first. He isn't talking to me. He's just here. I want so badly to communicate with him, but it's hard. In my mind I keep saying, "Tell me how to do this." No response. I beg for a sign that he can hear me. For what seems like a very long time I lie immobilized, looking at him. Finally I hear "Laura, you always knew what was on my mind. Just do it!" And all of a sudden the floodgates open. I can hear him, and I can talk to him.

What he says is very simple. He says that I can trust Uncle Albert. He also tells me that my Aunt Irene is with him. Aunt Irene has been dead for about five years. All I can do is nod to let him know I hear and understand. It feels as if he's draining me, drawing off my will and strength.

Then, before I know it, he's gone. It's a cool morning, and I'm under the blankets, sweating. All the energy has been sucked out of me to make room for accepting Josh. When I get out of bed my legs are trembling. The physical sensation lasts most of the morning.

I know this sounds like a scene out of a movie or TV show—*Truly Madly Deeply, Sleepless in Seattle, Ghost, Sherlock*, or *The Kominsky Method*, to name a few. But to Laura, this was real. Josh visited her many more times. Often when she was in her bedroom. Sometimes in her car. Once while she was walking on a beach. The "visitations," as she called them, were tiring but never as intense and draining as the first time. Soon she was looking forward to them. Only her therapist knew.

A turning point came on a Sunday morning about six months after the murder.

I am reading the Sunday *New York Times* in my living room. All of a sudden Josh is here with me. Aunt Irene is with him. I try to stand, a skeptic, outside of myself. Wondering. Doubting. Are they really here? Or is this my imagination?

Laura talked to them for a long time. At one point Josh suggested that she write down the things he was telling her. She was afraid to leave the room, afraid that they'd vanish while she was off fetching something to write on. But she went to her office, and when she came back with a yellow legal pad, Aunt Irene and Josh were still there.

A short time later, as Laura was writing what Josh was telling her, she realized that her fifteen-year-old son, Brian, was standing in the doorway. She had no idea how long he'd been there and what he'd heard. He asked her what was going on.

I ask him if he sees anything in the living room out of the ordinary. He looks around and obviously sees nothing. I decide to tell him. I say that Uncle Josh is sitting in the red chair. Aunt Irene is in the rocker. He stares at me for a moment, then sits down next to me on the couch. He stays there for another fifteen or twenty minutes. I'm interpreting Josh and Aunt Irene to Brian because Brian can't see or hear them.

By the time Josh and Aunt Irene left, floating out the living room window, Laura had been with them for nearly an hour. It was only then that Laura registered the fear and confusion in Brian's eyes. He'd lost his favorite uncle, the man who had filled the hole left in his life after Laura split up with his father, and now it must have seemed as if his mother were losing her mind.

Listening to Laura, I was shaken, too. Nothing in my own experience prepared me to make sense of hers. She was talking to a ghost yet describing the conversations so matter-of-factly that she might have been talking about conversations with the mailman.

There are no ghosts, I reminded myself. These had to be waking dreams, hallucinations cooked up by grief, abetted, perhaps, by lack of sleep and the medications she was taking. But she was so convinced and so convincing that, for the first time in my life, I was open, if just barely, to the possibility that Josh's restless soul really was reaching out to her.

I hoped that the spiritualists' meeting would give me insights, if not answers.

Spiritualism goes back to the mid-1800s, and one of its adherents was Sir Arthur Conan Doyle, the creator of rationalist detective Sherlock Holmes. Doyle's friend, the great magician Harry Houdini, spent decades debunking psychics and mediums. Those who practice spiritualism today believe that some people can act as channels through which spirits can communicate with the living. The term spiritualism conjures images of musty Victorian houses with darkened rooms, windows shrouded with heavy drapes, candles flickering, people gathered around a table and holding hands as they summon the spirits of the dead. Cue spooky music.

The setting for this spiritualist meeting was a fifth-floor apartment in an undistinguished modern brick building. I parked, rode up in the elevator, and was greeted at the door with a warm hug by the host, Reverend Ida. She was an older woman, generously proportioned, wearing a flowing coppery caftan with amber beads and earrings that seemed to glow. We'd talked on the phone earlier, so I knew that I'd have to wait until the second half of the meeting to learn about mediumship. First there'd be a psychic healing.

Reverend Ida ushered me into the living room, where about a dozen others were already waiting. Folding chairs were set up in a circle around a mirrored coffee table topped with porcelain angels, votive candles, and lava lamps. The air was heavy with incense. I overheard one of the men saying, "Some people. They have rocks in their heads and don't see the truth of healing, the power of the mind." He punctuated the thought with a clenched fist. I made my way to the opposite end of the room, afraid that if he were at all prescient, he'd take one look at me and see how much uncertainty and doubt was knocking around inside me.

We all took our seats and introduced ourselves. The people seemed utterly ordinary. There was a librarian. A nurse. An insurance agent. A retired attorney. Most of them came to these monthly meetings regularly.

Reverend Ida lit the candles, turned on the lava lamps, and lowered the overhead lights. We held hands and sat in silence for a few minutes as she began to chant. The words were about love and the spirit, so simple and repetitive that soon I was able to join in. Then she asked us to form a "healing circle" around Jeanine, a slender, pale woman about my age who was wearing dark jogger pants, a zippered sweatshirt, and a rust-colored turban. She sat slumped in her chair, her eyes rimmed with dark circles, her long fingers with stubby painted nails knitted together in her lap. Jeanine asked us to please be gentle since she was "wired." She showed us a tube that snaked out from beneath her loose green sweatshirt and explained that this was how she was getting her regular doses of chemo.

Reverend Ida instructed each of us to close our eyes and concentrate on sending healing thoughts and energy to Jeanine. Feeling very self-conscious, I kept my eyes open a slit. Everyone else stood with their eyes closed, their hands hovering over Jeanine's head or touching her back or shoulders. I reached out and let my hand rest lightly on her arm, trying to smother my inner skeptic.

This went on for about ten minutes, but it seemed much longer. When it was over, spots of pink had appeared on Jeanine's cheeks, and she was in tears. She thanked us. There were murmurs all around of "God bless you."

Several people commented on the breeze they'd felt during the healing circle. It was more than a breeze, one woman remarked. More like little tornados and whirlwinds whipping around the room. Reverend Ida said those were spirits. Several spirits, in fact. Others said they'd felt a tingle of electricity in the air. It was so strong, one woman said, that she was nearly swept off her feet.

"If you don't feel a healing tonight," Reverend Ida said, "you're never going to feel one."

I nodded and smiled, but I'd felt no breeze and not the tiniest tingle of electricity. All I'd felt was sympathy for this poor cancer patient and pressure to say that I sensed something that I did not.

But psychic healing wasn't what I'd come for, so I was glad when Reverend Ida eased the group into a discussion of the "astral plane," an intermediate world between heaven and earth where disembodied souls hang out. She explained that the living can travel there in dreams, during deep meditation, or even while conscious. *Like Laura,* I thought. Tonight, Reverend Ida promised, she'd guide us there.

One woman wanted to know if people like Jeffrey Dahmer would be there, too. No, Reverend Ida assured her, because he was evil. Not even, the woman pressed, if Dahmer's motives were pure? What if he truly believed what he'd done had been done for a good reason? Not even then was the answer.

Reverend Ida turned off the lights and left only a single votive candle lit. The flame and its reflection in the coffee table's mirrored top cast an eerie circle of light on the ceiling. "If you open yourself up to it and create a circle of light," Reverend Ida said, "the spirits will step into it."

The woman who was worried about Jeffrey Dahmer had another question. What if she opened herself up to the spirits, and someone she didn't much like when they were alive visited her? A perfectly reasonable question, in my opinion. Reverend Ida dismissed the concern. Another woman said she talked to her dead grandfather all the time in her dreams, and he was a whole lot nicer than he'd been when he was alive.

Dreaming that you talk to your dead grandfather was one thing. I looked around the circle and wondered if any of these people had experienced anything even close to what was happening to Laura.

The room fell silent as Reverend Ida turned the music back on and led us through a guided meditation. It began, "Close your eyes and envision in your hands a flower. Any flower. Feel it. Look into it. Then look up and see a beautiful field. A brook.

Deer and antelope frolicking on the other side. Go stand in the brook. Feel all of your cares and anxieties washed away. A beautiful monk comes toward you with a basket of flowers."

This went on. And on. It was warm in the room, and soon a man across the circle from me was softly snoring. A few minutes later Reverend Ida told us there was ectoplasm and electricity in the air. She said we should open ourselves up. Not be afraid. "We are safe within the circle of light." Then she summoned spirits to step into the light and announced, "The meeting is yours."

After a long silence, people on all sides started to talk. They brought images to one another. A silver teapot. A hairbrush. A single pearl. A man with a pick. Sometimes there was a name with the image, sometimes only an initial. There were messages, too, like "P says, do what you have to do." Or "J wants you to follow your heart." One woman brought the woman sitting next to her muffins with needles sticking out of them. No message, but she wondered, had someone close to her died who was into cooking and sewing?

Reverend Ida cautioned that the symbols were not to be taken literally. The person receiving the message would give it meaning. And, she said, she'd received a message for me.

The circle fell silent as she asked me if I knew a man who'd been crushed to death. Perhaps someone who'd fallen to his death? Because she saw concrete, slabs of concrete. "He's here, telling me . . . the message is . . ." She strained, listening, then lowered her voice. "I'm feeling pressure from two sides, but I will be able to reconcile them and stand up straight between them, on my own."

Everyone looked at me expectantly. I knew no one who'd been crushed to death, not literally. But people who'd been conflicted? Pressured in opposite directions? You could say that about Laura's brother Josh, needing to reach out to Laura but realizing it wasn't healthy for her to keep taking him in. It could have described me at that moment, feeling as if I should see meaning where I found none. In fact, that description—pressured from two sides—could be forced to fit just about anyone at any time, dead or alive.

Then Reverend Ida brought me a name. *Victoria*. It meant nothing to me, amazingly, since mine is a generation of Vickys and Susans and Nancys. Almost as an afterthought, she added, "And there's a message from Mom or Mommy. She says hello." A murmur of approval swept through the circle.

I almost laughed because it seemed so unlikely. My mother, a Hollywood screenwriter and a confirmed atheist, would have been appalled to have found herself waiting around for years on the astral plane to deliver a line as prosaic as *Hello*.

Finally, I was the only one in the group who hadn't brought a symbol or message into the circle. I apologized, saying I was new at this. But I thanked everyone and assured them that I felt light, luminous light. And gratitude for being able to bear witness. I was relieved when that seemed to be enough.

As the meeting broke up, I realized how ebullient they all were, their own spirits genuinely uplifted by the evening's experiences. Reverend Ida urged me to come back. I thanked her and said I would, though I knew I would not. She told me not to be discouraged, that I'd get the hang of it. And I suspected that was all too true, because how many meetings like this could anyone sit through and keep right on seeing and feeling nothing? I'd have soon found meaning in the messages and symbols people brought me. And maybe, in my dreams, I'd have been pleasantly surprised to discover that my mother had mellowed since she had died.

For these people, talking to dead relatives brought solace, and that was what Josh's messages brought Laura, too. At first. But after a few months, she realized that his visits weren't helping her get on with her life. Even worse, they were frightening her son. She couldn't let Josh keep coming whenever he felt like it. So she asked him to wait for her to call him, and that worked for a few more months until Laura stopped calling. Stopped needing to.

Laura never went back to work as a real estate agent, but a year after the murder she was able to move about in the world almost like a normal person, with only the occasional panic attack. It helped that by then Josh's killer had been apprehended. One of the last things she promised Josh was that she'd do everything in her power to see that his killer was convicted and went to prison for the rest of his life.

When Laura was getting ready to go to the courthouse to witness a pretrial motion, preparing to look her brother's killer in the eye for the first time since the murder, she excavated months' worth of shredded tissues that lined her purse—tissues that she'd stuffed there after the endless crying jags during sessions with her therapist. She sat through every pretrial motion, thirty-eight days of jury selection, the six-week trial, and nine days of jury deliberation. Her brother's killer was found guilty and sentenced to eighty-five years in prison with the possibility of parole after fifty years.

It's been twenty-five years since Josh's death. Laura and I never did write a book together. These days, she doesn't summon Josh, and he doesn't come unbidden. And even though my visit with the spiritualists was a bust, I'm reluctant to brush off Josh's visits as hallucinations or twilight sleep, the product of a vivid imagination fueled by wishful thinking. It's intoxicating to imagine that there was more to it than that.

I described Laura's experience to a clinical psychologist, and he used Freudian terms to explain her likely mental state. He said, "It has to do with what we call the self-reflective sense of self—the ability to step back and observe what you're doing and how you're doing it. When someone loses that distance, it speaks to a great likelihood of having this kind of vivid imagery. Their ego boundaries are a little permeable at the edges."

When I asked Laura what, in retrospect, she thought had really been going on, she spoke of entirely different kinds of fissures. "I was able to perceive Josh's spirit because I was so fragmented that his energy seeped into the cracks. As I healed, so did the cracks."

As for me, I still believe that when someone dies, it's game over. I also believe that whatever Laura's experience was, it was utterly authentic. I have no trouble holding those two ideas in my head at the same time. Grief is complicated, but it's not the end.

PLOT TWISTS

This Writer's Life

- Jeffery Deaver -

I WAS A NERD WHEN I WAS GROWING UP.

And a nerd when the word *meant* something. Not like nowadays, when being a nerd comes with a billion dollars in stock options and a Silicon Valley mansion, thanks to your inventing a social network platform or an algorithm for self-driving drones. I was a true nerd, a pure nerd: pudgy, clumsy, socially inept, ignored by the cheerleaders and pom-pom girls. I owned a slide rule (look it up on Google).

There was a reason that sports team captains in school picked me last for their teams. Even on the field, I would neglect the game and daydream, composing stories about knights and orcs and cowboys and poems that went something like this:

PLOT TWISTS

The score is tied; three boys on base.
I see the batter's happy face
As he grips the bat and looks my way.
All I can do is hope and pray
That he won't hit that ball to me.
But we all know how it goes;
He swings for me and breaks my nose.

But my status as nerd didn't really matter. I had something better than sports; I had the Glen Ellyn, Illinois, Public Library. That was where I escaped in the summers and after school, and it was there that I fell in love with books. Such miraculous little things . . . they could take you away from your daily cares, teach you about things you might otherwise never learn (Wikipedia and YouTube were not then even silicon gleams in an engineer's eye). Books also brought people together. Perhaps you were a new kid at school and didn't know a soul. Yet noticing that a fellow student across the schoolyard was holding a copy of Ray Bradbury's short stories or *The Lord of the Rings*, books that you, too, loved, you had an instant invitation to friendship.

I knew then that I wanted to make my living as a writer.

How to achieve that goal, though, was a mystery.

Among the various genres I tried my hand at was poetry. I loved the fusion of meaning and the sound of words. I didn't care much for confessional poetry and modeled my work after the likes of Robert Frost and Wallace Stevens and T. S. Eliot, who carefully crafted and structured their poems. After much work and many postage stamps, I was able to get some work published in literary journals and, in one case, a radical political publication (though why they wanted a poem about pining lovers I never did understand). Suddenly I was a published poet. I was also, I supposed, a professional poet, since I was paid for some of my work.

I was not, however, a profitable poet.

Many of the journals publishing poems, it turned out, had a grand scheme: yes, contributors made a few pennies per word, but if you wanted more than one copy of the magazine (to, say, impress cheerleaders and pom-pom girls—which doesn't work, by the way), you had to buy them, and they were quite expensive. One measures one's success as a poet the same way Internet startups are gauged: not by how much money they make but by how little they lose. In my best fiscal twelve months as a poet, I believe I lost only six dollars. A banner year!

Clearly, poetry was not going to allow me to lead a writer's life.

The mystery remained unsolved.

I decided to try combining my love of poetry with another passion: music. I would become a singer/songwriter, à la Bob Dylan or Richard Thompson. Just as I'd learned about the business of poetry, I learned several things about the profession of music. First was that the job description includes two requisite components: singer and songwriter. The writing came easily to me, and I churned out scores of lyrics. The singing . . . well, that was not my strong suit.

Second, and more troubling, was that I was too literary. This was brought home to me one night when I was performing as the opening act ahead of a popular folk/country singer. I was pleased to see him looking over the lead sheets of my songs—

pages of the lyrics and chord changes. He pointed to something on a sheet and asked, "What's that?"

I didn't understand and asked him what he meant.

He said, "That little thing there."

I replied, "Oh, a semicolon."

A pause. "Which is what?"

I explained the punctuation mark's vital role in the world of sentence structure.

"And you use those things in your songs?" He seemed amused.

That night proved typical: I gave a croaky, though grammatically correct, performance, while the other fellow blew the audience away with his natural talent and enviable voice.

Clearly, music was not going to help me solve the mystery of how to lead a writer's life.

What about short stories? I wondered, a form I loved to read. I had heard that one of America's esteemed literary and scholarly periodicals, Playboy, paid upward of $5,000 per. Out came the typewriter, and I banged out dozens of stories, most of which skewed toward the polemical, echoing Jonathan Swift. I'd hit the reader over the head with the mallet of social conscience. War is bad, corporate greed is bad, forests and whales are good. Blah, blah, blah . . .

The movie producer Samuel Goldwyn said if you want to send a message, go to Western Union (now he'd say send a tweet or put it on Facebook, I suppose). And I wish I'd heard of his dictum back then. Nobody, I learned the hard way, wants to be ranted at; an obvious corollary is that editors don't buy stories written by ranters.

I might have honed the craft of short fiction, but time was running out; student loans loomed, and I longed for such luxuries as food and shelter. I had gone to the University of Missouri School of Journalism, so I gave up fiction and landed a job as a magazine writer.

At last, I was making a living as a writer.

The profession and I were not a smooth fit, however. Like my previous forays into writing, journalism found me sailing amid rocky shoals. In this case, the problem was pretty much what I'd anticipated: editors wanted their writers to dig relentlessly for facts, to report the truth. They frowned upon making things up (these were the days before fake news became chic). Where was the room for creativity, for imagination? I felt stifled.

Discouraged, I abandoned my quest for the writer's life and did what everybody in the 1970s, be they cab driver or brain surgeon, did when confronting the least degree of job dissatisfaction. I went to law school.

I was by no means a terrible lawyer, primarily because I could write well, and law is largely about written communication: court documents, memoranda of law, and correspondence threatening litigation. I soon learned that I didn't have the steel to become a successful attorney.

I had one case in which my large, heartless multinational client—not to put too fine a point on it—was sued by a young employee who'd been fired. The termination was justified, and he had no complaint there. But he'd left a box of personal items behind in his office, and they'd gone missing. He was suing for their value, a small sum, about $500.

As a young attorney, I took the case more than seriously. I took it John Grisham seriously. On the appointed court date, I showed up with briefs, stacks of cases, and probably a musty old lawbook or two, as props if nothing else. The plaintiff presented his case, and then the judge turned to me. "The defense's response?"

In my best Perry Mason manner, I began to cite cases and statutes. The judge, who had no patience for nonsense like that, cut me short. She snapped, "What do you want, Counsellor?"

"Um, dismissal, Your Honor? On the grounds of gratuitous bailment?"

"Granted. Case dismissed."

I was ecstatic. I'd won my first trial. And then I looked over at the plaintiff, and he was in tears. Apparently among the missing items were one-of-a-kind photographs of his mother and his dog and other sentimental things. The glow of victory evaporated; I was stabbed with guilt. My inclination was to write him a personal check for the money he'd sought.

Clearly, I was not meant to be a Jeffrey Toobin or Alan Dershowitz—or even a Saul Goodman of *Breaking Bad* fame.

Where to go from there?

Let me digress for a moment. All of my novels feature at least two or three surprise endings. For these to work fairly, there must be a clue seeded early in the story so that when the twist is revealed, the reader says, "You know, I *saw* that but didn't think anything of it."

I've done exactly that in this essay. The clue was a sentence that appeared many paragraphs ago.

Among the various genres I tried my hand at . . .

I never said that poetry, short stories, songs, and magazine articles were the *only* genres I tried. From the very beginning of my quest to lead a writer's life, I was working away at another form: popular commercial fiction. Specifically, the favorite genre of my youth: crime fiction.

While still a full-time employee, I wrote my first murder mystery. I did most of the writing on my commute, which was close to three hours a day, plenty of time to churn out a fair amount of prose. I had one of the first laptop computers ever made. I don't know exactly what it weighed, but it had to be close to ten pounds. Yes, the manufacturer called it a laptop, but you could also call a ten-pound barbell a laptop, and it would put your legs to sleep just as quickly as that computer did. Many times, I left the train hobbling as my circulation slowly returned.

I kept at it, and despite the pressure of a full-time job—and numbness in the extremities—I managed to finish my first novel. I was proud as could be.

I was wary, though, too. Leading a writer's life meant producing a novel with some regularity and consistency. Was this book just a flash in the pan? I set it aside and over the next six months wrote a second. Then I went back and read them both, beginning to end. I learned that they were indeed consistent.

Consistently dreadful.

Chunky prose, convoluted and improbable plots, characters right out of a bad made-for-TV movie.

I threw them both out.

That was it. The mystery of becoming a writer was solved. I wasn't meant to *be* one. I would devote myself to the law and represent the poor, the helpless, the downtrodden. Or represent large, heartless multinational corporations and make a lot of money. The specific direction I took didn't matter. What was important was making the liberating choice of giving up my goal.

And where did I find myself a week or two later? Sitting at my desk banging out a new novel.

When I read through my final product, I decided that unlike those first two, this one was, in my opinion, probably the best commercial novel written that year. An opinion not shared by any agent or editor on the face of the earth.

Usually the manuscript went out and vanished into the abyss, never to return on the wings of the self-addressed, stamped envelope I had dutifully included. However, several were returned. When I received the hefty envelope in the mail, it was clear that it contained not a contract and a check for $100,000 but my manuscript. I opened it up, looking forward to a pithy and helpful letter about how to repair the novel and resubmit it. What I found was this: the manuscript had been dropped on the floor of the publisher and the pages jumbled and stuffed into the envelope every whichaway. There was dust and dirt and, those being the days when one could still smoke, a cigarette butt.

In place of that carefully crafted and helpful rejection letter, I received back only my own cover letter, upside down with a shoe print on the back. Being as naive as I was back then, I figured someone had accidentally stepped on the sheet. Now, being a bit more skeptical about publishing, I suspect the editorial staff drew straws to see who won the right to stomp on the manuscript before it was sent back.

Another rejection of the manuscript went something like this:

Dear Mr. Deaver:

Thank you for your submission. I feel I must tell you that I believe this manuscript to be unpublishable.

Very truly yours,

[Redacted] Publishing, Inc.

I of course focused on the positive: the "Thank you . . ." and the "Very truly yours." Which I took to be signs of encouragement and sent out the manuscript again. Over and over and over. With no success.

But that didn't matter. I'd caught the bug by then. I was going to get published—damn the clichés—come hell or high water. I thought back to famous rejection letters of authors who had gone on to great acclaim. This is anecdotal, but I understand that F. Scott Fitzgerald received a letter that read, "You'd have a good novel if only you'd get rid of that Gatsby character." And another one of my favorites; I'll let my readers figure out the author and the novel: "My dear sir, I'm afraid I must ask: Does it have to be a whale?"

But, since it wasn't selling, I shelved that novel, which I came to call, with affection, *The Unpublishable*, and wrote another one.

Something must have gone wrong somewhere because *that* manuscript was bought on first submission. It wasn't a *publishing event*; there was no big advance, and the *New York Times* did not review it. But I had a contract, and a novel with my name on it was in bookstores. There was no feeling like that in the world. Another novel with that company followed, and then I moved on to a bigger, better-known publisher with a three-book contract.

I delivered the first novel to them, and it received good notices, a movie option, and an Edgar Award nomination.

Then, a speed bump.

I had always told myself that if I were lucky enough to be published as a fiction writer, I would treat the craft as a business. Part of this meant never missing a deadline. But I was still working full time, and as the due date for the second book in the contract approached, I realized that I would be two months late in delivering it. What to do? As Baldrick in *Black Adder* would say, I came up with a cunning plan. I would dust off *The Unpublishable*, slap on a new title, and submit it to my editor. The six or so weeks it would take her to read it would give me the time I needed to finish the book I was working on.

She would contact me and say sheepishly, "Sorry, Jeff, I'm afraid this won't do. Do you have any other ideas?"

Whereupon, like an illusionist, I would produce a proper manuscript, awing her with not only my fine prose but my apparent superheroic stamina and speed.

She called me a week after I'd sent her *The Unpublishable* and reported that it was the best thing I'd ever written.

Go figure.

The challenge of becoming a writer occasionally extends off the written page. There have been several movies based on my books, and Hollywood is exponentially more mysterious than writing fiction. I love the comment by a producer that when he's looking for a book or script to turn into a movie, he wants something that's been wildly successful in the past . . . yet is completely original (which may explain the surfeit of sequels). The movies based on my books are *Dead Silence* with James Garner, *The Bone Collector* with Denzel Washington and Angelina Jolie, and *The Devil's Teardrop*. NBC is currently shooting a TV series based on *The Bone Collector*.

Hollywood is certainly ripe for experiences that might figure in this piece, since why and how a book is turned into a film are an utter mystery. But those tales will have to be penned by scriptwriters, those in the trenches. My involvement in all three movies and the TV show was cashing the check. Period. I respect filmmakers immensely and love movies, but I'm a person who does not play well with others in creative projects, and moviemaking is a form of entertainment whose engine is the collective.

An example of why I've chosen this path is a rather telling anecdote about the first movie—the one that came out as *Dead Silence*. The original book was *A Maiden's Grave*. The studio wanted the story but felt the title was too archaic and not literal enough. They wanted to call it *Dead Silence*. I pointed out that *A Maiden's Grave* was a vital motif in the story that echoed the past and foretold what would happen toward the end of the book. It was, in short, a perfect title.

Their response: Sorry, we want *Dead Silence*. In the book there were no maidens and no graves.

I pointed out that this same studio had just produced *Barbarians at the Gate*, about a modern-day corporate takeover, a story that featured not a single barbarian or gate.

They laughed at my clever rejoinder and said, "We still want *Dead Silence*."

I continued to resist.

Whereupon they said, "The other option is that we can find someone *else's* book to turn into a film."

And I replied, "*Dead Silence* has a nice *sound* to it." They missed the irony completely. And we moved forward with the deal.

Hollywood . . .

For three and a half decades, I've produced a novel and several short stories a year, and it was exactly twenty years ago that I quit my pesky day job to become a full-time fiction writer. There were many confounding trials and setbacks along the way—and there still are (like watching bookstores close and sales erode as people turn to streaming TV and video games). Still, there's no better profession. Think about it: I get to make up things for a living. Does it get any better than that?

I'm sure every author has a different approach to the challenge of how to lead a writer's life. It might be pursuing nonfiction or technical writing or graphic novels or the genres that I tried and discarded (or that discarded me!): poetry, songs, journalism, literary fiction, film.

In my case, the answer was stunning in its simplicity: coming to write the types of books and short stories that so captivated me as a young boy spending hour after hour in the Glen Ellyn Public Library many, many years ago. Just as in good detective fiction, the plot twist in which the mystery is solved was right before my eyes the entire time.

AN EXTRA CHILD

- Sulari Gentill -

THE *BOX* LIVED IN THE BACK OF A CUPBOARD. THAT IN IT-
self made it interesting. I suppose our flat-roofed house didn't
have an attic, so the cupboard served that purpose. In it were
stored those items that had no place in the light of day but
were valued or somehow important, even if the reason for that
importance had been long forgotten. As a child, I would hide
treasures in the cupboard and try to forget that I'd done so, just
so I could rediscover them after they'd had been imbued with
the magic that lingered there.

The box, however, did not need such contrivance; it was
truly an object of wonder.

It contained evidence of a life that had become a secret, lost
to an agreement to pretend.

I am the middle of three daughters, born in Sri Lanka in
a province known as Slave Island—so named because it was

once a port at which the slaving ships stopped on their way to America. My parents made me an immigrant before I was two years old. Of course, I was too young to care one way or another. The boundaries of my world still stopped at my family. After a brief stint in London, we spent five years in Zambia, where my sisters and I learned to speak English. By the time I was seven, I was Australian.

Ours was a typical immigrant family from South Asia. My parents placed a premium on education and were indifferent to sports. It made us a little odd in sports-mad Australia, but we became Australian nonetheless. We adopted the inflection and humor of our new country and navigated that line that all immigrant children walk, between the customs of where we were from and where we stood.

As the years passed, my sisters and I stopped speaking Singhalese, and, like trees, our new growth was ever further from our roots. We unfurled and flowered in the Australian sun, thriving in the dappled shade of gumtrees. Even so, I was aware that we were alone in this wide brown land. My parents were both from large families, but we lived half a planet away from grandparents or cousins or anyone who knew our history. There were no aunts and uncles to tell us funny stories about our parents, no collection of people with similar faces. At that distance, secrets were easily kept.

Perhaps my father sensed that the threads that connected us to the country of our birth were snapping one by one. The summer I was eight, he flew the whole family back to Sri Lanka. He rented a van, and in the weeks we were there, he took us to see every temple, monument, and ruin on the island—and Sri

Lanka is not short of temples, monuments, and ruins. He was a man on a mission, taking his daughters on a cultural boot camp, fertilizing our shallow roots in this place with a grand tour of the old country. How enthusiastically he would point to ancient statues of Sri Lankan kings and remind us that there was our mother's multiple-great-grandfather, our lofty heritage. Even as an eight-year-old, I could hear a kind of awe in his voice as he spoke of my mother's bloodline. I found it curious. I was fiercely egalitarian by then, but the idea of being some kind of princess had an undeniable and sparkly appeal. But it was fleeting. I was too much a tomboy to be mesmerized by a metaphorical tiara for long.

We called upon all the uncles and aunts, the cousins, the second cousins, the people who were *somehow related*, though no one was quite sure how. The vast estates of my mother's people—houses large enough to seem empty—and the humbler homes of my father's family. I was probably too young to entirely comprehend who my mother's family was in the context of the country I'd left as an infant. The descendants of kings, they were the guardians of religion, and from their ranks had come Sri Lanka's first prime ministers, governors, diplomats, and generals. Their sons were educated abroad, and their daughters were accomplished; they were patriots and leaders. Most impressive to eight-year-old me was a more recent ancestor whose head resided in the Tower of London, where it had been taken after he had been beheaded for leading a revolt against the British. Sri Lanka was a country in which who your family was mattered, where lines could be traced back thousands of years. As far as cultural baptisms went, it was not a mere sprinkling but an absolute dunking, undertaken in the hope that it would be enough to keep us at heart Sri Lankan, or at least keep Sri Lanka in our hearts; that our roots would be strong enough to survive in transplantation.

Six weeks later, we returned to Australia, a Western democracy whose kings and queens were foreign and relatively unremarked unless there was a royal wedding in the offing. Sri Lanka receded into a memory of our last grand exotic holiday, and the relatives we had met and embraced became stories again as we returned to the business of school and friends and suburban survival.

There were photos of that holiday, of course, printed and placed in an album specially bought. But it was not that collection, the images of us on beaches, in front of temples, with various groups of relatives, to which we were drawn. Perhaps it was because they were photos of foreigners on holiday, tourists . . . and we knew about the box.

It contained old photographs. Black-and-white, printed in smaller format and in different shapes from the standard four-by-six-inch prints of the day. Taken on box Brownies and in studios, long before we were born, they gave us a glimpse of our parents when they were not our parents.

The photos of my dad's family were taken with a borrowed camera when he was a young man. Posed photographs of his sisters in their best saris, my grandmother when her hair was gray rather than white, and my father smiling, confident, a brown-skinned Elvis on a tropical island.

The photographs from my mother's side were taken over a much greater span of time. Her family was wealthy enough to own cameras, to use them for more than special occasions. Pictures of Victorian children, my grandmother in curls and bows holding a hoop in front of the painted backdrop of an English garden. We were mesmerized by that photograph—the camera had caught something wistful and sad about that little girl. There was a studio photo of my grandfather inscribed to his then fiancée, hair slicked back, movie-star handsome. My grandmother as a young woman, bespectacled, unsmiling. Formal wedding photographs, a 1920s honeymoon in Egypt. Then a tribe of children on the family estate.

The story of our grandparents laid out before us.

These photographs invited our imaginations into their younger lives, into their stories, in a way that knowing them as our grandparents never did.

We spent many hours with these old photographs, demanding details from our mother as to their subjects and locations and occasions. In my family, my mother was the storyteller. She had an innate understanding of structure and pace, the ability to make the most mundane events sound exciting and magical. She was a spinner of drama, a master of the reveal, and so we would pester her for stories, and she became a kind of verbal text to the picture book we found in that box. She told us that the little girl in curls and bows had a younger sister she had loved dearly who was killed in an accident when the family chauffeur was drunk, that later her engagement to the devastatingly handsome young man in the portrait was broken off when he became a communist while studying in Edinburgh. That the two were eventually reconciled and married in a spectacular wedding that united two of the great houses of Sri Lanka. She allowed us to play with the exquisite dressing-table set that the then prime minister of Sri Lanka had given them as a wedding present and described the other riches gifted by foreign dignitaries and grand guests.

We knew that little girl, of course. She was our grandmother. Small, quiet, distant. She had traveled with us for part of our grand tour, and though we had become accustomed to her presence, to us she remained enigmatic. We had only snippets of memories of our grandfather, still handsome in old age. He smoked a pipe and seemed vaguely English, though he wore a sarong. Perhaps because we didn't really know them, it was easy to imagine them as young, the hero and heroine of a story to rival that of Elizabeth Bennet and her Mr. Darcy.

And then there were the photographs of the children. Girls in white dresses, boys in oversized shorts and collared shirts. Pictures taken on the estate, posing with bicycles, sitting in banyan trees, walking by the lake, and formal photos of the children together, direct, unsmiling gazes. My mother was the youngest by a long way, so she was not in all these group sittings, which is probably why it took me so long to notice that the numbers didn't add up. I knew I had two aunts and three uncles, one of whom had died as a teenager. That made six children born to the union of Elizabeth and Darcy. And, indeed, the group photos always had six. Even when my mother was not among them. I must have been about ten when I realized that in some of these photographs there was an extra child. A boy. Now, these were pictures of children I knew only as middle-aged men and women, and so I could not tell which of the four boys was the extra child.

There were many plausible reasons why there might be an extra child in a photograph. The pictures of my father's family often included cousins or friends or servants. And so, when I asked my mother, I was not particularly intrigued. I might have thought no more about it if she hadn't flat-out denied what was before me in black-and-white. "There's no extra child—you miscounted."

"No, Mum; you aren't in that photo, but there are still six kids."

"One of my brothers died when he was young. It must be him."

"No . . . there are four boys. I've only ever had three uncles."

"You must be making a mistake. . . . I hope you haven't been pulling out photos and not putting them back. Clean your room, by the way . . . and can you walk to the shops and get some milk?"

But ten-year-olds are persistent. I brought the photo to her and counted out my uncles. "Him!" I said triumphantly, once we'd eliminated the others. A thin boy with light eyes and ears like open cab doors. "Who is he?"

My mother picked up the photograph and stared at it for just a couple of beats too long. And when she spoke, there was something in her voice. A hesitation cut with sadness. "Must be some cousin . . . I don't remember who."

And that was that. She would say no more. I took the photo to my father and pointed out the extra child. "Do you know who he is, Dad?"

Now, if my father had simply said no, I probably would have forgotten all about it. But he said, "Who does your mother say it is?"

"She says it was some cousin."

"That must be right, then."

A ring-in cousin who visited so often he was in a number of different family photographs but whose name was forgotten. I was underwhelmed by the explanation, but it was what it was. If I'd had easy access to other family, I might have kept asking, but I was ten, and I didn't.

I did think about the boy from time to time. While I accepted my mother's half-hearted explanation, I never believed it. I wondered occasionally if he was a ghost accidentally caught on film or a criminal child who had been disowned. But mostly I didn't think about him. He returned to the box of photographs, an unclaimed child with no name.

In the end, it was my mother who told me who the boy was on the day that he died. My sisters and I had arrived home from school in our usual noisy straggle, all schoolbags and bickering. My mother had been crying. She met us with "I have to speak to you girls about something."

She told us then about the extra boy in the photo, her eldest brother, the first-born son of the little girl in curls and lace and the handsome young man who'd been a communist, the heir to wealth and status from both sides of his family, a future doctor or barrister or prime minister. But it had been a difficult birth, a forceps delivery that somehow damaged the baby, and he had stayed a five-year-old child. Celebration became tragedy. He grew up in a town where his father was the local doctor, surrounded by brothers and sisters in a grand house with many servants. My mother's family are not demonstrative people, but I do think they loved him. They certainly protected and cared for him, perhaps even indulged him. And then, when he was nineteen, that all changed.

His five-year-old mind, it seemed, was susceptible to the frustrations and rages of that age, which, when expressed with the strength and body of a young man, were becoming difficult to manage. In a fit of temper, he'd flung a pair of scissors that had struck my grandmother and drawn blood. And that was it. It was decided that he could no longer live at home, and he was sent away.

My mother told us of the asylum, which housed patients with all sorts of mental fragility. Where my uncle lived for the rest of his life, sharing a room with a man who believed he was the king of England. She recounted funny conversations, anecdotes that made the asylum seem like a privileged board-ing school.

When we asked why we'd never heard of this uncle, she said it was my grandfather's wish that no one know. My mother, the youngest child, had been barely four when her eldest brother had last lived at home. Her memories of him were few and faded: he would place her on top of cupboards when they fought—she a small child, he a grown man with the mind of a child. Like all my mother's stories, they were funny and light and beautifully constructed. They made us laugh and think warmly of the uncle we'd never known existed.

Once every couple of months my grandmother would visit the asylum, taking bribes for the staff and treats for her firstborn son. The last time we'd been in Sri Lanka, my mother had gone to see her brother for the first time in many years. Now she told us that he'd recognized her. She narrated the funny exchanges, the innocent honesty, the childlike questions, and then, with an instinctive understanding of pathos, she revealed that before they'd left, he'd warned her not to be naughty lest their father send her there, too.

That was probably the first hint I had that the asylum was not akin to some mythical English boarding school where everything was jolly.

I do remember being deeply troubled by the fact that my uncle had still been alive when last we'd been in Sri Lanka. We could have met him if we'd been allowed to know he existed. And now it was too late. An opportunity missed; a connection never made.

It was we who told our father that our uncle had died. My mother had gone to bed before he came home from work. This method of avoidance wasn't particularly unusual in my family. My mother was possessive of her family. She would not share them with my father; she barely shared them with her daughters. And, it seemed, she had never told him she had a brother in the Angoda Asylum.

But my father knew. He is six years my mother's senior, and as a child, he'd lived in the same town in the highlands of Sri Lanka. My grandfather had been the doctor on the hill, an important and wealthy man. Dad's family was poor, but he attended the same local school as the doctor's children until they were packed off to elite boarding schools.

In whispers, my father told us what he remembered of our late uncle. The handsomest of the doctor's brood, he was tall and green-eyed. Both features made him distinctive in Sri Lanka. Dad told us that as a young man, the eldest son of Elizabeth and

Darcy would wander the streets in the town that was his home, where everyone knew him, as the people of Maycomb, Alabama, knew Arthur "Boo" Radley. That he would walk casually into people's houses and request a drink or something to eat, as small children do. That the townspeople all knew he was a "bit silly" but harmless.

Later my father would confess that he'd first raised the subject of my uncle with my mother when they were newlyweds. She had denied having such a brother so absolutely that he'd never mentioned it again . . . though he knew. He complied with the pretense because it was the cause of such shame, and my mother's people were very proud.

At the time, I accepted this, though I did wonder whether it was my uncle or where they'd left him that made them ashamed. I desperately wanted to be his champion, but it was too late. Occasionally I would retrieve the pictures from the box in the cupboard and look at the extra boy in the family photos, knowing now that he'd had green eyes, that his mind was that of a five-year-old child, and that he was my uncle. But aside from that, the sadness of him faded.

It wasn't until well after my sons were born that my thoughts turned again to my late uncle. My eldest son is now eighteen, and while I love the young man he's become, I do remember, with a sense of bittersweet loss, the five-year-old boy he once was. There is something so beautiful about the mind and heart of a child that age: the honesty, the innocence, the wide-eyed wonder at the world, the beginnings of humor, that fierce, uninhibited love. It was a mind like this that my grandparents had consigned to the Angoda Asylum, an institution that a little

Googling reveals had more in common with the sanatorium in Miloš Forman's *One Flew Over the Cuckoo's Nest* than any of my mother's stories ever revealed, a place that housed the intellectually challenged together with the criminally insane, a place that gained a reputation for brutality.

My uncle lived at Angoda for over thirty years. He died in the body of a man in his fifties, but his mind was still that of a child. He would have been as hurt and scared and confused as a child. His mother went to see him once every two months. My grandfather could not bear it and stayed away entirely. I don't know how often his brothers and sisters, the other children in those photographs, visited, but I doubt it was more than rarely. He had many nieces and nephews, born to a more accepting generation, but they were not allowed to know of his existence.

I look now at those old photos. My dapper, modern grandfather who forsook the sarong for a suit and pipe. My grandmother, who was born to such wealth and privilege but who, even as a child in curls and bows, never seemed to smile. Perhaps she had some sense even then of the anguish life had in store for her, what circumstance and society would demand she bear. I look at that extra boy in the family portrait, and I wonder what he thought, what he felt, what he wanted. He remains a mystery. But he's no longer a secret.

FIELD NOTES
À LA MAIGRET
FROM PARIS

- Cara Black -

I BLAME MY ENTRY INTO CRIME WRITING ON INSPECTOR Maigret, the protagonist of Georges Simenon's novels about a Parisian police inspector. Georges Simenon, originally from Belgium, first arrived in Paris as an outsider. While Agatha Christie is known all over the world as the queen of crime, Georges Simenon has sold almost as many books—between 500 and 700 million copies worldwide of his 570 books.

His Inspector Maigret novels captured my imagination. Fascination with Paris is a family trait. My uncle and my father, two brothers from Chicago with not a French vein in their bodies, were devoted Francophiles. No clue as to why, but I think French cuisine and wine were probably factors. When I was a child, my father had read me Charles Dickens's *A Tale of Two Cities*, a nineteenth-century edition illustrated with scary woodcuts. In that story, Paris is peopled by revolutionaries, men in frock coats, and Madame Defarge knitting with a malevolent eye.

My uncle, who lived with us, had stayed on the Left Bank. "Studying art," he claimed, but really drinking a lot of *vin rouge*. He'd talk about how, after a night of partying, they'd end up at five A.M. in their tuxedoes at Les Halles, Paris's famous fresh-food market, where they'd eat onion soup next to the butchers working in their bloodstained aprons. How his teacher Georges Braque's studio was so cold, and the artist such a tightwad, that when my uncle asked the master to put more coals in the stove because the model was turning blue, Braque gestured for him to leave and kicked him downstairs. His stories offered an earthy side to the photos I'd seen in *Vogue*, with slim, tousle-haired women, effortlessly chic in Chanel jackets, carrying dogs in their handbags. The glamor and the grit seemed to go hand in hand.

You always remember the first time . . . the first time you felt Paris. For me, it was reading Hemingway's *A Moveable Feast*, exploring the gritty side with Inspector Maigret, listening to Edith Piaf songs. The city of light exuded sensuality and a hard, visceral beauty.

I first came to Paris in a long-ago September. What I owned lay in my rucksack carried on my back. My travelmate and I woke up in the École de Médecine student dormitory somewhere in the Latin Quarter. Two medical students, who were on call all night, had given us their beds. Needless to say, they expected to share them with us the following morning. I remember that peculiar feeling of a fluffy duvet, sun pouring in the tall window, and two grinning male students greeting us with soup bowls of bitter coffee and peaches. Peaches whose sweet juice stained our chins. We thanked them, maneuvering our way out by promising to come back. Somehow, we never did.

I never forgot the actual boots-down feeling of this place. Paris comes to me with the scent of ripe Montreuil peaches, the high heels clicking over the cobbles, the dripping plane-tree branches leaving shadows on the quai, the flowing of the khaki-colored Seine. Always that shiver from cold stone inside soot-stained, centuries-old churches, relics of history and mystery under a piercing blue sky. But feeling Paris is not the same as knowing it, and I have spent my life trying to connect to this city as one of my own, à la Maigret.

That first September, wearing a déclassé flannel shirt and jeans, I haunted the cafés where famous writers wrote. Those cafés encouraged my resolve that I would write someday. But it wasn't until years later in Paris, during another September, that I found a story. My friend Sarah took me to the Marais, then ungentrified, and showed me where her mother, at the age of fourteen, had hidden during the German occupation. Sarah's mother's family had been taken by the French police, and she'd lived, hidden, wearing a yellow star and going to school, until the liberation of Paris. Sadly, her family never returned.

The war had never felt close to me until that moment, standing on the narrow rue des Rosiers in front of a building where a tragedy—so many more than one in this old Jewish part of Paris—had occurred. It was the collision between the present and the past that floated in front of me as I imagined Sarah's mother's life. Almost as if the ghosts hovered out of reach, but there in the shadowy stone recesses of the building. I never forgot that shiver of encountering the past.

When my father heard the story of Sarah's mother hiding in the Marais during the war, he handed me a slim crime novel by Georges Simenon and said, "Read this. It's set in Paris."

But it's old-fashioned, I thought.

"It might be a way to tell this story you're going on about," said my father, tired of the obsession consuming me after hearing about Sarah's family.

So my life of crime began with reading Inspector Maigret's investigations. Could I approach understanding Parisians like an investigation, a case to crack, as in those slender Inspector Maigret novels that intrigued me? Maybe I could understand Parisians, blend in at least for a moment before I opened my mouth. Figure out the code they communicated in, discover if their flair disguised another reality. The seething passions below the surface that led to spilling blood. What better way than an investigation for someone like me—not as a voyeur but as an observer who noted details, caught a nuance, dug below the surface, always searching for motive, opportunity?

I identified with an investigator because I was always on the outside looking for a way in. And crime fiction sets Paris against a backdrop of gray, an overcast sky, and perhaps a corpse or two in the cobbled streets—discovered, of course, by Georges Simenon's pipe-smoking Inspector Jules Maigret.

Though Maigret's era passed long ago, it's not all history. His "old office" in the police department at 36 Quai des Orfèvres, the Paris Préfecture (often referred to as "36"), now belongs to a trim forty-something *commissaire* with a laptop; gone is the charcoal-burning stove. Maigret's unit, the Sûreté, is no more, but has been restructured and renamed the Brigade Criminelle, Paris's elite homicide squad. From time immemorial, officers have hung bloody clothing from crime scenes to dry under the rafters in the attic at 36. This tradition hasn't changed. Nor has the rooftop view, courteously shown to me by a member of the Brigade Criminelle. A vista with the Seine and all of Paris before us. Breathtaking. And beneath us are 36's underground holding cells, which date from the Revolution, if not further back.

That's become my job: to write stories about crime and murder *à la parisienne*, set in contemporary Paris. A way for me, an outsider, to explore and scratch that itch of curiosity.

The streets are the same as they were in Maigret's time, but today's Fifth Republic Paris is a blended wealth of cultural traditions from all over the world. For me, this means there are new enclaves and hidden worlds to encounter, no matter how well I think I know these cobbled streets.

To know Paris, as Edmund White and countless others have observed, one must be a *flâneur*, one who takes leisurely strolls through the city, letting unexpected moods wash over you and remaining open to discovery—in my case, with an eye for crime. One must take the pulse of a *quartier*, assessing its rhythm; know it by heart, from the lime trees flanking its boulevards to its nineteenth-century *passages couverts*. Only when I can feel that pulse can I start the rest of my research for a novel.

Writers, like detectives, must be curious, and ask, "What if?"—which I had been doing since I first stepped on the cobbles. Detectives follow their noses, as the old adage goes; when a word rings false, when the indefinable something-isn't-right moment happens—that is the moment to wonder, to ask questions. The exchange of a furtive glance, a figure ducking out of sight into the back of a café and failing to reemerge. In Paris, those who want to disappear can do so via the spare exit gate of a back courtyard, through the city's series of covered passageways, even over the gray zinc rooftops or underground through a cellar or an old World War II bomb shelter.

All a writer needs is that "What if?" and a story tumbles out. I imagine the line at the *tabac* by Pigalle Métro station evaporating, the group of teens breaking off into threes to pickpocket unsuspecting tourists; an artist in a tiny fifth-floor den closing her shutters to block out street noise; a man with a gun entering a jewelry store in the "golden triangle" off the Champs-Élysées, ready to commit one in a series of daytime robberies. How I long to get it right, to write about the city with the confidence of a native, to reflect the Paris of the 1990s, with its hidden courtyards and criminal underbelly—updating the Paris that Inspector Maigret haunted.

Over the years, I'd gotten to meet police, and in order to know more, I'd gone out drinking with the *flics*, the local cops. Lucky enough to receive such an invitation one night, I joined several at the bar across the Seine from 36, where they'd taken over a back table.

An intoxicated young man looking for a fight entered the bar and approached us at our table—a table of off-duty police officers. Who knows why? Bad luck, I suppose. He began a drunken monologue. If you've had such an encounter, you know the kind. This young man was the sort you wanted to leave the premises before he got belligerent. A few of the officers spoke with him and escorted him out. He sat down on the sidewalk, and one of the admin police, who resembled an accountant, stayed behind to join him on the curb across from *la maison*, as the Préfecture is called. This policeman spoke with the young man for a long time amid the smokers and passersby, talking him down rather than talking down to him. I'd gone outside for a cigarette and noticed them carrying on a conversation. I didn't get involved, as I didn't have anything to add, nor did I wish to accidentally provoke someone so inebriated. When I came out again later, they were still talking. The flic was kindly asking questions. Maybe the kid had broken up with his girlfriend, lost his job, or just had a really bad day; I never found out.

It was something the flic didn't have to do, with all his buddies inside drinking. Whether he enjoyed getting out of the bar, or the view of the Seine, or just talking with this kid, it struck me as something Jules Maigret would have done. Maigret, the knowing, sometimes fatherly figure who knew people would tell you their story if you just coaxed it out of them. Averting disaster, heading off a confrontation, recognizing the signs that a situation could spin out of control. Maybe that was part of what they taught at the police academy. By the time the young man (who was still, in my opinion, one slice short of a baguette, sobriety-wise) finally left, he had a smile on his face. I'll never know what happened to him after that, but I had the feeling he would just go home and sleep it off. He wouldn't feel denigrated or demoralized in the morning, only hungover.

Georges Simenon's novels are full of investigators, flics on their daily beat, the victims' neighbors, hotel concierges, capturing a time, a part of Paris, that exists now only in the imagination. A time when cell phones and numeric-entry keypads were unheard of—one could only ring the concierge's bell to gain entry after midnight. Everyone knew everyone else's business in a city with enclosed courtyards, high walls, and watchful eyes. I think they still do. Parisians smoked and drank morning, noon, and night. Men's wool overcoats and hats steamed as they came in from a wet winter evening to a warm café with a charcoal stove burning. People knew their neighbors. Snitches snitched. Girlfriends chatted with each other, and mothers-in-law complained—human connections abounded, often forming a web of lies and deceit.

In that complicated world, Maigret keeps at it—plodding, questioning, then throwing out those questions, lighting his pipe when it goes out, and the suspect in the chair opposite him knows it's only a matter of time. As does Maigret. He drinks at lunch, sometimes he gets angry, even orders sandwiches and beer in the afternoon. He takes the annual August *vacances* with Madame Maigret, unless a case comes up—but when doesn't it?—and detains him in hot, deserted Paris. But a few of his investigations find him out in the countryside, in hermetically sealed villages where observant eyes don't miss a thing. As in many cultures, an outsider arriving in a small French village is often met with distrust, even more so if they're different.

That hasn't changed.

I confess that when I first began writing my Aimée Leduc novels, I would think, *Okay. There's a murder, a staircase dripping with blood. . . . What would Inspector Maigret do?* That wasn't always much help, since Aimée is a PI, not a policewoman. But then I'd consider what she might do if Maigret appeared on the scene and questioned her after she found the body. That worked a little better. Of course, the police system in place now is different: Jules Maigret, as the head *commissaire*, would certainly not respond in person. Today, it would be the Brigade Criminelle and *le procureur* (the equivalent of our DA) who would hotfoot it to the scene and dictate the next steps in the investigation. My *flic* friends told me I had to change my way of thinking about the police process in a murder investigation. The way Maigret operated didn't make for a plausible scenario now. So I relearned in order to keep the details in my books accurate and came to the conclusion that Maigret had it easier than a head *commissaire* would today.

Is Simenon's work dated? Historical? Timeless? I'd argue the second two. I personally like my Paris streets dark and narrow, with glistening cobbles. The air thick with mist and suspicion. The Montmartre cemetery wall, the same as it was then, hulking with old, lichen-covered stone. I've imagined a corpse there more than once. My friend lives a block away, and returning late at night from the last Métro, walking uphill from Place de Clichy, the *cinéma* marquees dark, the café lights fading as I cross over to the cemetery, I hear the thrum of the old Citroën or Renault engine, the shift of gears, and smell the cherry tobacco. (I like to think Maigret smoked cherry tobacco, though I don't know that it's ever specified; perhaps there's a Simenon scholar out there who can tell me.) Flashlights illuminate the corpse sprawled on the damp pavement; Maigret nods to his lieutenant with a "Take this down," and we're off on an investigation. An investigation that leads to the hidden life behind the walls, intrigue in the *quartier*, and worlds we'd never visit otherwise. Worlds that make me feel like I belong.

The iconic Préfecture at 36 Quai des Orfévres is now falling to pieces, the *flics* say—well-worn and tired around the edges, ancient and unequipped to handle the new technology the force needs. They've moved to a brand-new building that's designed to gather all the gendarme divisions in one place. It's in the 17th near the Parc Clichy-Batignolles and the old train switching yards, abandoned for many years. Had France gotten the 2012 Olympic bid that went to England, this is where the Olympic Village would have been. I'm kind of glad that never happened. As some *flics* point out, the move has been long slated, but with the current budget crisis, there's an advantage to keeping the headquarters. The genius of being in the very center of Paris is that the city Tribunal is right next door. Prisoners awaiting trial literally go from their holding cells to the court through an ancient underground tunnel. A friend, a *flic* whose first assignment out of the academy was escorting those in custody from their funky cells to the court, aptly described the surroundings as "medieval" and foreboding, as they were in Maigret's time.

Boulevard Richard Lenoir is where the inspector lived with Madame Maigret. I confess to making a pilgrimage to their apartment building. While I know it's a fictional building, I couldn't resist scoping it out. I imagined myself saying, "It would be this street number and, yes, just as Simenon described." Years later, riding a Vélib, a cycle from the citywide bike share, I returned home late to find that all the stations near my lodgings on the Canal Saint-Martin were full. Zut! It was late and drizzling, and I was hungry and looking to rest my aching feet. Finally, I found a single empty spot for my bicycle: on Boulevard Richard Lenoir, right below the Maigret apartment. How I wished Madame Maigret were still up waiting for Jules, warming a pot of cassoulet on the stove.

Even though I've made regular visits to France for over twenty years, I'm still l'américaine. I've been a guest at several of the locals' weddings, heard about their husbands' affairs. . . . I'd like to think they trust me now. After all, I've been into their homes, which is considered an honor and no mean feat. But in many ways, I'm still the outsider, the investigator. And yet they've given me a window into their lives, a way to see, so if that's the way an outsider is, then I'm fine with it. I think if I ever do completely understand the French, the magic and mystery will be gone—but no fear of that. The first peaches of the season still drip and stain my chin, I'm full of wonder, and that duvet feels comfortable now.

LYDIA AND JACK

– Connie May Fowler –

WHEN I WAS FIVE, I TRIED TO KILL MYSELF.

The fluorescent tube buzzed overhead like a giant gnat that refused to die. Jaundiced light cast a yellow pall over tossed-but-not-forgotten foot pedals, bobbin cases, needle bars, snapped needles, bent needles, miniature screwdrivers, scissors, and fabric swatches upon which my mother had sewn a sampling of fancy stitches (I loved the zigzag stitch and often ran the tip of my index finger along its nadirs and zeniths, comforted by the highs and lows of its oppositional pattern) as I searched for a knife.

I suppose I could have zipped into the path of an oncoming bus (that would happen two years later), but at that moment, while my parents raged in the showroom of their sewing-machine store, the slitting of my wrists seemed reasonable, necessary, inevitable.

The knife was situated near the rear of the worktable, placed there, no doubt, so I could not reach it or the jar of peanut butter atop which it balanced. I rose to my tippy-toes and stretched as far as I could, grunting with the effort, my mother's treasured pinking shears cold against my belly, but the knife and the nearly empty bag of Sunbeam bread with its illustration of the impossibly pretty Little Miss Sunbeam—blue bow nestled in blond curls—remained just beyond my grasp. The tome that was the phone book sat beneath a pile of oily rags. I stacked it on the floor along with several sewing-machine manuals, a Florida atlas, and a coffee-stained dime novel. That was all I needed.

I held aloft the knife, enormous in my tiny hand. In the shiny reflection in the steel, one eye stared back. I stepped off my paper stool, glanced at the burgundy curtain separating me from my warring parents, placed the blade against the pale skin of my left wrist with its road map of springtime-blue veins, and sawed.

FIFTY-PLUS YEARS LATER, AS AN ADULT LIVING A QUIET LIFE on a Caribbean island, a mystery dogs me: How was a child of five aware of the concepts of slit wrists, bleeding out, the warm silence of death?

I NEVER WANTED CHILDREN. THE NOTION OF A TEN-POUND bowling ball ripping open my vagina strikes me as one of Nature's cruelest jokes. The responsibility that mushrooms the second the child exits said torn vagina is so monumental, it seems a thinking person would carefully consider and reconsider the pros and cons.

Perhaps it's different for millennials, but baby-boomer females grew up on the pablum that cast motherhood as a requirement for every woman, no matter her circumstances or desires.

Oh, the moment that child is in your arms, you forget all about the pain of labor.

There is no love like a mother's love.

A woman is incomplete without children.

It's your Christian duty.

The only women who don't want children are deviant women.

What else are you going to do with your life?

I am not a coward. I could have gotten over the ripping open of my private parts. But given my history of trauma, I sniffed a rat regarding the pro-motherhood platitudes. After all, my sister and I were so incessantly abused, we thought *What Ever Happened to Baby Jane?* was a comedy. A mother who beats a child while telling her she detests her (the mildest of my mother's invectives) isn't exactly an endearing portrait of maternal love, nor does it inspire confidence in the institution.

And that responsibility issue? My father died when I was six, leaving my mother to stew alone in her madness. As her behavior grew more violent and erratic, and as her alcoholism morphed into barbed steel, my sister and I (my brother, far older, was long gone) became her unwilling parents determined to somehow ensure we all survived the fury.

MY DECISION NOT TO HAVE CHILDREN PUTS ME IN THE crosshairs of several world religions. Humanity has waged inquisitions, committed ancient and modern-day massacres, and suspended the civil liberties of those who worship gods not their own. Yet people line up in solidarity on the issue of procreation. In a way, I can't blame them. Their texts were written and long worshipped during a time when populating the earth was a swell idea.

But given the cataclysmic realities of climate change, fewer babies might be a selfless, conscious act committed in pursuit of saving the planet. I think those of us who decline to procreate should be lauded as iconic, let's-avoid-the-apocalypse role models. On Mother's Day we should be sent flowers on behalf of the embattled Earth. But instead, with ancient beliefs de rigueur in these late days, we catch a lot of flak. Judgment, I'm afraid, is its own form of shrapnel.

My gender can be the most openly hostile. Women who insist they know what God thinks cluck, shake their heads, and make sad, pouty fish lips as they reach across desks in banks and college administrators' offices or dinner tables jumbled with wineglasses, chortling, *Don't worry, dear. It's not too late. You know, if all else fails, there is always adoption. I'll pray for you.* They cast sympathetic glances at my husband, even though *he* had a vasectomy years before we ever met.

For some people, no matter how woke a portion of the population becomes, it's always the woman's fault and never her— or her and her partner's—choice. Real men don't eat quiche, as the old platitude goes, and real women don't decide to forgo having babies.

Among the benefits of being old enough to be a grandmother—again, a familial status I'll never achieve—is the patina of age I bear like starshine. But the shine doesn't smudge away the awkwardness. When I'm asked how many children and grandchildren I have, and I answer zero, people often pause, look past me, recalibrate, and then whip out their phones to show me photos of beaming offspring. Undeterred, I whip out mine and just as enthusiastically share images of my incredibly smart, gorgeous, and student-loan-free dogs. *This is Pablo's favorite chair. He likes to take a nap in it after he poops.*

But at least those who think they know what I should have been doing all these years with my womb—that unseen moon, that mysterious planet with lunar cycles indefatigable and misunderstood—no longer insist that I must bear human fruit. Even they know that ship has sailed.

TURN OF THE SCREW: IT ISN'T COMPLETELY TRUE THAT I NEVER wanted children. When I was in my twenties, thirties, forties, I wanted them desperately once a month. But I am a writer. And writers, if we're any good at our calling, divine patterns. I didn't need to be Shakespeare to figure out that my child desires were tied to my womb's lunar cycles, cycles that did nothing to erase the sting of childhood traumas. What might have seemed mysterious or a biological mandate to some became crystalline and manageable, lines drawn between the celestial dots of my womanhood.

WHEN I WAS AN UNDERGRAD—LOST, VULNERABLE, TUMBLING, with no safe place to land inside my mother's wounded orbit—a professor informed the class that his wife desired to remain childless because, as an abuse survivor, she knew battered children always grew up to repeat their parents' sins. Not only did the professor possess great authority by virtue of his position, but, as a girl who'd grown up fatherless, I was poised to believe everything he said.

And I continued to believe him, even after it became apparent to most anyone who could breathe that he was picking off wide-eyed coeds for his sexual pleasure as if we were little more than rotting fruit moldering at the base of his tree. I defend my gullibility by virtue of the fact that his views on battered children were supported by everything I had read on the topic in my Introduction to Social Work textbook. Even today, social sciences spout the same blather, hawking statistics to bolster a misguided and most damaging allegation that is yet another blow to the bodies and spirits of the battered.

In 2004, as I gave a speech to a group of domestic violence workers, a different truth pushed its way to the front of my brain, dispelling the lie and prompting me to go off script. The only people the if-you're-a-battered-child-you're-doomed statistic counts are those who end up in the system. But what about that grand majority populated by folks who never become perpetrators, who go on to live exemplary lives? We are legion. We are friends, colleagues, neighbors, sisters, brothers: battered children who grow up to be overachievers, shining examples of humanity, leaders within our communities, people who never have run-ins with the law, who would never even think about harming a child. And, unlike nonreproductive me, most survivors go on to have happy, healthy children whom they love with their entire beings. They do not beat them.

Those of us who ascend the ashes of our shattered childhoods are not counted by social scientists or law enforcers or grant givers. This omission is not just a mystery; it's an unwitting crime that tarnishes our self-esteem and slows our ascension.

BUT LET'S BE HONEST. THERE ARE FAR MORE PERSONAL MYSteries surrounding my childlessness, mysteries that contradict, confound, taunt. *I never wanted children. Once a month, my hormones wanted them.* And now, something deeper, more complicated, another inexplicable turn of the screw. A wild woman lurks inside me—one unfazed by rational thought and untouched by feminine cycles—who truly, madly, deeply desires them. Worse, the desire is acidified with regret. In middle age, when mortality becomes less abstract, in the ebb and flow of my life's far-flung oceans, I am forced to admit that sorrow tugs at the watery edges. These are dark waters where nary a toe is dipped. The what-ifs are profound, unanswerable, unsafe. They open a door to a different eternity. When I gaze through it, I see a woman who is me but who is also not me, a woman whose reason for living is divided among beloveds she created. And then I wonder, can we exist simultaneously in two different stories?

I HAVE NEVER TAKEN A BIRTH-CONTROL PILL IN MY LIFE.

I wouldn't know what to do with a rubber other than transform it into a water balloon.

I confuse the rhythm method with the Stanislavski method.

In my early twenties, responsible young woman that I was, I went to a gynecologist for an IUD. With my mom recently deceased but the damage she inflicted alive and bouncing, and as I tried to finish college even as professors ran amok, I figured anything could happen. Better safe than shattered.

When the male gynecologist looked at my chart and saw that I was a single woman seeking birth control, his eyes narrowed and his folksy demeanor hardened to stone. This was his professional persona, I told myself, and nothing more. Frightened but determined and a wee bit plucky, I placed my bare feet in the cold stirrups and thought, *Giddy-up*.

Within seconds, the man jammed a speculum into me with such force that I screamed. Upon the IUD's insertion, my uterus convulsed in a wild, prolonged rhumba. As the pain climbed to twenty on a one-to-ten scale, he snapped, "There," whipped off his latex gloves, and tossed them in the trash. "Get dressed. Go home."

In the bathroom, while trying to change out of the cotton exam gown, I collapsed and called for help. The nurse cracked open the door, glanced in, told the doctor, "She's curled up on the floor, groaning like a little pig," and sauntered away.

Spiraled in a tight nautilus on the cold tile, I looked to the heavens for help. On the wall hung a poster depicting God's hand reaching down through the clouds to touch a pregnant woman's naked belly. Perhaps me lying on a disinfected floor below a rendering of the Almighty blessing a woman with child was God's wrath made manifest. Perhaps my mother's constant admonition that I was no damned good was simply her way of practicing honesty.

Eventually, my uterus still in revolt, I uncurled, pulled myself up, dressed, and stumbled out. As I passed the front desk, the staff glanced away. Mine was a different walk of shame.

THE IUD CAUSED ME TO BLEED SO PROFUSELY THAT FOR ONE week each month I could not leave my apartment. A different doctor ripped it out six months later, but to this day questions linger.

Is my childlessness luck or tragedy? Voodoo or science? Chaos or rational consequence?

And then the bitter pill: Did that man mark me?

ON THANKSGIVING MORNING 2018, WITH BLOOD SWIRLING in the bowl and staining the toilet paper, I know something is terribly wrong. Scared, I push away my reticence to seek medical help. I call the hospital and, despite my broken Spanish, get an appointment for the following day.

My husband and I spend the next twenty-four hours creating plausible excuses (I never tell him about various other anomalies that for the past two months I have hoped I was imagining): new skin cream upped my estrogen levels; the stationary bike is a bitch on the ol' cootchy; it's just one of those things that doesn't amount to a hill of beans. *No worries. I'm gonna live forever.*

DOCTORA GARCIA IS TINY—MAYBE EIGHTY POUNDS—HER VOICE the timbre of Minnie Mouse's, but she dives into the hidden nether regions of my anatomy with the zeal of a WWE wrestler. She discovers a polyp on my cervix and proceeds to excise it on the spot—no anesthesia, no sedative, just—in an impossibly high octave—*Hang in there.*

For the rest of the day, I'm trapped in a hailstorm of tests, questions, results. In Mexico, one doesn't wait for weeks and months for prognostications and surgeries. They are delivered pronto. In this *tormenta*, this storm, I keep expecting good news because one of my great failings as a human being is my insistence on optimism. Each time a white sheet of paper with my future on it is passed my way, I expect Doctora Garcia to gaze at me with her steady black eyes and say, *It's nothing. Just one of those things. Go home. You're A-OK, amiga.*

But instead, by test number six, my husband and I are close to the unspeakable: *cancer.* My uterus is twelve times thicker than it should be. Marring the surface of an organ I never used for its intended purpose are islets of atypical cells. The *tranquilo*, whose job it is to roam the hospital and make conversation with patients and their families to ensure universal calm, spends a lot of time with me. His name is Casanova, and he reminds me of a Mexican Mr. Rogers—kind, peaceful, with a wry sense of humor. Amid aimless chitchat about his children, my dogs, the crazy things gringos do, Yucatán's mind-boggling heat, I detect concern. My husband detects it, too. That's why he clamps his arm around my shoulders—to hang on to me, to never let me slip away, to make sure I keep at it: tests, tests, tests. I cannot tell him that what I want more than anything is to float out of the hospital's white walls and white noise and white glare back to my hammock under the ceiba tree, where disease and heartache do not exist.

IN THE DAYS LEADING UP TO MY SURGERY, I SPEND MANY more hours—worried mornings, frantic afternoons—at the hospital and am soon on a first-name basis with everyone from receptionists to housekeepers to doctors. They call me by my middle name, Anita, because my proper name, Constance, does not roll off their tongues with ease.

I love being addressed as Anita and am grateful, after a lifetime regretting it, that the nurse when I was born wrote down my name incorrectly: Anita instead of Oneida. No one pronounces Oneida (O-need-a) with certainty, and I am not one to readily correct mispronunciations. As with most things, I suffer silently, which might be what got me into this mess: negative thinking amid impotent optimism.

In the hospital's antiseptic hallways, the incessant whine of jackhammers muffling whispered conversations and ringing phones, I grab random shards: the unexpected joy of being Anita, Casanova teasing that soon he will create a room just for me, the internist declaring me in excellent health other than my uterine turmoil, saying *Hello* and *Good-bye* and *Nice to see you* and *Thank you* and *Have a good day* in Spanish to the receptionists; Doctora Garcia bear-hugging me, which is quite a feat given her size, and kissing my cheek as I leave; her ordering me, *Don't worry!*

But not worrying is impossible. Every chance I get, I pee and examine, looking for certainty, something that signals without equivocation *You are going to live* or *You are going to die.* I find only the hieroglyphics that the human body is so good at emitting, tea leaves composed of blood and urine and sloughed-off cells. *If I am going to die,* I think, *I have to know soon because I have so much left to* do. And this: *You cannot die yet. You must still solve the riddle of your mad mother's sadness lest your life be in vain.*

I walk into the living room and announce to my husband, who is treating his fear with vodka and mango juice and endless episodes of *American Pickers*, "I have cancer. I'm dying."

"You do not have cancer."

That's what I'm looking for: a declarative sentence that will solve at least one mystery. I sit down, grab the remote. *I do not have cancer.*

These games I play are deadly serious. I take no chances, not even with insects. Here, on this tropical island, tiny heart-shaped flies loll away their brief lives in my bathroom. The reason for their apparent affection for my bathroom is easily solved via an Internet search for "heart-shaped flies." According to Wikipedia, drain-fly larvae thrive unseen in my sink's plumbing. Adult drain flies, if left to their own devices, have a life span of approximately twenty days. Once winged, they're slow movers and, thus, easy pickings. Adjusted lifespan when I'm in the room? A few hours. Murder is a breeze. A paper towel and a firm palm. No guts. No blood. No bone. Only a smudge of black powder, as if the flies barely ever existed, as if time did not pulse between the spaces of that old utterance *ashes to ashes.*

But during my presurgery days, when I feel my mortality grow from shadow to substance, I allow them to live out their days undisturbed. No more paper towels casting the shadow of death. *Kill one more fly and you die.*

I worry, though, about the flies getting out of hand. Perhaps drain flies carry disease. Perhaps I'll die not from cancer but from drain fly–itis. Because my husband's mortality remains a gauzy spiral of smoke in the far-distant future, I ask him to do the deed. I know, karma-wise, that asking for a surrogate killer is iffy, but I'm desperate.

Okay, he responds, without asking why. But he never lifts a finger. Not a single fly dies by his hand. And I don't ask again. Perhaps he, too, is taking no chances. As a result, my bathroom becomes a twenty-day-cycle flytopia.

One afternoon after yet another hospital visit, on our way to lunch, we pass the small Catholic cathedral in Centro. I shoot inside—not a priest in sight—and in the shadows and heat, lacking a to-go cup, I douse myself with copious handfuls of holy water. I step back into the bright Cozumelean sunlight looking like a deranged contestant in an over-fifty wet-T-shirt contest.

"What are you doing?" my husband asks, fear and bemusement etching his southern Indiana drawl.

"Insurance," I mutter, wading into a herd of tourists so pitiful they wear balloon hats shaped like wiener dogs and pirate ships. Why they embarrass themselves so willingly is another mystery I'll never solve.

TRUTH: ALL THREE OF MY MOTHER'S CHILDREN BEAR WOUNDS of her violence, scars of her psychological war games. Our bodies, spirits, behaviors occasionally betray the secrets we keep for her as we try in vain to become children she approves of, children she loves. We are, deep into adulthood, children who will do anything to protect her, even in the face of death, from a reckoning. Our goal our entire lives has been to make sure she never pays for her sins.

Maybe that's why I'm childless. I cannot risk the possibility that the reckoning—the paying for sins not our own—might fall to them.

ONE OF MY EARLIEST MEMORIES IS OF MY MOTHER TELLING ME my brother had been dishonorably discharged from the army, that he was a coward who so feared military service that he pretended, while in basic training, to be a homosexual. She repeated this story until the day she died, trotting it out at Thanksgiving and Christmas and when neighbors stopped by for coffee cake and a smoke.

THERE WILL COME A TIME, A FUTURE POINT, POSTSURGERY, when I am aflame with multiple infections; when I am adrift in an obstinate, pelagic swath of unfathomable bad luck; when I will pray for healing to a god I'm not sure exists. This is when I will get a phone call informing me my brother is dead. My doctors will insist I am too ill to fly to Houston for his funeral. Multiple layers of grief and guilt will assail me.

I will hopscotch from my sickbed to the hospital and back again, and in the midst of my journeys my sister will phone, her voice cracking under the weight of heaving tears that buckle, crack, bellow. Our niece, she will explain, contacted Veterans Affairs to see whether they could help cover the cost of burying her father, who always bragged about his military service while my sister, mother, and I winced at his lies. My heart, amid my fevers, will seize. *Oh, my God, she knows the truth. Her father the coward! How can we make this right? How can we soften the blow?*

The VA, my sister will warble between sobs, told my niece it was obliged to offer various means of support, including funds to help bury her father, our brother, who served his country honorably, with distinction, for four years. He will receive a military funeral at the National Cemetery in Houston.

I, too, will cry, although tears will do little to help my brain comprehend cruelty and its echo. What mother spreads lies, especially such a despicable one, about her son? Why did she instill in us shame about our brother over a cowardice that, I will learn too late, never existed?

My sister and I will wonder if our brother knew about the lie. Did she spit it out in one of her rages? Did it curl back toward him through the grapevine? Did he believe the lie despite the truth because she insisted? Did he just keep going, a wounded wild animal determined to chase the light, hoping it would bleach the pain?

For my sister and me—the only two left standing—our pain will be the color of a cardinal's wing, slicing open old wounds, thick scars, stashed memories, causing us to once again recoil from shadows, belts, hairbrushes, bruises, open palms, closed fists, lakes, sunlight at a certain angle, orange trees, cockroaches, sewing machines, voices accusatory and violent and dripping with lies— all those things from our pasts that we will never be able to set on a shelf, look at dispassionately, and muse, *You know, it wasn't so bad.*

Because here's the God's honest truth: it was far worse than we ever owned up to.

WHICH LEADS TO ANOTHER MYSTERY: HOW DAMAGED ARE we? What will it take—one more truth from the past revealed— for either of us to turn that butter knife into a razor blade, our food into secret trash-can detritus, that fine day into a lightless cave?

I cannot escape what she did to me or the hollow despair I feel if I think too long about my solitude, how being childless ensures various forms of exile. Which was maybe what she was after all along: if she was mean enough, we would flee.

I HOLD A GLASS OF WATER IN ONE HAND, A PILL IN THE OTHER that will cause my uterus to dilate and cramp. The surgery is one day away. "I think we should make up fantasy children so that when people ask, we can lie."

"Why?" My husband doesn't take his eyes off his laptop.

"Because it's the first thing people want to know. Both Mexicans and gringos. And answering always makes me feel bad."

"How many do you want?" My husband glances up, unaware I have it all worked out, even details so fine they are like flagella on my brain.

"Two. A boy and a girl. They're twins. Lydia is a research scientist working on cures for childhood diseases. Jack is a champion surfer living in Hawaii."

"Really?"

I nod. "Yep." I sip my water, set it and the pill on the side table. "The kids don't visit often because they're so busy. But that doesn't mean we're not a close family. We Skype every Sunday morning. Rain or shine."

GINORMOUS, I BARELY FIT IN THIS ICEBERG OF A BRIGHTLY LIT operating room.

My medical team scurries and giggles and pushes Jurassic-sized pieces of equipment from the walls to my cadaver table, a table I am far too big for. The nurses, the techs, everyone: they are so tiny, tinier even than Doctora Garcia. Somehow—on the wings of some strange sedative, perhaps—I find myself no longer on a Caribbean island but in Jonathan Swift's Lilliput, a giant at the mercy of diminutive, green-scrub-attired Lilliputians.

Fear is the only thing that comes close to matching my monstrous size. Maybe the sedative is producing a paradoxical effect and before long I will howl for release, as if I am a hysterical Gulliver staked to the ground by tight lengths of crisscrossed rope.

The anesthesiologist, wielding a syringe the size of my *Hindenburg* thigh, explains that he needs to give me a spinal block, that it's going to hurt, that I have to curl into a ball so he can safely inject the needle, whose tip grazes the ceiling. *He's going to paralyze me. I will never walk again. Or breathe on my own again.* I do as I'm told.

"No, no. I need you in a tight ball. Tight! Tight! When I say don't move, that's it, not a muscle."

I don't know what to do with these directions. How can I roll into the proper position if I'm not allowed to move? Lucky for me, half the village of Lilliput rushes to my aid. I weigh a thousand tons, and my bum the size of Jupiter eclipses most of the room, but none of the Lilliputians seem deterred. Though they don't say it, I hear them. *One, two, three, push!* Over I go. The redwood log that is me is now perched on the edge of the cadaver table. I eye the descent. It is a long, long way down.

Despite the Lilliputians' success in moving the redwood log to the precipice, the anesthesiologist is grumbly and furtive and about to lose whatever patience he was born with. Evidently, in my inflated state, I'm incapable of turning my body into a ball.

I'm about to cry, "I can't do this. Please, let me go home!" when someone caresses my forehead and then my cheek with hands that are kind, gentle, assured, and nearly as big as Gulliver's. "Like this, dear, make like you are a shrimp." And the man to whom the hands belong softly laughs as he cradles me.

"He is your surgeon, Anita," Doctora Garcia squeaks.

"You are going to be fine," the surgeon says in a voice that inspires confidence in all of Lilliput, which eases my mind a tad because I could tell they were beginning to lose faith in me. "Come on, Anita, curl up like a little shrimp in the sea."

With a few expert gestures, as if I am human origami, he folds my body in on itself. My muscles and ligaments and skeleton respond fluidly and without my permission. Given the circumstances, I'm okay with that.

"What a good little shrimp!" He laughs again—this guy personifies gusto—and holds me tight, keeping steady my shrimp pose while the anesthesiologist injects the skyscraper-sized needle into either side of my endless Swiss cheese spine so many times I lose count.

It all gets weirder from here. Flat on my back, my left leg the size of a 747 hangs in the air at an agonizing, inhuman angle, as if its wing has broken free of its socket. Surely they do not expect my leg to dangle like that, suspended in pain, throughout the surgery. "Doctora Garcia! My leg! It's killing me. Please, put it down."

She can barely see over my cadaver table, but I see her. She is all business. No nonsense. The sheriff of Lilliput. "Your leg is not in the air. Both of your legs are straight and on the table." She does not smile. She does not give away any concern that her Gulliver has gone mad.

"Oh," I say, and as part of trying to trick myself into believing her, I begin a silent mantra. *You must calm down. You must get hold of yourself. You must calm down. You must get hold of yourself. Your legs are on the table.*

The tubed oxygen they position at my nose simultaneously burns and tickles. My diaphragm is partially immobilized by the spinal block, so I can't sigh, I can't take a deep breath, I can't cough. I try to fight off the drowning sensation, summoning strength I didn't know I possessed in order not to scream, "Help! I'm suffocating!" Although I do—in a desperate attempt to stay alive—wail, "Doctora, my heart is beating too fast."

"No, it's not," she squeaks, and the only thing that comforts me is that she seems very certain. In fact, she has taken on the air of a drill sergeant who has just about had her fill of my shenanigans.

Steady your mind. Shallow breaths. The Lilliputians are very good at medicine. And also *This is all a big, big mistake. I do not know what the surgeon is doing. Removing my womb? Dissecting my womb? Tossing it high in the air like a pizza pie?*

I do not exist from my rib cage to my toes. I'm all neck and head, which means the fact that I have no power over what they are doing to me from the neck down seems less important than it once did.

And time? Nothing more than a trickster. So I leave it behind, drifting to places where gravity is an outmoded notion clung to by people who don't know how to think.

Lilliputians caress me—head, hand, shoulders. I am grateful for their gentle laying on of warm palms, for I am very, very cold. They whisper into my ear, "How are you doing, Anita?" Sometimes people yell and I'm not sure if they are yelling at me or at one another, so I drift further and further into a soft, feathering darkness.

Every time I float into full immersion, someone wakes me. I am at their mercy. *Anita! Anita!* My womb is the star, and the Lilliputians are damned and determined that I shall be awake for its curtain call. My hidden planet, this determiner of my destiny, this source of things unknown, I realize, is displayed for all of Lilliput to see. Monday at the Movies. But I do not look. I do not want to know. Blood and organs and the surgeon's tools are not a trinity I can presently cope with. *Why, womb, hast thou forsaken me?* A howling from far shores.

I float in and I float out of amniotic waters of my own making. A desire morphs into wishful thinking: I will be rebirthed not as Gulliver the Trapped or Connie the Detested but as Anita the Beloved, a woman free of childhood baggage and whose two grown, fine children are extra special because they are twins. The Scientist and The Surfer.

This wishful thinking ferries me deeper into my cold, strange amniotic tide. I float along, unaware of anything the Lilliputians are doing. I like the not knowing, the ignorance that resembles the sweetest sleep.

But peace is not my destiny.

"Anita! Look! Look!" The surgeon's booming voice cuts through the darkness, scattering feathers and water everywhere. With one quick tug, he pulls me from the abyss. "Anita! Open your eyes!"

My lids slide open.

"You have given birth to a niño!"

Though I see this world through a mist, I make out his giant hand, hovering inches above my face. He holds an immense gray mass (my memory says it's gray, but this is an uncertain moment), and from the grotesque sphere trail many tails. I shut my eyes against the evil.

"Your son, Anita! You have given birth to an ugly son!" and all the Lilliputians laugh.

I watch from the ceiling as the surgeon slips the tumor and its trailing polyps into a clear jar. Someone writes my name on it. *Constance*. I mumble a heartless rosary, and my words fall like black rain upon the village. *Es un niño. Es un niño. ¡Qué mala suerte tengo!*

I do not realize tears have escaped the corners of my eyes and are meandering down my cold cheeks until one of the sweet, sweet Lilliputians wipes them from my face, whispering, "Everything is okay, Anita. You're doing good."

And the surgeon, perhaps catching on to my sadness, bellows, "Anita, look! Isn't she beautiful!" The Lilliputian guides my face to the right and points to a large monitor. I am not allowed to look away. I blink against the mist, and my heart gasps. There, blooming across the screen, a moon—golden and bronze—glows.

Why the moon? Why now?

"That, Anita, is your uterus. No more tumors. No more polyps. As gorgeous as the sun." The surgeon's voice quivers with pride, with notions that this is *his* uterus. *He* made it beautiful again.

I gaze at that golden planet, that distant celestial body radiating a Buddha's strength inside me, its curvature suggesting galaxies neither I nor Gulliver nor my surgeon will ever see. And then I think about my mother and how, for her own good reasons, she never wanted me. And how I will never make sense of her random cruelty. And how her children can attach labels all we want—bipolar, schizophrenic, sociopathic, incurably broken—and none of them will erase what she did, not the names she called us or the beatings we endured or the exile she banished us to. Yet still, I love her. *Look at that golden orb, Anita, floating with perfect gravity and grace within the sacred center of your body.*

The Lilliputians are quiet now, putting me and the room back in order. My surgeon and Doctora Garcia study *mi muchacho malo* floating in its clear jar, whispering to each other with curious intensity. I gaze across the length and breadth of the operating room. Giant contraptions that held my legs aloft and others that assisted in the exploration of my insides and hunks of metal edged in plastic with functions that escape me and machines on wheels studded with keyboards and screens—it all seems prehistoric—lie strewn hither and yon, as if a great battle has taken place. A battle for what? And who is the victor? The monitor that displayed my uterus is now a black rectangle, switched off, deprived of current, wheeled into a corner.

Do not forget.

I have been to the dark side of my own moon. It glowed like quicksilver, like gold, like a vast sea illuminated by hope's infinite mysteries. I gaze once more at the irony that is *mi muchacho malo*. What evil curse or stroke of bad luck or incompetent medical care or rational decision making resulted in my womb giving birth to a gray tumor with a corona of polyp-riddled tentacles . . . instead of a rosy-cheeked child?

Remember, Anita, you never wanted me.

As they wheel me out of the operating room and into re-covery, my mortality pulses. It is this acknowledgment of death and, perhaps, its inevitability, that draws a faint outline of new thinking, of earned optimism burnished by the pain of past tra-vails: maybe all of this, every single moment, the good and the bad, is a miracle. The seas and the forests and the animals and the humans and the planets and births that give way to deaths, and deaths that give way to life. We will never solve the puzzle, the why of our being or the minutiae of our hours that tattoo the map of who we are on our souls.

The recovery-room nurse lifts my blanket—though I have returned to my normal size, I remain bone-cold—and places on the bed a hose blowing warm air. The heat flows over me like a sheet of summer water, and within seconds my body and its shaking ease.

"*Hola*, Anita. My name is Alex," the nurse says, straightening the blanket over my feet that do not yet exist.

"*Hola*, Alex. *Gracias*." I watch as he takes my vitals. He records them with grim efficiency, not because there is a problem or be-cause he doesn't care but because he is doing a good and thor-ough job. I am, after all, his charge for the next several hours.

"Alex?"

"Yes, Anita?"

I reach toward my legs, which also do not yet exist. I don't know how long it will be before the anesthesia ebbs and they return. "When I get out of here, after I've healed up? I'm going to live. I mean really, really live."

"What will you do?"

I pause, thinking about precisely that.

"Dance?"

"Yes."

"Karaoke?"

"Yes."

"Take lovers?"

I blush.

"Travel the world? Maybe see Mars? Venus?"

I giggle and close my eyes, conjuring the image of my freshly razored uterus. There is nothing bad there. Nothing sad or shameful. Only me, hovering like Buddha above a lotus blossom, Buddha accepting of the fact that many of the mysteries of life are not only not fatal but are destined to remain beyond the powers of mortal deduction. I look at Alex, who is looking at me, waiting for an answer. Behind him, over his left shoulder, awash in that lovely, golden uterine light, I see them, concerned and full of love. Lydia and Jack.

THE LAND OF THE MORNING CALM

(and Other Military Mysteries)

– Martin Limón –

WHEN I FIRST HOPPED OFF THE PLANE AT KIMPO AIRFIELD in June of 1968, I had heard of Korea only in reference to the war that had ended fifteen years earlier, a war that left three million people dead, an economy smashed to smithereens, and a peninsula divided into a brutal communist dictatorship in the north and an authoritarian military oligarchy in the south. But despite this history of conflict and suffering, I was happy to be here. I'd been in the army almost two years, and while serving stateside, I'd watched as one buddy after another had been shipped off to Vietnam. Just four months earlier, the Tet Offensive had enflamed that country, and fighting had engulfed even the capital city of Saigon. There were ten times as many GIs in Vietnam as there were in Korea, so when I received orders for an assignment at the headquarters of the Eighth US Army in Seoul, I felt as if I'd won the lottery.

But my relief was soon tempered as I faced a number of mysteries involving both the US Army and the country that my nineteen-year-old mind would, in short order, begin to struggle to unravel. The first mystery was how to survive the unexpectedly high crime rate. Most of it GI-on-Korean crime. Some of it GI-on-GI crime. Much of it brutal. Occasionally deadly.

Korea claims a proud five-thousand-year history with language, art, and culture that not only have evolved independently of the West but also have largely differentiated themselves from its Far Eastern neighbors. Into this ancient stew, for some mysterious reason, the US Army saw fit to drop a gaggle of knucklehead teenaged GIs (me included) without any preparation, cultural training, or apparent forethought. Mayhem, as you might imagine, ensued.

But if the army is good at anything, it is good at counting beans. The chaos of the clash of cultures between the GIs and the Koreans was monitored daily by the brass via the military police blotter report. I know because I was one of the minions who did the monitoring. Near American military bases, of which we had over fifty scattered around the country, crime was rampant. Simple larceny, such as refusing to pay a Korean cab driver or, worse, beating him up and robbing him of a hard day's receipts, was common. Domestic abuse, also common, mainly targeting the uneducated and economically exploited young Korean women who made their livings in the nightclubs and bars and brothels that sprang up like poisonous mushrooms around the US compounds. Rape was endemic, happening not only to the prostitutes the GIs called *business girls* but occasionally to innocent farm women in rural areas where military units were performing war games. Fights and even muggings among the GIs themselves occurred more often than the generals wanted to admit, resulting in wounds and stitches and broken bones and lost time in the performance of soldierly duties.

A friend of mine once got into a fight with a Turkish soldier. Turkey had a very small contingent in Seoul as part of the UN Honor Guard. My friend was from Chicago and a pretty tough guy, and he kept reaching into his back pocket, threatening to pull out the switchblade he always carried. The Turks were known to also carry knives, and supposedly honor required, whenever they pulled their knife, that blood be drawn. Fortunately, the MPs arrived in time to break things up before someone's spleen was excised.

But sometimes things were worse. Sometimes there was murder.

One case in the late 1960s that made international news involved a GI accused of strangling a Korean bar girl. Pubic hair and other forensic evidence found in her bed convinced Korean authorities that a Caucasian male had perpetrated the crime. But in those pre-DNA-analysis days, they couldn't be sure of the identity, and according to eyewitnesses, the young lady had been known to entertain more than one American GI. Still, the most likely suspect was identified. Routinely, Korean authorities turned miscreant GIs over to the US Army for trial by court-martial on an American base. But in this case, public outrage demanded that the South Korean government try the American in a South Korean courtroom. Even though the evidence was thin, and many Americans thought the GI was innocent, the mystery had to be solved in order to assuage public opinion. After a highly publicized trial, the GI was convicted of first-degree murder.

Now, the first question was, what would the Koreans do about this outrage? The South Korean government, beholden in those days to US military support against the tangible threat of another devastating attack by the communist North Koreans, didn't really want to punish him as any regular criminal would be punished—by hanging by the neck until dead. The resulting publicity would mitigate against good US-Korean relations. The second question was, What American mom or dad would want to send their son to defend a faraway Asian country if the young soldier was subject to being convicted of a murder that many contended he didn't commit and then being hanged for it?

Quite a conundrum. But the South Korean government found a way out of the dilemma. They compromised. When the sentence was passed down, it was for a mere four years in jail. Four years for a crime that even in America in those days might've resulted in his being shoved inside a gas chamber to watch potassium cyanide pellets sizzle and then dissolve in a vat of sulfuric acid. The last thing he'd ever see.

Besides crime and punishment, another mystery that I had to deal with was figuring out what was seen as good for the Eighth Army versus what was seen as good for the rest of creation.

The Eighth US Army was the overall command that ruled the US military in Korea. It was insular; it did things its way. Often, it operated on the basis of what was called an "Eighth Army

Supplement to the Army Regulation." In other words, once I arrived in Korea, I was told to forget everything I'd learned previously. We did things here in Korea our way, not the regular army way. Which is why GIs often referred to the Eighth Army as the Eighth Imperial Army, harking back to the Japanese Imperial Army, which held sway on the Korean Peninsula from 1910 until the surrender at the end of World War II in 1945.

The most glaring example of a restriction that seemed to make no sense was ration control. In the United States, we live in a society drenched in capitalism. Buy, buy, buy is the constant refrain we hear from birth to death. So I was disoriented when I landed in Korea and was told that I couldn't buy things. Or not many things, anyway. In the PX, which is like a small department store, and the commissary, which is like a small grocery store, the honchos of the Eighth Army had imposed something called "ration control." A young, single serviceman such as myself was allowed to purchase only ninety dollars in goods—total—for an entire month, from the PX and the commissary combined. Also, certain items such as TVs, stereo sets, and other electronics were called "controlled items," and we had to prove that we still owned them when we left the country. The ostensible reason for these restrictions was to stanch the flow into Korea of duty-free—and tax-free—American-made goods. That way, fledgling Korean industries would have a chance to compete and grow. Otherwise, GIs would sell everything they purchased on the black market to the growing Korean consumer base, and those start-up companies would fail under the pressure of unfair competition. These rules were given the weight of law and strictly enforced, and miscreants could find themselves punished under the Uniform Code of Military Justice.

I once bought a girl a tape recorder. Small, made of plastic, it was about as cheap a model as one could imagine. When we broke up, I lost sleep at night wondering how I would explain that I no longer owned it. In the end, I wasn't punished, but only because I was leaving the country, and the GI clerk who was processing my paperwork glanced around, saw that no one was watching, and waved me on impatiently.

Another mysterious rule was even more powerful, unwritten but ironclad: never embarrass the command. If you couldn't figure out what would make the Eighth Army commander look good and what would make him look bad, you'd better put your brain in gear because if you embarrassed the brass, *your ass was grass*, as we used to crudely say.

When something went wrong, especially something as embarrassing as GI-on-Korean crime, the edict was *deny, deny, deny*. Until, of course, you were forced to admit it. I was often told that GIs were guests in Korea and therefore ambassadors for our country. These admonishments lasted all of about ten seconds once we raucous American soldiers were outside the military gate, parading down the streets toward the bars and nightclubs and red-light districts, free at last on an overnight pass.

But when we did get caught doing something wrong, the Eighth Army did its best to keep it quiet. All crime reports, known as serious incident reports by the MPs, were for official use only. This meant that they were kept on base and distributed on a need-to-know basis, and the information they contained was absolutely denied to civilians or outsiders of any kind. Especially reporters. Although no American civilian reporters ever poked around, as far as I could tell.

The US military was, and still is, a secret society, keeping its nefarious skeletons hidden in safes within vaults within crypts. Good luck with unraveling its mysteries or exposing its peccadillos to the light of day. Many have tried. Many have failed. Young GIs, if they knew what was good for them, left these mysteries unsolved and even unspoken. Like docents tiptoeing around the holy of holies, they whispered and pressed forefingers to their lips.

In addition to dealing with the often-unreasonable demands of the US Army, another thing I soon started to notice was the magnificent Asian world swirling around me. I wasn't in Kansas anymore, or even in Southern California, for that matter.

Probably the first thing I noticed was the food.

Korean food, of course, to my uneducated eyes, was a mystery beyond fathoming. It smelled bad, it was composed largely of odd-looking vegetables in some sort of red sauce, and more often than not it reeked of garlic and fish. What I didn't know then was that Korean vegetables actually belonged to different species from the cabbage and radish and greens that I'd seen in the States. Namely, Napa cabbage, Korean radish, and Asian turnips, all shaped oddly and looking quite different from what was available on stateside produce stands. These ingredients were chopped up and soaked in brine, along with green onions, salted fermented shrimp, red peppers, and, of course, garlic, along with other ingredients, to make a series of dishes known as kimchi. The advantage of preparing food this way was that it could be preserved without refrigeration, although setting the earthen pots outside during the winter made it last even longer. Kimchi, plus roasted mackerel, say, with steamed rice and a bowl of hot bean-sprout soup, made for a delicious, and nutritious, meal. But at first, to a dummy like me, it looked unappetizing and even dangerous. Keep in mind that in those days, people weren't "foodies." Exotic foreign dishes didn't appear on television. They were not only eschewed but frowned upon. I often heard the refrain, "I'm a meat-and-potatoes man." So, before I could enjoy a Korean repast, I had to solve the mystery of what in the heck it was. And how in the heck to eat it.

First, I sat down at a low table on a flat cushion. Then I picked up the metal spoon. Or it seemed like a spoon. It had a long stem and a round business end that was almost flat. I wondered how much broth it could hold. Not much, I soon discovered, but it was great for shoveling rice. And then the chopsticks. After being shown how to hold them, I tried but soon gave up. Still, one can do pretty well at a Korean table by just using them as spears. Soon I was jabbing the hot slices of bulgogi, marinated and thinly sliced flank steak, into my mouth. Followed by a spoonful of glutinous rice topped by a chunk of kkakdugi, diced turnip pickled in spicy brine. To my delight, I discovered that it was delicious. Thus encouraged, within a few weeks, I was using my chopsticks and spoon with something resembling alacrity.

Another mystery was the clothing.

As I rode in jeeps and tanks and trucks throughout the Korean countryside, I'd often see old men squatting under the shade of an old oak tree playing a game of *baduk*, Japanese Go, or *janggi*, Korean chess. They wore white cotton outfits of loose pantaloons and vests and more often than not carried gnarled wooden walking sticks and long-stemmed pipes with small bowls. But strangest of all was their headgear. Stovepipe hats with flat, round brims made of some sort of black, mostly transparent woven material. I came to find that the material was horsehair and that when a Korean gentleman retired, he cast aside his Western suit and tie and spent the rest of his life wearing the much more comfortable Korean traditional garb of a *hal-abeoji*. A grandfather. GIs sometimes put on this type of clothing and took photos of themselves as a sort of weak joke. The gnarled wooden walking stick was even more widely adopted. American soldiers called it a "short-timer's stick," mainly because the only guys who owned them had been in Korea for a while and routinely carved notches on the stick to indicate how long they'd been in country and thereby calculate how long they had left until they returned stateside.

On holidays and other special occasions, young Korean women often wore a *hanbok*, a brightly colored dress with a high-waisted full skirt that wrapped tightly across their breasts and flowed all the way to their ankles. This was paired with a short tunic with loose-fitting sleeves that reached to their wrists—not exactly form fitting. I came to find out that the sleeves had inside pockets for handkerchiefs and combs and other items and that beneath the skirt, the women often wore thick long johns, helping them cope with the frigid Korean winters.

Not exactly the bikinis I was used to.

On their feet were linen booties stuffed with cotton, most often covered by rubber slippers with an upturned toe. Excellent for making one's way across ice-covered streets.

Another thing that mystified me was the problem of language. The vast majority of GIs never made the slightest effort to learn Korean. The few words and phrases they picked up through constant repetition were barroom slang. Words such as irriwa, "come here," and karra chogi, "get outta here." Not exactly the king's Korean. Even in the carpeted halls of Eighth Army headquarters, the honchos didn't worry about the institutional lack of linguistic skill. They had plenty of educated Koreans working for them, some of whom spoke English as well as, or even better than, most GIs. That was good enough for the brass. After all, the prevailing attitude was that every Korean actually spoke English. When they protested that they didn't understand, they were just being obtuse. Faking it. "I know he speaks English," people would say to me, when I knew he didn't.

A very few of us actually did study the Korean language. There was ample opportunity. Night classes on base, English-Korean dictionaries sold in local bookstores, and plenty of off-duty time to wander a few yards from base and speak to locals using the new, halting words and phrases I had so painstakingly mastered. Once I could read the signs, once I could understand the shouted banter, once I could convince someone to stop and look me in the eye and explain something, such as directions or a local custom or the reason for a dispute, it was as if the world opened up. Vision in the land of the blind. Mystery solved.

But most GIs—from privates all the way up to generals—never bothered.

"What are you going to do with it?" people asked me when they saw me studying.

"Talk," I replied.

Korean and English developed on opposite sides of the earth. Linguists claim that the Korean language has only one rough counterpart, Japanese, which has a similar grammatical structure. However, the vocabulary is very different, and it is thought that the two languages diverged far back in prehistory. Contrary to popular belief, Korean has little similarity to Chinese. However, because of the long-standing influence of the Central Kingdom, Koreans have adopted many Chinese words and plugged them into their language, in a way very similar to how Greek and Latin have been incorporated into English.

Another thing that threw my adolescent mind for a loop was the unusual grammatical structure of the Korean language. Instead of the subject-verb-object sentence structure that I had grown up with, the Koreans are allowed to shuffle their subject or object around at the beginning of the sentence but are required to save the verb for last. If this didn't confuse me enough, I soon discovered that the verb is followed by an indicator word that shows the relative social status of the person speaking and the person being spoken to.

This is probably the greatest mystery of the Korean language, and it can be extremely confusing for foreigners. Personal relationships in Korea are hierarchical and strictly defined, based on the Confucian structure of obedience owed by the inferior to his or her social superior. It has been said that if you're not native born, you will never fully master the complex mystery of Korean social interactions, which meant any American GI who endeavored to study the language would spend virtually his entire time with his foot stuck firmly in his mouth.

The good news is that the Koreans forgive you. You're a foreigner, and they don't really expect you to get it. Sometimes, even they don't get it.

Another mystery we GIs had to deal with, and maybe the one that caused the most grief, was love. Early on, during our in-processing, a veteran NCO told us, "If you're going to fall in love, you'd better do it quick." What he was referring to was the paperwork required to seek permission to marry a Korean woman. It could take eight to ten months, and with only a twelve-month tour in country, that didn't leave much time. The reason for the extensive paperwork was twofold. First, the US Army wanted to make sure that we weren't marrying a spy, that our level of access to government secrets wasn't so high that marriage to a foreign national might lower or even eliminate our security clearance, and that we and the potential bride were healthy and had been fully counseled on the difficulties of international marriage by both our unit commander and the post chaplain. Meanwhile, the South Korean government wanted to make sure that we weren't marrying either a criminal or, worse, a communist. Also, they wanted to brief the potential bride on the dangers of living abroad and the difficulty of assimilation into American culture and to caution her against falling into the clutches of manipulative North Korean intelligence agents. The real reason for the runaround, of course, was to stall in the hope that the GI would change his mind and not take a woman from an ancient Asian culture back to the American heartland. It is my belief that the brass wanted to keep the statistics on GI-foreign marriage down so it didn't look as if the Eighth Army was running a dating service, something of which Congress, and your hometown Chamber of Commerce, might disapprove.

The final mystery for me was how to handle leaving. In the few short months that I'd been in Korea, I'd learned much and discovered a world completely different from the one I'd left in Southern California. A world not of year-round sunshine and endless freeways and smog thick enough to cramp young lungs but of thatched-roof farmhouses and earthen pots lining brick walls and families in wooden carts being pulled by snorting oxen and green summer rice fields and white cranes flapping angled wings into the sky. And I'd met people who saw the world very differently than I did. People who knew how precious existence was because they knew too many people who'd lost their existence in the war that had so recently ended. They knew how poignant the four seasons were: summer fading into fall, fall giving way to winter, winter exploding into spring. And how beautiful the distant hills and how gentle the morning mist and how life-giving the *danbi*, the sweet rain, when it falls like a slowly slackening curtain of beads.

How appropriate that the last dynasty of Korea, the one that ended at the beginning of the twentieth century, was named Chosun, the Land of the Morning Calm. It was bittersweet for this young man to have my eyes opened to a new way of life and then, so suddenly and too quickly, be forced to leave. Slapped wide awake from a fleeting dream.

THE CLAY THAT WE SHAPE

– William Kent Krueger –

"WE DON'T RECEIVE WISDOM," PROUST FAMOUSLY OB-served. "We must discover it for ourselves after a journey that no one can take for us or spare us." Which is a truth every writer, at some point, comes to understand.

When I was a child, if someone asked me a simple question, I never gave them a simple answer. What poured from my lips was always some intricate construct of pure imagination that had nothing to do with the truth. I was a notorious liar, and, to a degree, I still am. For most of my life, the why of this questionable behavior has been a mystery to me. But a few years ago, I wrote a novel that changed everything, that took me on the journey Proust so wisely observed no one can spare us, and that helped me see the truth behind the lies I'd been telling myself and others all my life.

When I was six years old, my mother was admitted for the first time—but not the last—to a mental institution as an inpatient. I didn't understand everything about her condition then, and probably still do not, but what I knew was that my mother had been suffering for a long time. I still remember the vacant look in her eyes, how she often stared for extended periods at nothing, and how, when she spoke, I sometimes couldn't make heads or tails of her meaning. I remember my father rushing her to the hospital once with a bloody towel wrapped around her wrist. I remember the long drive from our home in Texas to Wyoming so that my siblings and I could stay with our grandparents while my mother received treatment at the Wyoming State Hospital in Cheyenne. My father returned alone to Texas to continue earning a living, and I spent the next several months dreaming of his return. One of the most poignant memories I have of that time is how, when he finally came to retrieve us, despite all the happily-ever-after scenarios I'd imagined, and in which he'd played a central part, I didn't recognize him at all.

My mother was an extraordinary woman in many ways. She had ebony hair and penetrating blue eyes, and even as a child I understood that she was a beauty. Her voice was a clear, lovely soprano, and her hands could work magic on a piano keyboard. She'd graduated from Drake University in Des Moines, Iowa, with a dual major—music and drama. My father often remarked that he'd fallen in love with her the moment he'd laid eyes on her, and how, when she was on stage in the many theater productions she starred in at Drake, she was a magnet for the eyes of the audience. But my mother had another extraordinary talent, which I didn't become fully aware of or appreciate until I was much older: she was clairvoyant. She knew things. When the telephone rang, she could tell you who was calling. She was aware, even at great distances, of when something was troubling someone she cared about. She grew up Protestant but was always searching for a broader explanation for the things she saw and felt that others didn't. So she dabbled in many religions and esoteric philosophies and became an adventurer in metaphysics.

She also drank. She was, I understand now, an alcoholic. And when she'd had a few drinks—she often had martinis waiting when my father came home from work—she changed. Those soft blue eyes became chips of ice, and her tongue became a cutting thing. I remember her arguments with my father, beating her fists against his chest while he stood stoic under her drunken, ineffectual pummeling. When she was like this, she was another person, someone I didn't know, a fearsome wraith, and I did my best to stay out of her way.

During my growing-up years, my mother was often emotionally distant. But she was also physically distant, admitted to mental institutions on four separate occasions. These absences were spaced several years apart and lasted from a few weeks to a few months. Her diagnosis was paranoid schizophrenia, and usually the treatment was a mixture of electroshock therapy, psychiatric counseling, and Thorazine or similar medications. Her institutionalizations were not cheap, and medical insurance didn't always cover the cost. As a result, for most of my childhood and adolescence, my parents were saddled with significant debt.

I loved my mother, but for much of my life my feelings toward her were tangled up with fear and resentment. I also had a deep, unfulfilled longing for some understanding of her inexplicable behavior and the havoc that it wreaked on my life and the lives of everyone I cared about. It wasn't until I wrote a novel called *Ordinary Grace* that I began at last to see with some clarity how her lifelong struggle with reality, and my lifelong wrestling with the truth, were two strands of the same rope.

Ordinary Grace is set in the summer of 1961 in a small town deep in the very beautiful Minnesota River Valley. It's the story of a Methodist minister whose beloved child is murdered. That's the compelling mystery component. But at heart, it's really the story of what that tragedy does to this man's faith, his family, and, ultimately, the entire fabric of the small town in which he lives. It's a first-person narrative told by the minister's son, who, from the perspective of a man now in his fifties, looks back on that momentous summer when he was thirteen years old.

In many ways, I drew on my own life to create *Ordinary Grace*. In the story, Ruth Drum, the minister's wife, is a woman who doesn't want the kind of life that's been forced on her as a result of her marriage. She's a beautiful woman with a lovely voice and a love of music. She really has no interest in being a minister's wife or in being a homemaker—she's not very good at these things—which was the role women were expected to play when I was growing up. In writing the character of Ruth Drum, I simply tapped my own memories of my mother.

For readers, stories have the potential to do much more than entertain. They instruct; they enlighten; they encourage; they inspire. For authors, the blessings are much the same. In writing *Ordinary Grace*, a story that reflected my recollections of what it was to be thirteen years old and all the emotions I felt regarding my family at that time, I came to a number of enlightening realizations that not only helped me let go of old grievances but also opened a door to understanding the *why* at the heart of my fabrications.

Here's a little story to help you understand the kind of dynamic that often existed between my mother and me as I was growing up. The summer I was eleven years old, my father moved our family to a rented farmhouse in northwestern Ohio. He'd grown up in a city, and it had always been his dream to give his children what he imagined would be the freedom of a rural existence. My brothers and sister and I loved that old farmhouse and our first taste of country living. We got to know the kids on neighboring farms and joined the local Boy Scout troop. Every day after my father left for work, we hopped on the school bus, and though we lived a good distance from our nearest neighbors, we didn't feel isolated in the least or denied any pleasures.

It was a very different experience for my mother, something I didn't understand until I wrote *Ordinary Grace*. When I began to look back more carefully on the history we shared, I saw how challenging, and ultimately destructive, that rural existence must have been for a woman like her. She was vivacious, a lover of music, of theater, of parties. And yet she spent almost every day alone in that farmhouse. She had no one to talk to, nothing to occupy her time but the household chores. What she often did was read, and she finally decided she wanted to be a writer.

On matchbooks and on the back cover of magazines in those days, an organization called The Famous Writers School advertised for students to enroll in a correspondence program operating out of New York City. Some pretty well-known names were attached to the school: Bennett Cerf, who'd founded Random House, along with Faith Baldwin, Rod Serling, Bruce Catton, and others. My mother sent away for an application and a test to see if she had the right stuff. I still remember her sitting at the kitchen table in her bathrobe, a cup of coffee at hand, along with an ashtray and a Salem cigarette from which a snake of smoke curled upward, while she worked on the test, which was a series of questions such as "Complete this sentence: Noisy as _____."

Fifty-seven years later, I can still remember my mother's response: "Noisy as a loose shutter in a storm." Which I admired then and even now think wasn't a bad response.

As I recall, she never sent the application.

Deprived of what sustains it, the spirit shrivels and eventually dies. I remember watching as the spark of life inside my mother grew fainter and fainter in that isolated farmhouse, the vacant look more and more pervasive, her talk more and more just ramblings, frightening because of their incoherence. A few days before Thanksgiving, after we'd caught the school bus, my father took my mother to a sanitarium outside Columbus for her second institutionalization.

Although my father visited her every week, sometimes several times in a week, her children didn't see her again until Christmas. She wasn't allowed to come home, but a kind couple who lived near the sanitarium and who planned to be gone during the holidays offered their house for our gathering. I still remember my fear and lingering anger as we made the long drive to Columbus to pick up my mother. Fear because my last recollections of her were so disconcerting and anger because she'd broken an important promise she'd made to me before she succumbed completely to her illness. We were alone together one afternoon in our farmhouse kitchen, when I'd caught her staring out the window at nothing but the bleak, bare fields, and she'd turned and seen me watching. She'd knelt and taken my face in her hands and said, "I love you, and I'll be better. I promise I won't hurt you again."

But she had hurt me. She'd abandoned me—abandoned us all.

When she came out to greet us for that Christmas visit, in a red dress with a white angel pinned to her lapel, the others ran to her, but not me. After she'd hugged them all, she came to me. As she had in the farmhouse kitchen, she knelt and took my face in her hands.

"I know," she said. "I know. But I'm back now. I'm really back. And I promise I won't leave you again."

I remember seeing that lovely spirit once more animating her blue eyes, and her hands so gentle as they cupped my face, and I fell in love with her all over again and believed what she told me.

But she did leave us again, another institutionalization only four years later. And another a few years after that.

So my memories of my mother have always been balled up with fear and anger and resentment, recollections of abandonment and promises unkept.

My mother had been dead several years before the story that eventually became *Ordinary Grace* began to take shape in my imagination. I'd been looking for an idea that would allow me to go back and remember a particularly poignant summer in my life, the summer I was thirteen. I wanted to use all my recollections to create the story, to write it in such a way that pieces of my own experience would help to shape its course and the tone of its telling. Without realizing it, I was embarking on a journey that would help me understand not only my mother but also myself and the reason that fabrications—stories, lies, however you want to characterize them—are an important part of who I am.

By the time I'd finished the manuscript, I felt a deep sympathy for my mother that I'd never experienced before. In immersing myself in the imagining of the story, as good storytellers must, I began to see with a more open heart the challenges she faced. I saw that the life she'd dreamed for herself as a young woman, a life she'd believed would include music and theater and an audience for her talents, had never materialized. I felt her burning resentment, which I came to believe had kept her from embracing the reality of her marriage and her family and which, I'm certain, often left her feeling terribly isolated. What a lonely existence that must have been.

But it was also a lonely existence being her child. In writing *Ordinary Grace*, as I looked back for truths that had eluded me, I began to see why this child of hers might have been prone to fabrications. When her frequent periods of emotional distance or her long hospitalizations took my mother away, I created my own realities in her absence, stories in which the world was not all chaos, where one thing led rationally to another, a world where I had some control and where, in the end, everyone had the hope of living happily ever after. Is it any wonder that I write in a genre in which mysteries are solved and what was wrong is set right? The truth, I understand now, is that stories have always been my refuge. My mother dealt with the disappointments of her life in one way. I've dealt with the disappointments of mine in another.

A good story, I believe, should be a journey, not just for the characters involved but also for the readers and, maybe most important, for the storyteller. At the end of that journey, everyone should be in a different place in their understanding of the world and of themselves. The conclusion of *Ordinary Grace* is one of my favorites in all the stories I've written because the place most of the characters have come to is one of understanding and forgiveness. I get mail every week from readers who tell me how much their journey in reading that novel has meant to them. For me, writing it was one of the most wondrous journeys of my whole life, and one that brought me at last to a place of understanding and of forgiveness.

Storytellers' best tales often rise out of their own lived experiences. Although an experience may offer only the seed of an idea, what grows from that seed can be truly extraordinary, even great. Think about Harper Lee and *To Kill a Mockingbird* or John Steinbeck and his wonderful stories of the Salinas Valley. F. Scott Fitzgerald mined both his childhood in Saint Paul and his difficult relationship with Zelda to create some of the most memorable stories in American fiction. The clay of our own existence, of our own lives, of our own thoughts and dreams, of the people we've known and the places we've lived, is the clay that as storytellers we so often use to create our offerings. They may begin as shapeless masses, but as we allow ourselves to do the hard work of remembering, and the harder work of understanding and maybe even forgiving, that formless clay takes on shape and purpose and meaning. And isn't that one of the blessings of art, that it can offer some hope of meaning in a world that too often seems filled with nothing but chaos?

ORIGINS AND DESTINATIONS

– Ausma Zehanat Khan –

ORIGINS

I WAS THIRTEEN THE FIRST TIME I SAW THE REFUGEE CAMPS on the outskirts of Peshawar, but it was a long time before I understood what the camps represented. I asked my father who the inhabitants of the camps were. He answered, "Your brothers and sisters." When I asked why they were living as refugees, he mused, "Because of lines drawn on maps that mean nothing to the people of these lands."

Children can be blithely uncaring about their parents' past, and it was only as an adult that I became eager to learn where my parents were from and why, during the course of their lives, they ventured so far from home. Because of the journeys my parents undertook, my own life has consisted of periods of stability mixed with uprootings and migrations. I've often wondered how my family's origins, and my parents' quest for new frontiers, have shaped the journeys I've taken in both my life and my writing. To answer that question, I've tried to unravel a mystery: where my family is from, where I might belong as a result—and why I feel a sense of belonging to so many different places.

My parents are ethnic Pashtuns. (Urdu-speaking Pashtuns such as my family call themselves Pathans, but the Pashto-language identifier "Pashtun" is more widely known.) They were born in northern India during a turbulent period in the subcontinent's history: its drive for independence from the British.

In 1947, the British departed from India after a period of rule that lasted nearly two hundred years and partitioned the subcontinent into India and Pakistan. Drawing these borders was accompanied by cataclysmic bloodshed that left between one and two million dead and also by mass migration on an unparalleled scale, with an estimated fifteen million people uprooted and displaced.

My parents migrated to Pakistan under the shadow of Partition. My mother came as a child, her family settling in the Punjab; my father, an adolescent, traveled alone to what is now called Khyber Pakhtunkhwa. My parents believe that somewhere in their family histories was another migration, from Afghanistan to northern India, that led to their families settling in Shahjahanpur. They suspect that their tribal roots lie in Jalalabad or Kandahar, as episodes of Pashtun migration from Afghanistan to northern India were not infrequent. But there are no family records of these journeys, no mention of when they may have taken place or in what context—as merchants or as raiders, perhaps? Beyond the names of my great-grandparents, our history is silent. What I do know is that my parents have been Indian, Pakistani, British, and Canadian, with untraceable Afghan roots. To their bones they are Pashtun Muslims. I have been Pakistani, British, Canadian, and now American, but I have kindled that flame of Pashtun Muslim identity inside me from my earliest memories, undiminished by the mystery of my family's origin.

The gap between then and now seems immense, impossible to fathom, even harder to retrace. In this process of searching to overcome it, I have written several novels that follow my family's history, excavating the lost past to better understand how it shapes my view of the world and why I write the stories I do—a mystery series in which the main character, Esa Khattak, is a Canadian Pashtun detective with a deep sense of connection to his family's roots, and a fantasy series set along the Silk Road, recalling the lost glories of the civilization of Islam and touching upon cities my parents journeyed through to brush against this history. I wanted to know this history, a history that passed me by despite the many summers I have spent in Pakistan. To that end, my parents told me stories, and more than a decade ago, I recorded some of my father's memories.

SHAHJAHANPUR LOST

My father was born in Shahjahanpur, close to the border with Nepal. He has spoken of places where he traveled with my grandfather, who was the administrator of a school and whose own father was a judge. He remembers, as a boy, a dog that was cared for in the courtyard of the local mosque and how he would look for opportunities to slip out to the mosque for a chance to play with that dog. Hearing his stories, I wanted to roam the streets of Shahjahanpur, look at the house that had been signed over to squatters in the aftermath of Partition, retrace the path my father took on his bicycle when he was chased by a gang of monkeys, and see the place where his pigeons were set free by his older brother because he wasn't applying himself to his studies.

My mother was also born in Shahjahanpur, and she still hopes for the chance to visit India, though her longing is tied to other mysteries. She doesn't know exactly when she was born. Like many of those displaced by Partition, she was assigned an arbitrary date of birth; new documents established her identity, and now she often says that Pakistan gave her everything she has.

KHYBER PAST

When I asked my father about his origins and what he would consider his hometown, he named the city of Peshawar, where he attended Khyber Medical College and where I spent some time in my childhood. This is another gap in the family history where I thought to ask questions too late. Now I wonder about my father's connection to Peshawar and about his work during the early days of his training. He taught pharmacology at the college in the 1960s. During the summers, he would take his students to administer vaccinations in the tribal areas. Where did he go? What were conditions like in those Pashtun villages in the north? Was he able to treat women? How were his efforts received? Are there any descendants of those families who might remember him or have stories to share about his early life and work? Maybe because I look so much like him, one day I'll run into someone who knew him in the streets of Peshawar, and they'll tell me, "Your father took the bus from his college, and then he trekked into our village." His is a journey I long to uncover and retrace.

MY THOUGHTS MOVE TO AFGHANISTAN. I WONDER ABOUT migrations whose paths I can't follow. Do I have family in Jalalabad and Kandahar that, through a strange genetic coincidence, I might resemble? Someone took a picture of my younger brother during a visit to Peshawar. He was wearing *shalwar kameez*—for men and women both, the traditional attire of a long tunic worn over loose pants—in the midst of a group of our cousins and second cousins, all similarly dressed, all ruggedly fierce and handsome, half of them green-eyed, and it was as if my brother had risen from the mountains himself, always part of that history, as if oceans and migrations had never divided us or separated us from our family. Perhaps my ancestors fought the British; perhaps that Pashtun blood coursing through my veins is why I was impelled to set one of my novels in Afghanistan, reimagining cities such as Kandahar and Herat into places I renamed Candour and Hira without leaving their history behind.

In my writing, I have returned to what my father said about "the imaginary lines drawn by empire" that slashed through the Pashtun heartland. My main character says something like this to a French Interpol agent, a woman who has seen a resemblance between my Pashtun detective and the Afghan refugee children who populate the refugee camp at Moria on the Greek island of Lesvos in my novel *A Dangerous Crossing*. She asks if she's imagining the resemblance, and he answers, "Do you remember the imaginary line the British drew to delimit their sphere of influence—the Durand Line? Sometimes it's hard to know on which side of it you belong." A reflection of my father's words, a reflection of what it means to be Pashtun.

MY JOURNEY HOME

When we visited Peshawar, I became enamored with it, wandering around the university with my family and then through the bazaar, where everyone seemed to be carrying a Kalashnikov. Wrapped in a white *chador*, I accompanied my father and his friend on an evening walk. The friend commented on the soft summer weather, and, not understanding that this was a conservative culture where girls didn't say such things, I replied in Urdu, quoting one of my parents' favorite songs. *Mausam hai ashiqana* . . . this is the weather for falling in love.

We stayed at the home of another family in Peshawar, and my teenaged eyes were dazzled by the introduction of one dashing Pashtun relative after another. Late at night, on an upstairs terrace, jasmine was in bloom, and we sat around a beautiful handwoven Pakistani carpet as tea was served with oranges and sweets, and film songs drifted up from radios playing on the street. I've forgotten who was with us in that company—who our host's children were, whether there were other girls there—but the rest I remember in such vivid detail, including that feeling of nostalgia, that I made it a pivotal scene in *Among the Ruins*, where Esa Khattak waits for a woman who might be able to help him solve a murder. He is on a rooftop terrace in Esfahan that reminds him achingly of his grandfather's home in Peshawar. Every journey forward is a step into something bright and welcoming, but every separation from the past is a loss.

These hidden connections must exist for every writer. I still feel that haunting desire to return to Peshawar in my father's company, to see it through my own lens, a lens that has become clearer with time.

DESTINATIONS

My parents must have felt the same longing. After they migrated to England, there was a long gap before they were able to return to what they still considered their home in Pakistan. My mother had borne three children during this period away; she was a young woman who was just learning English, without the extended network of family support that she was used to, and she was eager to return to her hometown. My father persuaded her that the most affordable way for them to travel to Pakistan would be to drive from England through most of continental Europe and then through Turkey, Iran, and Afghanistan before crossing the Khyber Pass. They had three young children in tow. As faithful Muslims, they wanted to travel through Turkey and Iran. As Pashtuns, they had Afghanistan in their blood. I was a child on this journey, and my parents' memories of the trip have faded. My siblings and I have patiently tried to retrace their route on a map, with only my mother's recollections to guide us.

One of my mother's favorite memories of this trip is a story about the attempted crossing from Afghanistan to Pakistan, a journey too dangerous to undertake now without a military escort. Back then, my father warned my outspoken twenty-something mother that if they were stopped by police or the toll-takers known as *chaukis* anywhere along the road, she shouldn't attempt to speak or to ask any questions. In his words, "Pashtuns don't expect women to speak." He also told my mother to cover her head. My mother had been wearing a pantsuit during this drive through Afghanistan and had intended to change into her *shalwar kameez* only after we had driven through the Khyber Pass. She didn't have anything with which to cover her head, so my father advised her to keep her head down and not to look at any man who might approach the car.

But my mother is not one to remain silent, nor is my father one to insist on silencing her, so she didn't obey this restriction when the moment came. It was late evening, and somewhere outside Ghazni, our car was stopped at a checkpoint. The man who stopped us wore a plain *shalwar kameez*, and he didn't speak to my mother, didn't look at her, per Pashtun custom, addressing only my father. He advised that the border was closed and that the customs check would have to be completed in the morning. My mother wanted to push through to Peshawar, so strong was her desire to reach home. Angrily, she muttered to my father in English, "These border guards are lazy. They don't want to work; that's why they've shut the border early."

Keeping his eyes studiously on my father, the man—who was a customs officer—answered in English with perfect composure, "Doctor *sahib*, we open our border at seven in the morning, and we close it at five o'clock at night. We do this because you are entering a tribal area where we cannot guarantee your safety. You have a wife and small children. I suggest that you check into a hotel for the night."

Naturally, my mother was mortified. And this, as my father later told me, was the only time he felt his roots dig deep—embarrassed that the unwritten laws of tribal culture had been infringed upon in the presence of a fellow Pashtun to such discourteous effect. But he followed the officer's advice, and later, he politely told my mother, "I did say it might be better for you not to speak up." My mother could hardly protest.

I understand now that my lifelong desire to drive through Afghanistan must originate from this encounter. I've been through the Khyber Pass twice. It's a dream and a miracle and a mystery layered upon other mysteries. My parents can no longer remember the name of the town where we were stopped or the hotel where we stayed. We've narrowed it down to somewhere between Ghazni and Torkham. So this secret place of family legend, and the name of the polite Pashtun customs officer, must remain unanswered questions. But if I have the chance one day, I will travel this route in hopes of reconnecting with the past and following in the footsteps of my young and adventurous parents. Perhaps I'll meet the descendant of a customs officer who might recognize a photograph of my father and have his own version of this story to tell.

SPLINTERS OF IRAN

I dream in Mughal diamonds and lost histories I know are mine. Their tapestries are threaded through my books. My parents' journey took them through Iran—Iran as it was before the Revolution—but the route they took is difficult for them to recall. Strangely and beautifully, I have found myself connected to Iran both through this journey of the past and also through unexpected ways in the present. I traveled the northern route through Iran as a child. I wrote a crime novel centered on Iran's current political context that digs into the history of the fabulous crown jewels that link Iran to India through the convulsions of Mughal history. And I am currently in the midst of writing a fantasy series that centers on the cities of the Persian empire. My connection to Iran has grown deeper in the past two decades, as I married into an Iranian family and have been immersed in Persian/Iranian culture. My husband is an outspoken critic of the present Iranian regime, which is an obstacle to retracing my parents' journey through Iran, though my longing to do so is intense.

If I traveled to Iran now, my path would splinter off from my parents' journey. My desire to see Esfahan, Shiraz, the museum that houses the crown jewels, is woven throughout my stories. But there is one place where past and present journeys intersect.

Some years ago, I studied Arabic in the West Bank as part of a study-abroad program. I lived in a hostel in Ramallah with Palestinian girls, and with other foreign students in the program. The Swedish roommate of a Palestinian friend introduced me to the novels of Amin Maalouf, a French Lebanese writer. She gave me a book called *Samarkand*, which is a story about the poet-philosopher-mathematician Omar Khayyam, who was born in Nishapur (Neyshabur in present-day Iran) and later journeyed to Samarkand. I was so entranced by the history of Persia encompassed in this novel, and by Maalouf's description of the fabled cities of Central Asia, that I promised myself I would visit both Samarkand and Nishapur one day. Many years later, I was able to fulfill half of my promise. I traveled to Uzbekistan, visiting Tashkent, Samarkand, and Bukhara. Checking into my hotel in Tashkent, I found myself standing in the Omar Khayyam lobby.

When I mentioned my fascination with Omar Khayyam to my mother, and my sadness that I would never be able to visit Nishapur, she told me to bring her an atlas. Uncertainly, her fingers traced the northern route we had taken from Turkey to Afghanistan on that journey that is not only shrouded in mystery to this day but has become almost mythical in my mind. My mother described our sojourn at the Caspian Sea, where the shore was composed of white seashells as far as the eye could see. The memory of it is one of my few clear memories of this trip. My mother says the memory was real. "We stopped at the shores of the Caspian, where you collected seashells. It may be we stopped at Nishapur as well."

I assigned this memory to a character in the book I wrote about a journey through Iran. In the same novel, I connected the past to the present by describing the illegal trade in artifacts from the Nishapur/Neyshabur dig. These artifacts included ceramics I had viewed in person at museums in New York and Toronto, slip-painted in white and adorned with the same calligraphy that whispers through my stories.

And because my sense of connection to Iran was so strong, I wasn't done with the Nishapur I may or may not have visited as a child. As I thought of it, longed for it, it became a place of refuge for the heroes of my fantasy series, who find sanctuary in a place called Nightshaper, the Poet's Graveyard, where a famous poet's tomb has been destroyed by marauding forces. Both the heroes of these stories and the forces that have vanquished the cities of the Silk Road are derived from my ethnic heritage as a Pashtun. The place of sanctuary I describe in *The Black Khan* is the tomb of Omar Khayyam: "He pointed to an odd structure on the other side of the ridge. It resembled the waters of a fountain, if the rising play of water had been etched in cool gray stone. It reached upward, a hyperbolic cone, its many-planed surface intersected by panels of sky. The stone was inlaid with lapis lazuli tile, Nastaliq script smashed by hammers in a furious outpouring of hate."

Some twenty years ago, my parents decided to visit the place of their birth in India. But when they applied for a visa, they were required to renounce their Pakistani citizenship. My parents' first reaction was outrage, their second, bewilderment and loss. They refused to give up their Pakistani citizenship, and despite his desire to do so, my father never returned to India. With his declining health, that opportunity no longer exists. And while the Shahjahan period is lost, one day my mother and I may return there, though there will be little she remembers.

If things change in Iran one day, perhaps I'll be able to make the same journey I made as a child with my parents. I've since been fortunate enough to retrace different parts of that journey, brushing against my heritage and history as a Pashtun and as an heir to the beauty of the civilization of Islam. My work as a writer has been infused with both. I know the different paths I've taken to arrive at my destination. I also know why the destination matters. But I still long to solve the deeper mystery of my origins.

A TRICK OF THE LIGHT

- Kristen Lepionka -

WHEN I FIRST TOOK POSSESSION OF THE APARTMENT ON Bryden Road, I got three keys: front door, mailbox, and basement. The first two I put on my key ring. The basement key went into my file cabinet, taped to a copy of the lease agreement, because I had no intention of using it. Ever. The basement was what I could only describe as a *murder room*. A door that locked from the outside, a single bare lightbulb to illuminate the entire space, cranky plumbing, an ancient boiler that groaned and hissed like a person in agony, and an illegible orange spray-paint scrawl on the cold cinder block that ran the length of the stairwell. The day of the open house, I went halfway down the steps, took one look around, and decided that I never needed to go into the basement again. I just had a feeling about it. I was twenty-five and not especially big on intuition—I was busy enough trying to keep my shit reasonably together—but the feeling I got from the basement was almost a physical barrier, a neon sign of the mind that said hell, no. It wasn't enough to make me not want the apartment, though.

I fell in love with the place from the moment I saw it— original floors, clawfoot bathtub, fireplace, washer and dryer in the unit. The landlord was some kind of local political bigwig who'd outsourced the search for a new tenant to a real estate agency in the neighborhood. The representative watched me with pupils shaped like dollar signs as I drifted through the spacious unit, imagining what my life would be like when it really, finally started. It was clear to both of us that I was going to take it.

A long hallway ran the length of the unit, starting at the front door and ending at the bathroom, with four doorways in be-tween. Each room was painted a different color: living room (burnt orange), office (dark teal), bedroom (a purple so deep it was almost black), dining room and kitchen (baby blue), bathroom (yellow), a patchwork that mimicked the look of the neighborhood itself, with its colorful mansions next to falling-down duplexes and vacant lots. I told myself that I'd never had a basement in my other apartments, so it wouldn't be a loss if I decided this basement didn't exist. You accessed it from the building's tiny lobby, a door just inside the front door that, the leasing agent assured me, was always kept locked. But that wound up not being true. Sometimes I'd come in and find the basement door propped open to a rectangle of darkness. Who propped open a door but kept the light off? When that happened, I would close the door immediately. It was more of an automatic reaction than a conscious choice, and to be honest, I didn't spend much time thinking about it.

Not until other things started happening—things that were harder to ignore.

Coincidence. Our language, for all its complex grammar and arbitrary rules, is sometimes woefully inadequate. "Co-," meaning together, and "incidence," meaning occurrence. There's nothing mysterious about that, but we use the word to mean something more. There's a touch of the mystical involved when we call something a coincidence, a touch of the unexplainable. It goes beyond simply existing at the same time, as the word would have you believe. A phone call from a friend at the exact moment you think of her. Waking up with an obscure song in your head, then hearing that song through the window of a passing car later that day. It doesn't necessarily mean anything, or does it? One can write these instances off as happenstance, but that gets harder to do when they start to multiply—when the purpose of that call from your friend is to tell you something that you somehow already know; when that obscure song is suddenly everywhere. That's the stuff that sends a chill creeping through your bones. We still say coincidence to describe it, but I believe it's so much more than the things occurring together that the definition would have us believe.

I still loved the apartment after I moved in. I loved the grand thoroughfare of Bryden Road, the tall, tall trees, the diversity of the residents in Columbus's Olde Towne East neighborhood. I loved the way my scrappy young-person furniture looked in my apartment. I loved having so much space to myself. I loved not living in a cookie-cutter complex somewhere, with *industrial surplus*–colored Berber carpet and matte white walls. There were some things that I didn't love, though. The occasional voices in the alley directly below my bedroom window to which I would sometimes wake, not entirely sure from where the sound was coming. Or the intermittent far-off pop-pop—*was that . . . no, surely not . . . a gunshot?* The kitchen faucet, which seemed possessed, spraying water everywhere except into the sink. The fact that my cat, who'd lived with me in four other apartments and was no stranger to moving, seemed terrified to leave my sight and sat right outside the bathroom and wailed when I took a shower.

Most of these things seemed beyond my control. The sink, though, wasn't. Post–lease signing, the political-bigwig landlord outsourced the maintenance of the apartments to his dippy son, Adam, who was terrible. He was nosy and unreliable, had promised to repaint the kitchen for me before I moved in but didn't, and then ducked my calls for a month. I left him a voice mail about my sink; he left me a plastic bag of washers with a Post-it attached—*For the sink!*—as if a lack of access to washers was the only thing that had prevented me from repairing it myself.

One afternoon, I happened to get a face full of hot water from the possessed faucet at the exact moment I heard Adam come into the lobby; a coincidence, a sign, surely, that he was supposed to help me that day. I went out, still clutching a damp dish towel, and demanded action.

"HEY, MISS KITTY!" he screamed at my cat when he came in. The cat hid under the couch—who could blame her?—as I tried to usher Adam into the kitchen. He was very chatty and wanted to stop in every room along the long hallway to survey my decorating. He asked for a beer, and when I said I didn't have any, he had the nerve to inquire about the beer and string cheese he had left in my fridge before I'd taken possession of the apartment—not as in he'd left it as a gift but rather because he had forgotten it while he'd been there *doing something other than repainting my kitchen as he had promised.*

I had zero patience for Adam.

He finally fixed the sink. But this—this—is where the weirdness truly began. As he was walking back down the hallway towards the front door, he said, "Has that toilet been running a lot?"

I stared at him. The toilet wasn't running, but it had been. I'd taken to moving the lid and manually lifting the float to get it to stop. In that moment, I felt certain that I should tell him "No." The word surprised me as it came out of my mouth.

Adam nodded and said, "Let me know if it does. Or if you have any more issues with the plumbing. That's just our friendly ghost!"

Adam was laughing a little as he said it. So I laughed, too, feebly, and let him leave without asking any follow-up questions.

I told myself that Adam was just a weirdo. There was evidence to support it: the string cheese, the washers, *hey, miss kitty!* A haunted toilet seemed like the type of thing such a person would joke about. Plus, if you'd asked me at the time if I believed in anything woo-woo, I would have said no. I knew people who'd *seen stuff* (don't we all), and I had recently enough escaped from a doom-and-gloom Catholic upbringing full of cloying incense and stations of the cross, but the idea of energy trapped here after death—no, that wasn't something I subscribed to. Wasn't any *haunting* much more likely to be a trick of the light, a story half remembered, a coincidence, nothing more? But the feeling I had was similar to the same flashing neon *hell, no* my mind's eye had seen in that basement.

Not too much later, I got a piece of mail. *James B. Martin— deceased*, the envelope said. It was from the IRS (which should probably know better than to send letters to dead people, if we're being honest). I'd actually gotten mail for him before, including solicitations to renew his subscription from the *Economist*, which probably could not be blamed for not knowing better. I threw the solicitations away, as I did the rest of the mail for previous tenants. There was a lot, virtually all of it junk. Except the letter to the friendly ghost.

I ran into my apartment to do a Google search for him.

Martin. James B. Martin, 27, of Bryden Road, Columbus, died Friday afternoon, August 26, 2005.

THERE ARE THINGS THAT ONE SHOULD NOT GOOGLE. EVEN A decade ago, when the Internet had yet to take over our lives, this was true. Unexplained pains in the torso, the crime statistics around your new apartment after you had already moved in, the obituary of your very own friendly ghost. It didn't say how he had died, or where. But I started to wonder if the basement didn't merely seem like a murder basement; maybe it was one.

I shamelessly tore into the letter, but it was a boilerplate document about estate closing with no action required of anyone. Then, having committed this small act of mail fraud, I felt guilty and, frankly, a little nuts. Why? Because when the friendly ghost was just an abstract concept, he didn't really bother me. I could easily write off Adam's claim as the blathering of an idiot. But now that the friendly ghost possibly had a name, I couldn't stop thinking about him. Maybe this was a coincidence, too— that my landlord's annoying son mentioned a ghost and, unrelatedly, a tenant of the same apartment had died a few years ago? That was possible, right?

If I didn't believe in ghosts, I certainly didn't believe in manifestation, in calling forth the thing that you think about most often.

IT WAS SUMMER, AND THE OLD BUILDING HAD CENTRAL AC— in the sense that there were vents in the floor and air sometimes came out of them, though the air wasn't especially cool. There weren't even vents in the bathroom, but the toilet tank sweat constantly, droplets of water slinking down the porcelain surface and splattering onto the floor.

It must be the water temperature, I assumed. Cold water, hot room.

But despite the hot room, the hexagonal tiles on the floor and the walls of the shower were always cold.

Antique hexagonal tile must not absorb heat at all, I assumed. A miracle substrate!

It all came to a head on a Sunday afternoon in late summer. At this point, I'd been casually ignoring the weird conditions in my bathroom for about four months, keeping myself busy with outdoorsy, young-person plans. In short, I hadn't spent a lot of time at home. But I'd gotten a sunburn at a festival the previous day—the part in my hair had transformed into an angry red slash across my scalp—and on this afternoon, I was having a low-key day in.

Until two things happened.

First, I couldn't find my colander. It had been in the sink, and then it was gone. I discovered its absence as I was about to pour my boxed macaroni down the drain. I set the pot back on the stove to consider the situation. The apartment was large, but it had a limited number of places for a plastic colander to hide itself. If it had suddenly become possessed of free will. These were the types of thoughts I was dealing with that summer. But, ultimately, I knew reality from wild speculation. If I didn't believe in ghosts, I definitely didn't believe in colander-stealing burglars or sentient kitchen tools.

I looked high and low in case I'd put the colander back in some odd location. Laundry room? Closet? Front porch? I was young and free; who knew what I could've gotten up to! Bathroom? Why not! I was laughing to myself as I went in and flipped on the lights. Nothing to see here. Except there it was, the colander, upside down in the sink.

I picked it up, put it down. I was no longer hungry. I abandoned my noodles and went directly to my computer to document the strangeness of this moment in an e-mail to a friend. And while I was waiting for the Wi-Fi to connect, I happened to look up.

I don't think anything caught my eye. In my memory, I looked up idly toward the doorway of the office leading out to the hallway. In my line of sight was an IKEA desk lamp with a blue-green embroidered shade. The moment I laid my eyes on it, that shade spun around exactly one time . . . and stopped. Not a slow, wobbling movement, nothing that could have been caused by a gust from the air conditioning or a fan or the motion of my walking by and sitting down. No, it was a quick and very precise spin, and it was the single freakiest thing I have ever seen.

I've probably never moved as fast as I did after the lampshade spun around. I grabbed my keys and phone and ran outside, where it was sunny and bright and hot, and I called Adam to finally ask him what the hell was going on.

The landlord's son laughed when I told him about the lampshade. He was surprised, but also not surprised, to hear from me. Apparently, that sounded just like James, who'd been a friend of his. He told me no, James had not been murdered in the basement, but he *had* died in the building. He had slit his wrists in my clawfoot bathtub. (That's when it occurred to me that Adam's willingness to discuss the matter was probably the real reason his bigwig father had not allowed him to speak to prospective tenants before the lease was finalized.)

"We aren't legally required to tell the tenants!" Adam whined and went on to tell me that James had been a former seminary student and that an exorcist had been called. The two tenants who'd lived in the apartment in the three years since James's death had reported some *problems*.

"You know, like with the toilet, the plumbing," he explained, which did not explain things at all. "But the lamp, wow. That's wild."

We hung up, with Adam promising to come by and look at the toilet the following day. I stood in the street for a while, not entirely sure what to do with myself. I didn't believe in ghosts. But I did believe in what I'd just experienced, so maybe I believed in ghosts after all.

When I finally mustered the courage to go back into the apartment, my cat meowed pitifully at me. I said, just to see, "Is anyone here?"

Nothing happened.

I gave the lampshade a full inspection. It was screwed tightly to the base; it didn't move at all when I tried to spin it myself. Nevertheless, I unplugged it and took it outside to the garbage.

Then I got the basement key out of my file cabinet and, sweaty-palmed, opened the basement door, bracing myself for the jolt of experiencing what I'd felt the first time I'd looked down there. But this time, it just looked like a basement. Still, it was one I wouldn't want to spend any time in and one I locked firmly behind me, just a regular old basement.

The following day—no, who are we kidding, several days later—Adam stopped by to look at the toilet, but of course it wasn't running. The condensation on the toilet tank had dried up, too, and the hexagonal tiles were chilly but not ice cold. This could have been explained by the fact that the hot weather had broken and I had the windows open, a cool breeze ruffling through from the backyard.

Or maybe there was another explanation.

"You probably scared him off with all your screaming," Adam said, and he laughed. "I mean, I'm assuming you screamed."

I didn't remember if I'd screamed, though I probably hadn't— rigid, petrified silence is more my style. But, regardless, I never had another issue with the plumbing. Nor with sentient kitchen tools or spinning lampshades. My cat, while still refusing to enter the bathroom, stopped wailing pathetically from the hallway.

That might be the biggest coincidence of all—that the weirdness in my apartment ceased immediately. Let's say the spinning lampshade was unrelated to the missing colander, and both things were unrelated to the plumbing, which was unrelated to the deceased tenant, which was also unrelated to the immediate hell, no I had felt about the basement; if each of these co-occupations of the same space is written as mere coincidence, doesn't that make it even weirder?

I know how it sounds. I'm putting myself into a column here, one titled people who believe in ghosts. I know I'm in good company, but I also know that there are plenty more people who are firm nonbelievers and uneasy agnostics on the subject. To me, it doesn't feel so much like a matter of believing in something as it is trusting my own senses. I also know what I saw, and I know that there was no rational explanation for any of it. Call it a ghost, a spirit, energy, the universe, an army of invisible butterflies; say I moved the lampshade with the current of my anxiety or the power of my own mind. Regardless of how it happened, it definitely happened, and it forced me to reevaluate the way I thought about woo-woo.

Once you believe that energy can exist beyond batteries and electrical cords, once you've actually witnessed with your own two eyes that it does, then you realize the true vastness of the possible, and one possibility is that there may never be an explanation for any of it and that coincidences are really just the beginning. And therein lies the mystery.

THE MYSTERY OF DECEPTION

— Lynn Cahoon —

I WAS CLOSING IN ON MY FORTIES. I'D JUST LEFT A VERBALLY abusive marriage. I'd been raised in a home with violence. I was done with men and relationships. I just wanted a little fun. A little relaxation time while my son finished high school. Then it was off to Seattle for me, where I'd rent a little condo and figure out what I wanted to do with my life. I had just started playing with the idea of being a writer, and I was taking classes after work at the local college, working toward a master of fine arts in the creative writing program.

Everything was an adventure.

But then my life was uprooted again. And I was a prime candidate for what happened.

A friend and I started going to an upscale bar on the weekends. I drank merlot because she did. (I found out a few years later that I enjoy white zinfandel a lot more.) Even in my wine choices, I was picking something because someone else liked it. We tried cigars and shooting oysters. It was a life I'd never imagined living. Then I'd go home and work two jobs to keep the lights on while I raised my son.

One night, a man with a stellar singing voice and a twang of Southern started hitting on my friend. She blew him off; she was looking for a man with more tangible assets—read: money—to keep her in the lifestyle she'd come to love during her first marriage. When he turned to me, I was surprised.

We spent the next few hours after my friend left talking and laughing. He sang to me. Looking back on this night, I don't remember actually offering to drive Adam home, but I must have. He was new to the area and hadn't found a place, nor had he bought a car.

Trust. It's built on one little action, one situation at a time.

I drove him back to the no-tell motel where he was sharing a room with a coworker. Definitely not the Marriott, but I wasn't worried about that. I wasn't shallow. I gave him my number.

He called; he was charming and offered to cook me dinner at my house the next day. At work, I grinned like a fool. I'd found the perfect man. Maybe it was the filter that I'd had about men and people in general that made me skim over the warning signs.

We started dating. I was entranced by his "Southern charm." He held the door open for me. He asked about my day, told me funny stories about his boss and the men he worked with. He listened when I talked about the failure of my first marriage. He talked about breaking up with a long-term girlfriend.

He liked what I liked. Country music was a shared passion. I told him about the concerts I'd attended, and we made plans to attend more that upcoming summer. Life was looking up.

By the end of the month, he was living with me. I can't remember who came up with the idea first. He wanted to help me pay my bills, which was a struggle for a single mom of a high school senior, even with two jobs. He wanted me to quit the second job so we could spend more time together. And with our joint income, we would be fine. We seemed to be getting along well. He worked nights. I worked days. I felt safe. I felt taken care of. I felt loved. I was part of a couple again. He and I became a we.

Our lives were normal. Or so it felt. Adam fell into my routine easily. He encouraged me to see my friends. He encouraged me to get out of the house, to do activities my ex-husband hadn't allowed, such as visiting the art museum or attending quilt shows. Because he worked nights, I continued to take classes at the local university. We'd have an early dinner together, and then he'd go to work and I'd do whatever. I was happy.

I thought my luck had taken a turn for the better. I had a man in my life who not only loved me but listened and supported my dreams for the future.

Except . . . my friends were worried. They kept telling me that it was too soon. Something felt off for them. As I introduced people to my new boyfriend, I found that they either loved the guy, or their warning bells went off as soon as they met him.

He did things to make me feel special. He brought home flowers. He woke me with kisses when he got in each morning. When I commented on his manners, he'd laugh and say his mama had brought him up right. My male friends asked me when I'd become a princess when I paused to let them open doors.

He'd trained me to expect the courtesy. Then he started training me to accept other facts in our lives.

Our lives got busier still when I received an unexpected visitor at my office. One who just added to the chaos.

I was working for a social services agency in the financial assistance program. A social worker from child protection came to talk to me. He asked me why I hadn't mentioned my sister to him or told him about her children. When I showed my confusion, he told me that if I didn't take the kids in, they were going to be placed in foster care. My sister needed time to get her act together. So, soon after Adam moved in, we added to the family. I took in my nieces for almost a year. Adding two elementary-aged kids to the mix also added homework and school functions and play dates. Adam encouraged me in this step. He helped with the girls, but he was at work most evenings. He was the perfect father figure. We went swimming and enjoyed other activities as a family. If Adam was busy, it was just the three of us girls. My nieces fell in love with him.

Adam started going to the bar on his nights off. I was concerned, especially with the kids in the house and what this might do to our family unit. The kids had already been moved out of one home.

He assured me everything was fine.

I kept life going. Work, classes, being a substitute mom to two kids and raising an almost independent son who treated me more like an ATM than a mom, but something felt off. Adam was still attentive, still considerate, still an overwhelming presence in our lives. I figured it was just a phase. That he was meeting new friends in the area. That he needed man time.

Then one morning, before work, we had a long talk. I was surprised when he told me that although he loved me and saw a future for us together, he needed some space. Some time.

I didn't like the idea, but I thought he'd come to his senses. I was raising three kids, taking night classes, and keeping the household going. I was too busy to argue. Every time he changed the rules, I thought it was because what I'd known about men was filtered through the craziness of my old life.

I didn't see the signs.

Later I learned that he'd already started dating other people, even when I thought we were a couple. We'd stopped being intimate about a month after he'd moved in, but I told myself it was because of our schedules. I didn't have time for romance, anyway. It's curious how much in the love game I accepted as reality. I never considered that his admission was less about my welfare than about his freedom.

The truth was, he just wasn't into me.

I know. You've heard this story before. It's on all the cable channels, and the endings are usually the same. The woman is found dead in her car, miles from the house. Or buried in the backyard after years of his claiming that she took off one night after they'd fought about her wanting a different life. I've always wondered how women in bad relationships didn't see the monster they were living with. I'd gotten away from one monster when I divorced my ex-husband. Had I jumped into the frying pan with another one?

Adam and I spent long hours on the Internet. AOL chats were the in thing back then, and we built a group of friends from the chat room. We met up off line to talk and drink. He traveled to other towns for work and met "friends" there. This was just a phase. Our situation was working fine as more than roommates, less than a couple. Well, almost fine.

From the time he moved in, he'd insisted on my depositing his check into my bank account. He didn't want me to keep track of what he deposited because he wanted to share the money he earned to take care of the family. I signed for an ATM card for him so he could access his money. I thought it was only fair. And that way, I didn't have to keep pulling out cash. I realize now that he had no identification in the name he'd been employed under.

He needed a car, so I took out a loan because his credit was bad. He got a pager (on my credit) so work could get hold of him. Trust. I believed him when he said his credit was bad, which was the stepping-stone for the next lie.

We went out on nights he had off . . . if he didn't have other plans. Then he started limiting where I could go in town. I wasn't allowed to go to the country bar that was his hangout. Where he had his friends. I told him I was taking line dance classes at that bar and didn't want to drive to the next town. He grudgingly gave me limited access to "his" bar. This was probably one of the first incidents where I stood my ground.

It didn't matter because I was making my own friends. And I was busy with the house, the kids, and my classes. And I was beginning to see a pattern.

The finances got tighter as he started spending more than he was bringing in. He kept telling me that he was up for a promotion at work. We, meaning I, applied for a credit card with him as an authorized user. I refinanced my house, pulling out the equity to pay off bills, and took out even more credit cards. Then he signed us up for a cell service. The bills were always in my name.

When I pushed for more information on his past, he admitted that he'd been in jail in Georgia. That was why he had to keep this night job for which he was so overqualified. Which was something he mentioned often. He was so much smarter than his boss or any of the other guys. His probation officer had set up the job for him. However, he never met with the officer, claiming they kept in touch via e-mail. He invited one of his friends over to our house, someone from his past, his childhood home, which turned out to be California. She was now living in the area. She pulled me aside and asked if I knew everything. Since he'd told me about the DUI that had landed him in jail, I assured her that I did.

I was wrong.

I didn't know half of it. She called him Patrick. Not Adam. Since I had a first name I hated from my childhood, I understood changing it. I agreed, I understood, I swept the inconsistencies under the rug. Even if we weren't lovers, we were friends. And I trusted him. Little actions building up. But his story was wearing thin.

The older niece started racing bikes. I bought her the uniform, the helmet, and the expensive bike. Adam took her to practice and all the competitions, her sister with them. She loved the sport, and I saw her grow in both confidence and self-awareness. The three of them would take off on Saturday mornings and come back later that day, hungry, dirty, and tired from the dirt track. I loved that he was helping her find her passion.

By this time, money was even tighter. He started hiding bills from me, claiming he'd paid them. When I found the $5,000 cell-phone bill, my heart sank. I had to admit it: I was in a financial mess. I was going to lose my house. There was no way I could pay all of the bills.

July 4th was filled with fun. We went to the beach and swam for a couple hours. Then out to my mother's for a barbecue. Finally, we went to a small town for the fireworks display. I started throwing up after the fireworks. I was so sick, a friend had to drive me home. She suggested that maybe he'd tried to poison me. I was stuck in bed for three days. He claimed I'd gotten food poisoning at my mother's barbecue party. The problem was, no one else had gotten sick. He brought me flowers while I was in bed recovering. I stopped eating food that he provided for me.

I realized that maybe Adam wasn't the man I'd met that night in the bar. Or maybe he was, and it was my filter that had screened out the bad parts. I started quietly making plans. Ways to get him out of the house. When I approached him again, he threw me against the wall, his hands around my throat. He would leave when he wanted to leave and not before. I considered calling the police, but I didn't. I was shocked at the action and not thinking clearly. He came back to my room a few minutes later and apologized. He told me he was stressed about the new girlfriend and the baby. That he'd messed up, and he didn't know how to get out of it. That he still loved me.

I kept looking for easy ways to get him to move, since my ultimatum hadn't done the trick. He went out of town to work on a construction site. When he came back three weeks later, I had a new boyfriend.

I'd met Jim, now my husband, months earlier, and we'd had our first date during the summer break when Adam was out of town. Mutual friends had filled him in on what was going on with my life. He decided he was going to help out and jumped into the fray.

All I knew was I really liked him, and I had a feeling that Adam wasn't going to like this strong, assertive man in my life. But for the first time in months, I felt safe.

My new boyfriend kept pointing out reality to me.

One step at a time, I reclaimed my life. I took back the credit and ATM cards. I deposited one last check of Adam's into my account and paid off all the late fees he had racked up. I turned off the cell phone and got a new one under my name. And finally, realizing he'd lost the war, he moved out and into a house his girlfriend's mother had rented for them.

My house was my own. My nieces went back to their mom and started a new school year, both of them happy and safe. And I had a new life. I was in horrible debt, but I was in charge of my own decisions for the first time since Adam had moved into my life.

The week before the New Year, I got a call from the girlfriend. She told me in shaky breaths that the police had come and arrested Adam under another name. Patrick hadn't been his first name but his legal last name. The name he'd grown up with. He'd called his mother over Christmas, thinking that he'd mend fences with the offer of a grandchild. She'd turned him in. He'd broken parole, and since she had put up the bail money, she was in danger of losing her house.

I went to the county courthouse and watched his arraignment. Gone was the swagger. He answered to a name I'd never heard. The man I'd lived with, had shared my life with, was gone. He'd never really existed.

When they asked if anyone was available to pay his bail, he looked around the courthouse. I stood. His eyes lit, and for a minute, he looked like Adam again. My voice was strong as I responded, "Cold day in hell."

Then I walked out of the courtroom and down the marble steps into the frigid winter afternoon. I called my boyfriend and told him I'd gone to the courthouse. As I told him what had happened, what the charges were, and how I'd left the room, a calm came over me. It was over. For the first time in a year, I could breathe. Now I just needed to clean up the damage.

Two years later, I got a summons. Adam/Patrick was trying to get custody of the child he'd fathered. I was being called as a character witness against him by the girlfriend. We'd never gotten along, and she'd pulled some pretty nasty crap on me, even after Adam was out of the picture, but the baby didn't deserve to have a liar for a father. I agreed to testify on her side.

I felt like an idiot sitting there, telling the courtroom how I'd been duped. How he'd spent my money, lied to me, lived in my home, all the while dating and sleeping with other women.

After I'd told the story of that year, Adam/Patrick stood to cross-examine me. He was serving as his own attorney. He walked over to me, staring into my eyes. His new girlfriend looked at me as if I'd lied under oath to get back at him for leaving me. For not loving me like he loved her.

He said that the girlfriend/baby mama had said he was abusive to her. That he'd hit her. He leaned against the banister separating us, and I scooted back in my chair. Then he asked the question: "In all the time we were together, did you ever see me hurt her?"

I took a deep breath and answered honestly, "I've never seen you hit her, but I heard it through the wall. And I believe her."

"Why would you do that?" he challenged, his blue eyes narrowing.

"Because you came into my bedroom and tried to choke me. You hurt me."

The courtroom got quiet as he stared at me. I had finally spoken up. I'd finally revealed what he'd done. He shook his head as if he was disappointed in me. "No further questions."

The judge excused me. As I passed by the baby mama's lawyer, he held out his hand. "Thank you," he whispered. "Thank you for being brave."

I ran from the courthouse, wanting to be out of that city. Away from Adam (or whatever he wanted to call himself) and back home, where I could feel safe. I didn't feel brave right then. I felt scared.

As a mystery author, I enjoy writing the final scene. Where everything is back to right. Where the bad guy is in jail and justice has been served. In real life, this lovely sense of closure doesn't always happen. We don't always get to say the snappy comeback to the idiot who degrades us. Or put the bow on the ribbon shutting the box that we can now put away, knowing the pain is over. Many times, real people carry around the open box with their pain leaking into their lives. But in books? The good guy wins.

I have been in a relationship where I've given up my power. The mystery of relationships teaches us that each couple's truth is their own. But looking from the outside in, I'd never thought I'd be the one duped so completely.

Adam had developed a completely different personality when he arrived in Idaho. His mystery was based on the good guy he thought he was, or wanted to be. At least, that was what I assumed was under all of the lies and deceit. But the more he fell into his new good-guy personality, the more lies he had to tell and the more he went back to his real personality. The one that didn't care who he hurt. This was the mystery that came back to bite him when he let his guard down.

Living with someone who believed that deception was a normal part of life made me trust less. The mystery of deception kept me from seeing the warning signs. I'd always wondered how women in bad relationships didn't see the monster they were living with. Now, I know.

What did I learn from this situation? That even when all is dark, there will be light. And that strong heroines learn to save themselves.

THE LONG SHADOW
OF WAR

– Rhys Bowen –

I THINK I WAS DESTINED TO WRITE ABOUT WORLD WAR II.
It has haunted my subconscious for my entire life. After all,
I was born into the middle of it, and I survived a near miss
during a bombing raid in Essex, just outside London. While I
was too young to remember details, my heart rate still quickens
if I hear a siren wailing or see a searchlight strafing the sky. I do
remember the matter-of-fact way everyone got on with it, did
their duty, and didn't panic.

My father and my uncles all joined up, because it was their
duty to do so, and were sent overseas. At home, we saved every
scrap of paper, vegetable peelings for pig swill, and items of
metal that could be used to build planes. We lived on a quarter
pound of meat per person per week. And after the war ended,

conditions were almost as grim for a long time. New clothes on ration, new furniture on ration, cars almost nonexistent. But people were cheerful. They didn't have nervous breakdowns or rush to their shrinks. It was this "England expects" attitude that I wanted to recapture in any story I wrote. Of course, there were always a few people who didn't feel this patriotic swelling of the heart and used the war to profit on the black market. They, too, were remembered when I wrote about those years.

My father was away fighting in Egypt and later in Palestine. He did not see me until I was three. My uncles were in the navy and air force, and fortunately they all came home safely. So I was born into a world without men. What a shock when they reappeared!

Long after the war, we were still feeling the effects in my home and throughout Britain. Food rationing continued until the 1950s. I remember tasting my first banana. What a disappointment! And I was old enough to remember when sweets came off ration. There was a run on the sweet shops, and they sold out in minutes. The hardships faced by a child!

Every town had its bomb sites. You could not walk far without coming across the remains of a bombed building, the blackened shell of a burned-out church. And war memorials. Every village had its central memorial, often an obelisk etched with the names of the locals, boys and men, who hadn't returned. I grew up conscious that a great war had been fought and that we had been victorious. We were the good guys!

I've written about so much of this. But this isn't about my novels; it's about the mysteries of war—how I survived and moved forward with my life and how it still continues to impact me so many years later. I rather suspect that my biographers will say I had the perfect childhood for a writer. Being born in the middle of a war, I had all those memories, all those experiences. What they don't know is that I was overprotected. Imagine being a child who never played with another child until you were three. My mother was a teacher and not allowed to quit her job, as there were not enough teachers. I was raised in isolation by my grandmother and my blind great-aunt, who was called Min by the family. (Yes, the Brits give family members silly nicknames. Her real name was Sarah Ann.) Min was a great storyteller and also a willing participant in my games of pretend. She was always the old witch/bad fairy/evil queen, and I was always the princess/good fairy. Can you imagine how magical it is to escape into the mystery world of fantasy when your country is being bombarded?

When I wasn't playing with Min, I amused myself. I longed for more human contact, a real playmate, as was evident in my need to invent an imaginary family. They were called the Gott family. Four sisters: Gorna Gott, Leur Gott, Goo Goo Gott, and Perambulator Gott. (You can see that I didn't know what real children were called!) They had to do everything with me, from having their own places set at the dinner table to going on our shopping expeditions.

And when I wasn't playing with the Gott family, it was my grandmother's button box that occupied me. Those buttons became families who rode around in matchbox cars, lay in matchbox beds in hospitals, or sat in rows in a matchbox school.

My world was filled with wonder but also with change and uncertainty.

After the war, we moved to a big, drafty house in the country. (To this day, my much younger brother and I both swear it was haunted.) Again, I was isolated from other children, and I continued my games of pretend adventures: circus star on my own trapeze and girl sleuth chasing down criminals as characters did in the books I was reading. An isolated child does a lot of reading to fend off the loneliness.

I started off being attracted to reading mysteries because of their puzzles, their settings, adventures, the chase, and then the satisfaction of justice served at the end. As a young girl, I discovered the Famous Five: four children and a dog who went camping alone, discovered secrets in a smuggler's cave, and apprehended criminals. Oh, how I longed to do that! Now I see how unrealistic they were. The burglars, or smugglers, or whoever they caught always came along quietly. In today's world, children know that the bad guys would probably pull out a gun and shoot them all. So sad!

As soon as I was allowed in the adult section of the library, my world changed, and so many mysteries . . . about mysteries! . . . were solved. That was where I met Agatha Christie, whose puzzles and settings attracted me to her books, pulled me into her world. Big country houses with a body or two. Sweet English villages with poison-pen writers. And such clever murders. How I could identify with them in my own drafty house and small village setting. They were my friends when we were healing from the war. They were also my gold standard for many years. Still are, actually.

I grew up, went to college, and then went to work for the BBC in London as a studio manager in the drama department.

I started writing my own radio and TV plays, some of which were actually produced by the BBC. I was lured down to Australia to work for ABC. I met my husband, married him, and came to California. That was when my thoughts turned to writing fiction. I established a successful career as a writer for children and young adults. Then one day it dawned on me: Why was I not writing what I liked to read? All this time I had read and devoured every mystery novel I could get my hands on. Why not try to write one?

When I decided that I wanted to write mysteries, I created my own version of Agatha Christie. My sleuth was a Welsh police constable in the mountains of Snowdonia, where I had spent many happy hours as a child. I even called my village Llanfair, which means St. Mary's, in homage to St. Mary Mead. Like Agatha, I had a cast of quirky villagers.

By then I had paid my dues as a writer and found a publisher without much trouble, creating a series of cozy mysteries. But then, as the series progressed and I got to know my characters better, a darker element crept in. Real life, real problems began to be part of my stories. In one book, a Pakistani family takes over the local grocery store. The daughter becomes friendly with Evan and his wife, Bronwen, then comes to confide in them that she has overheard her parents discussing taking her back to Pakistan to marry her off to an older man. My editor was horrified when I turned in this manuscript. "You can't say that," she said. "It's too inflammatory."

I told her it was happening all the time in Britain. Strict Muslim parents clash with their children, who have been raised as normal British teenagers. The girls are often tricked into going back to Pakistan—to a big family celebration—that turns out to be their wedding. Then they are stuck with no passport and no means of escape. I had to write about this. It was real, and the world needed to know. I assembled a whole stack of newspaper cuttings and presented them to my editor. "See," I said. "This is happening all the time." She allowed me to keep the plot thread and the parallel story of the girl's brother being radicalized.

It's interesting to me how my work has evolved from storytelling for pure entertainment to a vehicle for social justice. I don't mean that I've started to preach in my books. I still want to be first and foremost a storyteller. But as I become more familiar with the characters in my series, I start to see the bigger picture, the problems in their world, the injustices they may encounter. And I see the relevance to our modern world and the prejudices we still encounter. I want to make my readers see parallels to our current environment and maybe want to do something about our modern injustices.

My theory is this: if I have created real characters, true to their time and place, then they have to be aware of the world around them. True events were happening at that moment and in that place. In the Molly Murphy books, set in New York City in the early 1900s, maybe there was an election, a snowstorm, a train crash. Events became part of the stories. Very early in the series, I realized that Molly couldn't vote! Her best friends are passionate suffragists. Molly joins in a march and plans meetings, much to the disgust of her husband. Yes, this was fiction, but I had a responsibility to share with readers the unfair disadvantages to women. They needed to know that in New York state a woman had virtually no rights. She could not vote. She could own no property. She was the property of her husband, who could legally beat her as long as the stick was no thicker than his thumb. He could have her committed to an insane asylum with just his signature and that of one doctor. Think of how many annoying wives were disposed of in this way. Did you know that one of the signs of insanity was the reading of novels?

And so my Molly Murphy became a champion of women's rights. I hadn't intended her to. It just happened. Another mystery: why so many of these terrible situations were kept secret. As a writer, I could help to change that.

When I moved on to my Royal Spyness series, I looked forward to writing books that were pure fun. Light social commentary and jabs at the class system in Britain. A penniless minor royal in 1930s London trying to make her own way in a difficult world while being given annoying little tasks by the queen. However, as I wrote the books, I became more and more aware of the background conditions. The Great Depression meant many people were out of work, some still with injuries from the Great War. Soup kitchens were a common sight at major railway stations. Beggars on street corners. And of course, this contrasts sharply with the aristocrats whom Georgie meets: the Bertie Woosters of the world, drinking champagne out of slippers, spending winters in their yachts on the Med. Fictional characters, true, but they reflected a part of our world that few would ever know. A population essentially untouched by the horrors of war.

And what about the struggle in Europe between communism and fascism? Europe was poised on a knife's edge until fascism, in the persons of Hitler, Mussolini, and Franco, took control. But I could have no foreshadowing. My characters saw Hitler as a comical character, that funny little man with his mustache. After twelve books, we had not yet reached a time when we know that Germany is rearming. The second World War was coming inevitably closer, yet we lived as if everything were returning to normal.

I was faced with a writer's dilemma. As war came closer, I realized that there were many aspects of that history that could not be touched in what are considered comic novels. Could I send Georgie to Germany to rescue Jewish children? I couldn't see how I could find any fun in that kind of situation, and thus my readers would be shocked to find a dark book had come into my series. But I was still dying to write about World War II, and the time had come to finally do what I had thought about for years.

I believe that one of the reasons so many people seem to be attracted to reading about that war is that it was the last time we had a clear sense of good versus evil. Every war, every confrontation we've had since then has been colored in shades of gray: Vietnam, Iraq, Afghanistan. During each conflict we have questioned whether we were doing the right thing by getting involved and sending young people into battle. Battles that were once between armies have turned into ugly skirmishes, rooftop snipers, civilian casualties. With World War II, everybody knew we must stop evil before it swallowed the world. Everybody was prepared to do his or her part, however small it was, and everybody had that great sense of purpose and togetherness. And of course, that period is full of so many good stories because it was a time of heightened emotions, of heart-wrenching good-byes, of ever-present danger. No corner of Europe was quite safe.

In times like ours, when there is division, uncertainty, and terrorism, it is comforting to read about a period when we fought and the right side won. After 9/11, everything changed. We were no longer safe even at home. These new conflicts that we call war are so different. Perhaps that's why we turn to books. When war comes to small English villages, disrupting peaceful lifestyles, and even quiet and simple people do great and noble deeds, take great risks, make great sacrifices, we can relate. We like to be reassured that in the end, good will triumph again.

I always felt that I would write about the war but wasn't sure what I could say that had not already been said a million times. Then, a few years ago, I got my first inspiration. I read that there had been British who had aided the Germans. Even more, a circle of British aristocrats who were pro-German and felt that we had a lot in common with the Germans. They were actually working behind the scenes to assist with the invasion. I was horrified. And embarrassed. I tried to understand their motivation and discovered that it was misguided but altruistic. Their feelings were that Britain could never win, and the longer we held out, the more of our historic buildings, even entire cities, would be destroyed. They felt that the Germans were so similar to us that we would have been treated fairly, especially because Hitler admired us. Utter rubbish! Were we not able to see the way that other occupied countries were treated?

Knowing this made me want to write about it even more! I plotted out a novel about British aristocrats and secret spies and sent it to my then agent. She told me bluntly that nobody was interested in World War II and that it was insulting to write about British country houses when so many people were dying in hellish conditions in Europe. Reluctantly I put the project aside. But the idea never fully left my head.

Later I got a new (and wonderful) agent. Years went by. I was fully occupied writing my mystery series. And then several things happened. My research took me to the Duke of Windsor—formerly the Prince of Wales and then King Edward VIII—and I found that he was a big fan of Hitler and that Hitler had a plan to put him on the throne as a puppet king after a successful invasion. That was why he was sent to be governor of the Bahamas—because those islands are near the coast of America and can be patrolled by US submarines.

While I was researching all this in 2016, the United States was going into a horribly divisive election. I felt that our own current political climate had started to show worrying similarities to that of prewar Europe. Extremism and racial hatred were rearing their ugly heads. The press was being discredited and stifled, just as it had been in prewar Germany. The motive for writing about the war became more compelling. I wanted my readers to become aware of the parallels between my historical story and the real world. An element of preaching, I suppose, but more an element of warning. And so I returned to that story that had been so rudely rejected, and I reworked the focus a little. I made it into a spy novel, with Bletchley Park and MI5 involved in seeking out a traitor. But I centered it around a stately home and an aristocratic family. The novel my first agent thought was offensive won three major awards. Readers did want to know, and they cared.

While I was teaching a writing workshop in Tuscany, I learned about the German occupation of Italy, the brutal retaliations if a German was killed or German property damaged. Whole villages were assembled in the central square and entire populations gunned down: old men, women, and children. Armed with this information, my second World War II novel was much more stark and brutal, the story of survival as well as of love.

And then another book, this one set during the first great war, a subject largely overlooked by writers. I wanted to focus on the home front and not on the trenches, examining how society copes when a whole generation of men has been killed. Who does their jobs? Who becomes the blacksmith, the carter, the publican? And what happens to the women forced into roles they would not have thought possible? Another story of loss and grief and ultimate triumph. All were messages I wanted, needed, to convey. There is no mystery in killing each other over an imaginary line drawn on a map, but there is a great mystery in how we survive, become stronger, and move forward.

I do believe that if one is passionate about the subject one writes about, it shows in the writing. When I write about the wars my country has had to endure, it is in part my own story. I see these wars through the eyes of my family. My grandmother, whose husband was drafted in World War I when he was almost forty and had four small children. My mother, who had to say good-bye to a new husband and endure three long years without him, most of the time not knowing if he was alive or dead. And my relatives, for whom nightly bombings became commonplace.

So many mysteries hide secrets. I want to tell a good story, but I want the following generations to know what it was like, what people went through, and to decide it must never happen again.

I DON'T KNOW THIS WORD

– Rachel Howzell Hall –

I WAS THREE YEARS INTO MY THIRTIES, AND I KNEW LOTS of words.

Elysian.

Lollygag.

Bloviate.

Catawampus.

But then I came across a word I didn't know.

Had never heard this word uttered before.

Since those doctor appointments had started three months after my thirty-third birthday, I'd learned *fine-needle aspiration*, *palpate*, *ultrasound guidance*, *transducer*.

I also knew *cancer* because everyone knows that word.

But this word?

No.

That September afternoon was the first time I'd heard it. That afternoon in September, I'd spelled that word like this:

f-i-l-l-o-d-e-e-z

During our telephone conversation, Dr. Brooks said that word. I stopped her and admitted that I didn't understand. How, exactly, had pathology classified the five-centimeter tumor growing in my right breast? And can you spell that for me, please?

P-h-y-l-l-o-d-e-s.

A new word. Worse than *defenestration*. Worse than *paresthesia*. It was *nefarious*. Yes. This word was nefarious and described the cancerous mass created by rogue cells.

As I learned new words that related to my body, other words, nonmedical words, slammed into other soft places around my body. I would come home from a doctor's appointment, and these words would be waiting for me in my mailboxes, both physical and digital. Words from editors that threatened to shred my will and disrupt my need to write after being poked and prodded all morning. I was surrounded by bad editorial words.

> "It's just too *upmarket* for the kinds
> of African American fiction we
> have been publishing successfully."

I was the spelling-bee champ of 59th Street Elementary School. The author of my first published novel, *A Quiet Storm*. I was a married and pregnant thirty-three-year-old fundraiser for the foremost civil liberties organization in the country. And that fall in 2003—and many falls later—I would hear many mysterious words with strange spellings and hidden meanings.

Connective.

Atypical.

Unusual.

But the word of the day that September: *phyllodes.* That was my tumor's name, and it was being fed by the estrogen created by my pregnancy. And it was growing rapidly, Dr. Brooks told me over the phone. The tumor needed to be removed immediately or else . . .

My husband, David, asked, "Or else . . . what?"

More words.

Metastasis.

Mastectomy.

Low grade.

Stage.

What the fuck? I was still young, and sure, I'd already had a myomectomy (another new word after another mystery solved), but . . . but . . . what had I *done*? Why was this *happening*? Why *now*?

During the sixth month of my pregnancy, after David kissed my forehead and said, "See you in a minute," I was wheeled into the operating room. Flanked by two heart monitors, I learned more words.

Twilight sleep.

Demerol.

Drains.

Margins.

A prayer stayed on my lips. *Lord, help me get through this. Help my baby get through this.* These words I knew. These words I understood. In the surgery suite, the anesthesiologist told me to count backward from 100.

99 . . . 98 . . . 97 . . .

> "We are finding that what sells
> for us right now is the hard-hitting
> Sista Souljah-type material
> with a street-lit feel to it."

I survived surgery. Obviously. But then, three years later, my ever-vigilant health-care team found precancerous calcifications growing in my left breast, the one that had behaved all this time. I realized then: my body was unknown to me. It liked making crazy crap that could kill me. And now, I added another set of words to my ever-expanding vocabulary.

Atypical hyperplasia.

Not always a forerunner to breast cancer, but for me, with my past? If they remained, those calcifications would very likely become cancer.

Why wouldn't they?

Those calcifications had to go.

Of course they did.

Mammograms and imaging and contrast dyes had become as familiar to me as the three-inch scar that was now a feature of my right breast.

Fear—that emotion now as familiar as joy, anger, and love.

My daughter, at that point three years old and healthy despite the drama surrounding her birth, had kept me busy. Working at the ACLU, that had kept me busy, too.

Trying to land another book deal . . . this hurt more than the operations and the scarring. Made me sicker than magnets and tubes and dyes.

> "It's been a struggle to convince booksellers that there is an audience for a story about this life."

After the surgery to remove precancerous calcifications, I enrolled in UCLA's high-risk program. For five years, I would receive comprehensive care—a geneticist, nutritionist, psychologist, oncologist, nurse practitioner. I was started on Tamoxifen, an antiestrogen chemotherapy that, in my case, would reduce the risk of breast cancer from developing. Five years: the length of my treatment. I was thirty-seven years old.

Do I have a long life ahead of me?

Will I receive those rewards I'd planned for myself at fifty?

Confronting my mortality, popping a pill that would (hopefully) fight my body's need to destroy itself. How was I supposed to deal with this?

Write.

I didn't know the answer.

I didn't know much of anything except this: I knew words, their mystery and their power. I'd use them somehow to survive, to enjoy the life that I'd been given.

Keep writing. Keep chasing that high of publication. Riding in the backseat of a hired town car en route to the airport. The high of signing books, of staying in nice hotels on the publisher's AMEX.

Just. Keep. Writing.

In my midtwenties, I was introduced to the writing life by working at PEN Center in Los Angeles, an organization committed to protecting the open expression of writers around the world. I subscribed to *Poets & Writers* and read *Glimmer Train*, attended readings and salons. Hung out with writers. Talked about writing. And like many young writers, I, too, wanted to land on the "30 Under 30" lists, to be featured as the next publishing wunderkind. I, too, had read those issues of *Granta* and had fantasized about long lines of readers waiting for signed copies of my great American novel. Fantasized about telling Oprah and the audience at the National Book Awards why I had chosen this story. Now, though, I could glimpse my fortieth birthday on the horizon. I couldn't hit "30 Under 30," but "40 Under 40"? Also, it was just a matter of time before the awards and the fancy dinner parties because I knew how to put words on paper, and I'd had enough traumatic experiences to write hundreds of books.

This life . . . my life . . .

Art is personal.

A black woman in America—that's who I was. Unlike atypical hyperplasia and a phyllodes tumor, my blackness could not be surgically removed. Being a black person and writing about regular, working-class black people with working-class problems (but without that street-lit feel, without that hard-hitting shit) was not cancer. But it wasn't a sought-after life in publishing back then.

This life . . . my life . . .

Right after college graduation, my words weren't ready yet. I hadn't *lived*, not really. Though placed in the correct order and spelled correctly and ending correctly, those words read flat and were far from nuanced. Read aloud, those words didn't sound like me—they sounded like Toni Morrison, Stephen King, Donna Tartt, and John Grisham. Hell, I didn't even know what *my voice* meant. In my twenties, my vocabulary had been informed by *Cosmopolitan* and *Glamour*, "Draw me like one of your French girls," and "Run, Forrest, run!" My parents were healthy. I was healthy, and my body acted the way it was supposed to act. I could eat what I wanted without fear of weight gain. My complexion was flawless. My hair shone.

That all changed in my thirties. Ten years of holding my breath, of not knowing what mysteries my body would bring forth, not having the ability to describe my fear and frustration . . . those ten years gave me wrinkles. Those years made me sag, maybe not physically but psychologically, emotionally.

My *voice*, though, was being formed and honed by those hard words. I was learning, firsthand, of crafting pointed responses to women who insisted I breastfeed because "breast is best" and didn't know that I wore a draining tube postlumpectomy. I was learning, firsthand, of faking cheer and strength when all I wanted to do was cry and crawl into bed. My seams were being ripped, all things smooth pilling and my stuffing trailing behind me. A different woman now than the young thing who had big, bright eyes and a closet full of spandex.

Wrinkles and imperfections are good. Talk to an artist, and she will tell you that she loves drawing interesting, imperfect faces, old bodies with crags and scars. Actresses with unmoving faces—from too much cosmetic surgery or too much Botox—won't land many acting jobs that require emotion.

A young writer just starting out may have something to say but may not have the wisdom to make that something interesting.

Ray Bradbury said, "If you want to be a great writer, then write a million words, and when you're done, you will be."

I didn't know then what I know now: all of this—drafts, rejections, query letters, more drafts, dead stories, trunk stories—would help me learn how to tell a story for readers outside English professors and writing groups. Back then, I didn't know that I had a while to go before hitting that millionth word.

> "Unfortunately, the project you describe does not suit our list at this time."

Throughout my treatment, the rejections came fast.

I sent out queries even more quickly.

No. No. Not now. Not at this time.

I heard those words, and they came at me like lightning. But then, I learned more just as fast.

Editorial consultant, BRCA, remainders, low-fat diet?

I BOUGHT A MERCEDES-BENZ E350.

I had planned to buy this car with my big book advance or on my fiftieth birthday, whichever came first. At thirty-seven years old, though, I knew there was a possibility of never receiving that book advance or reaching that milestone birthday. My so-called gift with words would not help me obtain something I'd dreamed about since turning sixteen years old.

This car was a survivor's gift.

A fighter's prize.

AT THIS TIME, I ALSO WONDERED, *WHAT ELSE DO I WANNA DO before my body wins and I'm forced to leave this world?*

Write a mystery. A police procedural.

But I didn't know how to write that world. Cops, robbers, dealers, murderers. Yeah, I'd lived around violence and anger, cops and dealers, gunfire and alley beat-downs, but I had no confidence in my ability to capture eighty thousand words of it.

Fear—of failing, of rejection, of not knowing—had kept me in place for so long.

After battling cancer and still being forced to stay in the ring, I understood and had experienced true fear. Ain't nothing like signing consent forms acknowledging that you and your unborn child may not make it through the operation. Nothing like relying on a pill the size of a thought to keep cancer at bay. And it wasn't as if I had a book contract. And at that time, it wasn't as if I had an agent, either. No one to disappoint. I'd already self-published two rejected novels on

Amazon's Kindle platform. Could always do that with this police procedural.

What was the worst that could happen if I tried this?

What I wanted to happen was this: Terry McMillan meets Walter Mosley.

That's who she'd be.

But who was "she"?

Didn't know. Just . . .

Her name was Lou.

I knew that.

And I knew that she was my survivor's gift. She was my fighter's prize.

> "I love the voice and
> characters and enjoyed
> reading these pages."

Jill, a literary agent in San Diego, wanted to read fifty pages. Then the entire manuscript. Then she called on the second day of February 2012 and said a word I hadn't heard in so long.

Yes.

At that moment—and many moments after—I didn't understand that simple *yes.* I searched for hidden meanings. Turned it over in my head, searching for burrs and weeds. Even today, I sometimes squint at "yes." Keep one foot on the ground. Hold my breath. Refuse to enjoy the moment, to enjoy the "yes" because what does that word, a key to possible moments of joy for me, mean?

Words hurt. Words confuse. And I loved—and loathed—them.

Jill's "yes," though. It didn't yank me, and I believed her. She'd love Lou Norton and my depiction of Los Angeles. Lou Norton, a native Angelena like me, who'd grown up working class. Lou had seen awful shit in her life and had straddled different worlds. She knew what it meant to hear gunfire with a brilliant blue sky above her, to see tall, swaying palm trees tagged with BPS or Rolling 60s. She had also sat in a booth next to LL Cool J at Roscoe's Chicken N Waffles and searched the depths of her fake Gucci bag for the crumpled piece of yellow paper needed to get her clothes off layaway.

I had used my pain to create Lou—a homicide detective, she was empathetic, vulnerable, exhausted. A fully formed woman facing the sometimes impossible, a lady Sisyphus who makes it up the mountain only for that rock to careen down the other side and into her car. I didn't give her sickness or disease to contend with. I didn't want her traumatized by her body. I couldn't be that cruel.

Jill would help me find a home for Lou Norton. She would find me another "yes."

NEW WORDS LEARNED WHILE ON SUBMISSION:

No.

Engaged.

Relaunch.
Track record.
Connection.
No.

ON THE DAY BEFORE MY FORTY-THIRD BIRTHDAY, I COM-
pleted my five-year Tamoxifen regimen. I'd done it—survived
my battle with disease and survived my chemotherapy. No more
mysteries except for writing them and learning more about this
Lou Norton character. Two months later, though, my right ovary
exploded, and my nine-year-old daughter found me writhing
in pain on the bathroom floor.

This life, my life . . . The surprises would never *really* stop,
would they?

What was gonna happen next?

What fresh hell was waiting for me in between writing stories and soccer/swim practice and *Walking Dead* episodes and
playing *Skyrim* on my Xbox?

Lou's first adventure of the two-book series would be published in just fifteen days.

Kristin, my new editor, made the offer for two books, and she
had all the best words. Then they sold the UK rights, and I had
a British publisher—Titan UK wanted me to come across the
pond for a tour.

This was happening.

Twelve years had passed between the publication of *A Quiet
Storm* and *Land of Shadows*. My entire thirties had been traumatic

and exhausting, with bursts of promise and joy. I would now have the writing career I'd fought for, with a body that had been cut up and restored too many times to count.

Over in the UK, there was one word I couldn't say.

The producer for BBC Radio Four, *Woman's Hour*.

Gangbanger.

Here in Los Angeles, that's the word we use for gang members. *He bang* means *He's a member of one of our urban men's groups.* Sure, it also meant group sex, but not in *Land of Shadows*.

Not for British listeners.

There was something about that word—which in the UK meant violent group sex—that spooked the Brits. For me, the word had no power—in my part of the world, *gangbanger* was as ubiquitous as *Kool-Aid* and *Doritos*. It was just a word.

Still, I was asked not to say *gangbanger* during the *Woman's Hour* interview.

Easy.

Don't say gangbanger. *Don't say* gangbanger.

Moments into the interview, that word tumbled out of my mouth. Not that I realized that it had. Afterward, my husband met me in the greenroom, smile on his face. "You said the word. Like, twenty seconds into the interview."

Some words cannot be silenced with just an hour's notice.

I HAD A DOCTOR'S APPOINTMENT FOR WHO-KNOWS ON June 4, 2014. Oh, yeah—bad cramps. A weird thing since I had no uterus. That morning, my doctor was telling me that I most likely had endometriosis, another side effect of ending Tamoxifen therapy, and that condition didn't require a uterus. It simply grew wherever the hell it wanted to grow.

More words. More fixing things. More hoping for normalcy.

She suggested that I try another drug called Lupron Depot to combat the bad cramps I'd been experiencing.

More drugs.

Tears burned my eyes, and I wondered, what side effects would this therapy bring? And what therapy would I need in two years to combat those side effects? And on and on and . . .

What had I done to bring this—?

My cell phone rang from my purse.

My doctor was talking to me about my next appointment.

The call rolled to voice mail.

Doc tore the prescription from the pad and handed it to me. She wished me well and said, "See you in six months."

Alone again, I checked my phone.

Jill!

Would this be good news? Or the news with words I'd come to know best?

Not now. No. We're passing. Revise and resubmit. Thanks, but . . .

By now, I was used to disappointment—from both my body and my writing. That morning, I couldn't decide whether to rush to my car to call Jill back . . . or take the scenic route through Canada.

Eventually, I slipped behind the steering wheel and took a deep breath. I selected Jill's number and clenched for bad words made softer by Jill's expertise.

Kristin at Forge had just offered to purchase two more books for my now four-book series.

Lou would survive.

I would survive.

Yeah, there would be more words to learn—*oovectomy, abdominal adhesions, sudden-onset menopause, shopping agreement, no, not now, maybe later.*

And credit-card bills and accumulated debt with so many surgery fees and imaging costs and . . . and . . .

Okay. Fine. This was my normal.

I'd punch back.

I always punched back.

Most times with words. By refusing to surrender.

A scary, wonderful, messy life that bled past the edges of everything. A life that took in too much at times, that seemed unfair and strange and stupid. Lou, Miriam, Rikki, Stacy, Danielle, and every character I will write today and tomorrow help me unload some of this life, help me make sense of it all. And readers, not all of you but a lot of you, appreciate my words about this life.

Because your life may not be altogether different. Because you, too, have heard hard words, winced at their sting. You've shimmied and shimmered—until you're grounded with strange, mean, uncaring words.

Uptight.

Stupid.

B****.

N*****.

C***.

A child of the church with musical ability, I was surrounded by song and melody. Alto in youth and school choirs. Violin player. Handbell ringer. Self-taught piano player. As an adult, my favorite religious songs had become more complex—from *Jesus loves me, this I know* to *God with us, the living truth.* Going through this . . . this strange, scary, convoluted journey, I needed gospel music, songs that spoke to my pain and fear and anger. And I listened to songs—Fred Hammond most times, "You Are the Living Word" and "No Weapon" and "I Will Trust" on repeat. Listened and sifted through the words for promises that I would be okay, that no weapon formed against me—even my own body—would prosper. On my drive to work, these songs infused me with hope, with promises that it would all work out in the end. *The end?* What kind of end?

Those songs—powerful words made to be sung—on Fred Hammond's albums still bring tears to my eyes. How his words ministered to me, how his words that played an active part of my healing prick me and shape me fifteen years after my obstetrician palpated that suspicious lump. I cry because I remember how I survived, how I climbed into my car each day and drove to work, pretended that I was okay, prayed that I'd be okay. Hummed those songs, Fred Hammond's words beneath my breath as the room dipped into silence and I could hear the crunching of those bad words in my head.

Just a few months ago, I heard those words so many writers hear.

No.

Numbers.

Not right now.

Sorry.

Months ago, those words broke me. I'd worked hard on a new story—I'd taken everything that I'd learned from writing the Lou Norton novels, the James Patterson story, the science-fiction short story, and the stand-alone seven-sinners novel and had created another interesting heroine with a twisting path and a smart mouth. After finishing, I was convinced that it was the best story I'd ever written, and I was certain that it would sell.

That afternoon, I cried in my office at work. Kept the door closed until my eyes whitened again, until my breathing straightened, until I could fake it. Took about twenty minutes.

Later that day, as I drove my almost-fifteen-year-old daughter home, I shared with her my story of rejection. And as I talked to her, I cried again and told her that this hurt and that I was tired and that I couldn't do more than what I'd done. I told her that I wished that I didn't have to write, that maybe I wasn't as talented as I thought. I told her that maybe I should find something else to do—she and my husband had given me a sewing machine for Christmas. Maybe quilting would be my thing now. Quilts are nice.

After handing me a napkin to dry my eyes, my kid held my hand and said, "I'm sorry, Mom." She kissed me on the cheek, then let me listen to Rachel Maddow's show on the radio without hassle. When we got home, she disappeared into her bedroom to do homework. Her Intro to Comp and Literature class had just started *Brave New World*, and she'd already told me that the words and ideas in Huxley's pages scared her. She was learning new words, too.

I cooked dinner because life went on. I told myself, while sautéing salmon, that I had experienced worse, that I'd published more books than the one book I'd prayed for. If I never landed a book contract again . . . My eyes burned—the thought of never landing a book contract again was not a new thought, but it was a thought that I hadn't thought I'd think again, you know? Here I was, though, hours after rejection (again), cooking dinner (again) and wondering if my writing career was over (again).

Before bedtime, my daughter came to the den to say goodnight to David and me. Along with a kiss on my forehead, she also gave me a present: one of her new binders. She had printed out and glued past reviews and stars from my novels onto the binder. She'd written, "Don't stop, Mom." And I cried again—there were so many words that I'd forgotten. So many words I'd discounted. That night, after a brutal day, Maya had helped me to remember.

The next morning, I prepared for work. Dumped leftover salmon and potatoes into a plastic container for lunch. Gave the dog her dental stick. And then I grabbed a new notebook and a pack of pens from my storage bin. I had plenty of stories that needed to be written. So many things I had to say. Quilting was great, but writing . . . Nothing compared to a nice pen drifting over clean white pages. Nothing compared to finding new ways to use twenty-six letters to give body to a thought in your mind.

Words hold tremendous power—they shape lives, end lives. They set mood—on paper, in songs, in a conference room. We second-guess their meanings and their mysteries, and sometimes, we still do not understand.

I am now in the last year of my forties. I am still learning the meaning of lots of words, simple words. I am still remembering words, simple words.

Enjoy.

Relax.

Appreciate.

Breathe.

Breathe.

THE BEAMS
KEEP FALLING

– Steph Cha –

MY FIRST APARTMENT WAS A DIM TWO-BEDROOM ON THE ground floor of a one-hundred-year-old building in New Haven, Connecticut. I was twenty-one and starting law school, still fresh out of college, where I'd spent all four years living in filthy dorm rooms. I had almost no role in finding the place and would not have known what to do if I had been looking on my own. I don't think I realized it at the time, but I didn't know anything when I was twenty-one.

I'd met my roommate, Maka, at an admitted students' weekend that spring. We'd been planning to find an apartment with another girl in our class, but she ended up rooming with someone else when three-bedrooms proved hard to come by. It was this third girl who found our place for us, since she lived close enough to New Haven to apartment hunt in person. She gave us the address, the price, and her general observations. We needed an apartment, so we went ahead and took it, sight unseen. At least neither of us was particular.

The building was called the Taft, and we moved into apartment 1A in August 2007.

It wasn't an especially nice apartment. It was old, and there were always weird noises—temperamental pipes, a periodic squeak that sounded like new sneakers on a waxed floor. There were maintenance issues, too. A whole month when both of our toilets kept breaking, and we had to use the bathroom of the restaurant/bar on our floor, a place called Hot Tomato's with a popular half-price martini night. Occasionally we had mice. But it was my home for three years, the first place I lived as an adult that felt like mine.

Our bedrooms were upstairs. Downstairs, we had a kitchen, a living area, and a tiny dining space: a four-top table crammed between the stairs, the door, and a giant pillar that went through the whole apartment. (I don't think we ever figured out what that pillar was for.) I spent most of my time downstairs, and most of that time on the couch.

I've changed in a lot of ways over the last twelve years, but one constant in my life is that I am extremely sedentary. I don't leave my house if I don't have to—I prefer to be home, where I don't have to get dressed or brush my teeth if I don't feel like it—and I more or less live on my couch. I'm on my couch right now, as a matter of fact, in my pajamas, flanked by my basset hounds.

I was the same way in school, especially in the winter months, when I hated to go outside. I never worked in libraries or coffee shops. There were weeks when I barely left that apartment, and when I was there, I was almost always on that couch. I didn't own a desk, so that was where I did most of my bullshitting and all of my work. I studied and did my homework there and wrote the first draft of my first novel. I kept odd hours (I still do), so I would often stay up super late and fall asleep on that couch, never making it upstairs. I'd say this happened around one out of every four or five nights.

The couch was my roommate's. I think it was from IKEA. Basic beige fabric, not beautiful but very comfortable. It was in our living area, right by the one downstairs window, which faced out onto a dingy alley and a brick wall. I walked through this alley most days—the back entrance to the Taft was in this alley, and it was closer to our apartment than the main entrance, which was through the lobby. It was a high-traffic alley, as it cut through a central downtown block, and when I was on the couch, I was something like three to five feet away from it, with just the window and the wall in between. We had an air-conditioning unit in that wall that carried sound in from the alley. We would often hear people walking through, occasionally recognizing the voices of people we knew.

One night, three months after we moved in, I was up late, reading or working or just dicking around on the Internet, but in any case sitting on the couch. It was after three in the morning, and my roommate was long asleep upstairs. I had my pants off, as I often did, and was lounging around in just a T-shirt and underwear when I heard someone talking in the alley.

I wasn't tuned in at first. It wasn't that unusual for there to be voices outside, even at night, and I had no reason to listen in on whatever he was saying. But then I heard the word *Asian* and then "I want to fuck your Asian ass." That got my attention. He was talking to me.

At that point, I realized I'd been hearing his voice for a while. I can't be sure, but I thought he'd been droning on for several minutes. His voice was low, and he was telling me what he wanted to do to me.

The window was closed, as were our blinds. We hadn't put in a curtain, thinking the blinds gave us enough privacy. It turned out, though, that if the lights were on in our apartment, anyone willing to press their faces right up to our window could peer in and see past the flimsy blinds.

I don't know if I can really convey how jarring and terrifying that moment was, when I went from relaxing in my own home to being conscripted into the sexual fantasies of a strange man, a man whose face I couldn't see but who spoke to me from only a few feet away, close enough that I could hear him clearly, though he never raised his voice.

I think if I had been fully dressed, I would have gotten up and gone upstairs right away. But I didn't have pants on, and he was saying these disgusting things to me, and I didn't want him to see me running through my apartment in my underwear. Instead, I positioned my laptop to cover myself and waited silently for him to go away.

He kept talking. I don't know for how long—it felt like an hour, though it's entirely possible it was only a few more minutes. I couldn't tune him out, and I couldn't concentrate on anything else, so I heard every filthy word that came out of his mouth.

I was so scared, I didn't say a word, and I moved as little as possible. (Once, I shifted, and he begged, "Oh, don't turn over.") I think I would've stayed like that, waiting him out, except that he started talking about wanting to come in, asking me to open the door so he could fuck me.

At that point, I reached for my phone and called the police. I told them there was a man harassing me from the alley outside my window, and I made sure I was speaking loudly enough that he'd be able to hear. He stopped talking after that, but I waited several more minutes to get up and move around. When I thought enough time had passed that he must be gone, I called out, just in case, that I had called the police, and they were on their way. Only then did I go upstairs to wake up my roommate and tell her what had happened.

The police came, and the man was, of course, long gone. As relieved as I was that he was no longer pressed up against my window, I was upset that he had gotten away. I had nothing to offer the police to help them identify this man. Who he was, where he'd come from—it was all a mystery to me. Meanwhile, he knew exactly what I looked like and where I lived.

I talked to Maka. I called my boyfriend. I cried. At some point, I fell asleep. The next day, I ordered Mace-brand police-model pepper spray from a home-security website. I told our apartment manager about the incident and requested that the back door be kept locked at all times. Maka bought us a curtain.

None of this reversed the feeling of violation or softened the truth it exposed: that my safety was at the pleasure of men, that even the most pathetic man could make me feel like a helpless nothing girl.

For some time, I fantasized about all the other ways that scene might have played out. I thought of all the clever, cutting things I could have said, the words that might have shown this man who he really was and sent him off in tears. I saw myself turning around and lifting the blinds to look him dead in the eye. I imagined grabbing a kitchen knife and running out to meet him in the alley.

I think if I'd heard this story from a friend, I would have quietly taken for granted that I might have done one of these things if I were in her situation (probably not the kitchen knife). I'd never been averse to confrontation, and I thought of myself as someone who stood up for herself and for others. I was only twenty-one, and I had already had a number of arguments with gross drunk men. Of course, those had taken place at parties and bars, public spaces where I didn't feel like I was in danger. This was the first time I'd had to face the threat of a man alone. It only took a few words for him to pour acid on all my nice illusions.

If there is one good thing that came of this, it's that I've never felt the need to ask why a woman might not fight back against a rapist, why she might find herself unable to face him or report him after an assault. I've known some formidable women who have suffered at the hands of men and who have not gone Kill Bill on them as I otherwise might have expected.

I am formidable, but I remember how I was paralyzed by that voice, a voice belonging to a man who couldn't even touch me, whose face I never saw. Whenever I hear people ask, "Why didn't she fight? Why didn't she say something?" I know they've never felt that kind of fear. It is humbling, and it is revelatory, and while I would not wish it on anyone, I do wish that those who have never felt it would have the humility and the compassion to keep their fucking mouths shut.

ONE DAY, A FEW WEEKS AFTER THE INCIDENT, I WAS COMING home through the alley, and I saw a man crouched against the wall of the Taft. I was about to go in through the back door when he spoke—either to no one or to me. He mumbled something that I couldn't be sure I heard correctly. What I thought I heard were the words "I want to fuck you," the refrain of the peeping Tom in the alley, in what I thought was his voice. The man was positioned beneath my window.

He was young, under twenty, I thought, white or Latino, in a hoodie. I didn't get a very good look at him and would not have known his face even minutes later. I bolted from the alley and went straight to Matt's apartment, which was on my block. I didn't return to the Taft until after Maka came home.

I DIDN'T CALL THE POLICE. I WASN'T AT ALL SURE THAT I'D heard him correctly, and the chances were too high that he was just a random drunk. Still, I told myself it was him, and even now, when I picture the man harassing me from the alley, I picture him as young and sad, sitting outside with nothing better to do. This second encounter freaked me out, of course, but I think it helped me more than it scared me, being able to attach that voice to a human body.

The pepper spray took a month to ship—would not recommend HomeSecurityStore.com—and by the time it arrived, I had moved past the worst of the terror. I threw the pepper spray away not too long ago. It had expired, and I never had to use it.

THERE'S A LITTLE PARABLE EMBEDDED IN THE MALTESE FALCON about a man who runs away from his life after a near miss with death in the form of a beam falling from a high building. As Sam Spade tells Brigid O'Shaughnessy, "He felt like somebody had taken the lid off life and let him see the works." He builds a new life for himself, but Spade can't help but notice that it's essentially the same as the old one. "He adjusted himself to beams falling, and then no more of them fell, and he adjusted himself to them not falling."

I think about this passage a lot. It's such a perfect, succinct description of the way we process our brushes with danger and, if we are lucky, move on with our lives. I didn't move out of the Taft, as I thought I might during the first days after the incident. I stayed there and went back to my routine, hanging out on the couch with my pants off, relying on the closed curtain to protect me from dirty men in the alley. But one thing I can tell you about being a woman: we don't forget about the beams. Because the beams never really stop falling.

About one in five women are raped or sexually assaulted at some point in their lives. (I know this number seems high to a lot of folks, but consider that most women you know would never tell you if they were raped. I have a lot of close female friends, and I think 20 percent might be a low estimate.) I have been lucky; I have never been assaulted. But all women have to think about the specter of sexual violence, even if we often let ourselves believe it's farther away than it is. We have to watch for the shadow of a beam falling because those beams are falling on somebody every hour of every damn day.

In June 2016, less than three months after Matt and I bought our house, I moderated an event with fellow crime writers Ivy Pochoda and Alafair Burke at Book Soup on the Sunset Strip. It was a seven P.M. event, and the plan was to get drinks beforehand and dinner afterward, so I decided to play responsibly and take an Uber to West Hollywood.

The driver was a guy named Brian. He was in his late twenties or early thirties, close to my age. He was very friendly and talkative right off the bat. I learned that he was living on the Westside and going to school for psychotherapy, that he had recently moved back home to LA after a relationship had fallen apart in another state. He had grown up in the Pacific Palisades, and it turned out that his brother had gone to my high school—I learned his full name this way.

He was so forthcoming, and it was still sunny out, and he had his arm in a sling. I wasn't even thinking about this at the time, but I'm guessing all of these factors helped put me at ease. We had about a half hour together in traffic, and I was happy to engage in the conversation. I was also in a buoyant mood. I was on my way to a bar to meet Alafair and Ivy for drinks, and Michael Connelly—a man I admire greatly and had at that point met only in passing—was joining us. When the driver asked questions, I was eager to answer them. I told him I was a novelist and that I was doing this bookstore event, and I definitely could not help myself and name-dropped Connelly. I also mentioned my husband, just in the course of conversation, and Brian asked the normal questions: how long we'd been together, how long we'd been married, things like that.

He talked about his injury, which he'd gotten doing something athletic, I don't remember what. He said he loved to surf and hike, and he asked me what I did for exercise. I told him that I didn't really exercise, that my husband and I were both pretty inactive, sedentary people. Then he asked how often we had sex, and because I'd categorized him as friendly and harmless and was in the rhythm of talking and answering questions, I just flat-out told him. It took me a few more seconds to process what had happened, and by then he was asking me how many times a week I orgasmed.

At that point, I stopped talking. I fired up my Google Maps to check how far we were from my destination and was mortified when the app started shouting out directions—I didn't want the driver to realize I was counting the minutes left in the ride. He tried to engage me a couple more times, even offering that he was studying to be a therapist and that I could just let him know if he crossed any lines. I didn't say another word to him.

I ended up having a good time in West Hollywood, but as soon as I got home and told my husband what had happened, the fear and anger came back to me, and I broke down and cried. I gave Brian a two-star Uber rating—I guess I was scared that he'd come for me if he saw that he'd gotten one star—and then filed a complaint with Uber, detailing what had happened. I thought at first that there was a chance the conversation had started out innocently and had taken an inappropriate turn and that Brian might be offended and horrified that I had reported him when he thought we were friends. It took me a while longer to understand that he'd known exactly what he was doing. There was no mystery there once I had figured him out. I was a woman alone, happily married, happy in her career, on my way to hang out with renowned authors. It must have been clear to him that the thought of his dick hadn't once crossed my mind. He'd had this brief window when I was in his power, and he had used the opportunity to put me in my place.

That night, after my husband went to sleep, I sat on our couch downstairs, and I looked out the window of our new house. Our living-room curtains were raised, as they often are, and I could see the street, dark while I sat inside, bathed in light. I started thinking about whether someone outside could see me and how close he could get without my noticing. Brian knew where I lived.

WRITING
ABOUT WAR

– Jacqueline Winspear –

IT WAS A SATURDAY MORNING, THE DAY WE WENT INTO THE town some two miles away to do the shopping. The "town" in question was more like a village, but because the city/town/village/hamlet designation in England is based upon the size of the church, and our community had a very large ancient church, it was known as a town.

My father worked on Saturdays, and we had no car, plus you couldn't get those big Silver Cross prams onto a bus in those days, so my mother pushed the pram with my baby brother tucked inside and me, four years of age, walking beside her. Not only would we do the grocery shopping, but my mother also returned library books for the elderly people on our street—which was most of the people on the street—and chose new books based upon their reading preferences. And, of course, there were other errands to run before we began the long walk home.

My mother and father were London people who had moved to rural Kent to get away from the World War II bomb sites that would not be cleared for decades. In fact, the last bomb sites were dealt with when construction began for the 2012 London Olympics. And frankly, as newlyweds in 1949, Mum and Dad couldn't find a place to live because housing was at a premium. Tens of thousands of people had been made homeless due to years of bombing, and it would take many years to provide decent accommodation for those who had lost so much. So families lived together, and newlyweds moved in with a set of in-laws, which my mother didn't take to at all. And if truth were told, she had to leave London to get away from the memories.

On that day, more than fifteen years after the war ended, we were walking toward the grocery store when I needed to use the WC, so we turned up the lane by the side of the post office toward the "public conveniences." Then the fire siren sounded. With a partial force of volunteer firemen, the town siren was used to summon them to the fire station, and it was the same siren used to warn of an air raid during the war. The second that siren began its wail from a low cry to a full-blown crescendo, my mother grabbed my brother from the pram, took me in her arms, and cowered in a doorway. I remember seeing the animal-like fear in her eyes as she looked up, scanning the sky above, yet people on the street went about their day, not noticing a young woman paralyzed with fear while grasping her children to her.

"It's all right, Mummy," I said, tugging her sleeve to get her attention. "There's no bombs; it's all right. It's only the firemen."

You see, though young, I knew instinctively what was ailing her—that the siren had dragged her back through the years to a time when people were told to "Keep Calm and Carry On" despite seeing death and destruction every single day for years on end. And I knew this because she had told me her stories as if I were an adult and not a child. But in that moment, when I reminded my mother that we were safe, that it was only the fire siren, it was not an intellectual knowing that I experienced, an observation I could put into words and explain at such an age. It was something I knew because I felt it—and even at such an age, I'd already witnessed something of war's lingering demons clinging to another person I loved.

I'VE OFTEN WONDERED WHETHER MY MOTHER TOLD HER STO-ries time and again as a sort of exorcism, replaying images of being sent away from home as an evacuee or being bombed out of a house—a story I heard time and again because, as she was being carried away by a policeman, she ignored his warning to keep her dust-filled eyes closed and opened them only to see the neighbor's little girl—who had been playing hopscotch on the street—bloodied and dead, her body torn to shreds. Though my mother worked on the local farm in the early years of my childhood, I was her closest companion, and perhaps she forgot that I was so young when she told these stories—certainly there was never any baby talk in our house. I remember bringing home my reading book from school and my mother rolling her eyes at the page where I had to read about the duck going "Quack, quack, quack." If she'd had her way, I'd have been on *Anna Karenina* by age seven.

The truth is that it wasn't until I began writing my series featuring Maisie Dobbs, the former World War I nurse who becomes a private investigator, that I began to wonder if I, too, was not delving into war as a kind of exorcism, perhaps using story as an emotional connection to those who had been through war, weaving together truth, fact, and fiction to explore what happens to people at such a time. But it was later, following the 2014 publication of my World War I stand-alone novel, that I realized I was perhaps a bit more transparent than I'd imagined. Maureen Corrigan, book reviewer for NPR's *Fresh Air*, broadcast a tenth-anniversary retrospective of the Maisie Dobbs series, ending her review with "Winspear has returned—via a good new stand-alone, nonmystery novel called *The Care and Management of Lies*—to the wartime period that clearly continues to haunt her."

Haunted? I thought. *Me?*

And it occurred to me that she could be right.

AS THE DAYS AND MONTHS PASSED, THE QUESTION OF MY haunting began to bother me more and more, and I wondered about other writers who gravitate toward war as a theme. I wanted to know what it was about war that drew them in and how they felt not only about their own stories of conflict but about the research they'd delved into to create a wartime world. I suppose I wanted to know if we were all haunted in our way.

In his book *War Is a Force That Gives Us Meaning*, former war cor-respondent Chris Hedges writes, "[War] is peddled by myth-makers—historians, war correspondents, filmmakers, novelists, and the state—all of whom endow it with qualities it often does possess: excitement, exoticism, power, chances to rise above our small stations in life, and a bizarre and fantastic universe that has a grotesque and dark beauty." If that is not the basis for a stunning work of nonfiction, an award-winning film, Pulitzer Prize–winning journalism, and, yes, bestselling fiction, I don't know what is. But I know that as a child, I would listen to fam-ily stories of war and be transfixed. Later, as I entered my teen years, I became passionate about ending war. At age twelve, when my friends had posters of pop stars, I was pinning Viet-nam photojournalism to my bedroom wall. I remember one image in particular, of an American soldier with a white dove perched on his hand. At the time I was too young and naive to realize that these things were staged, but it caught at my heart and brought me to tears.

Many writers who have experienced war have used the creative act of writing to explore how people are engaged in and impacted by conflict, while others have been inspired by bearing witness to those who have suffered through war. Rhys Bowen, author of two bestselling novels set in World War II and a new World War I novel, *The Victory Garden*, shared something of a wartime experience that arguably informs her interest and engagement with the subject. "I think that the Second World War has always been part of my subconscious," said Bowen. "I was born toward the end of it; don't remember details, except I was taken to a back-garden shelter when bombs were falling and had an absolute panic attack. But growing up in the post-war years, one was so conscious of great things that had been achieved, soldiers coming home weary but triumphant, and great sufferings endured."

MARTIN PARSONS, FOUNDER OF THE RESEARCH CENTRE FOR Evacuee and War Child Studies at the University of Reading, England, suggests that it takes three generations for an immediate experience of war to work its way through the family system—especially if the wartime experience was in childhood. I read his book *War Child* when it was first published. I remember getting to that part and sitting back to consider the fact that perhaps my mother's experience of war was working itself through me and, in other ways, my brother, too. Many years before, I had read Ben Wicks's searing book *No Time to Wave Goodbye* about the 1.5 million children evacuated during World War II from Britain's cities into the countryside. I'd bought the book for my mother, but she couldn't read past the first few pages—it brought back too many painful memories, so she cast it aside. But then there was my grandfather.

My first novel, *Maisie Dobbs*, was dedicated in part to my grandfather, a veteran of the Great War. In fact, I am named for "Jack" Winspear. But I was only two and a half years of age when I saw how war could injure a person from within—how "shell shock" can cause such distress decades after war has ended. Distress and demons. Granddad was still suffering from wounds sustained at the Battle of the Somme in 1916, one of the most devastating battles of that terrible conflict. He had already seen action at Ploegsteert Wood and Ypres—names that echo from history books today—and he came home shell-shocked, gassed, and with terrible leg wounds. He was a dear man around whom we had to be quiet and who was still removing shrapnel splinters from his legs when he died at age seventy-seven. My father's childhood in an otherwise happy family home was marked by his father's ill health as a result of the war.

The postwar winters were hard on my grandfather because his poor lungs could barely cope with the damp and smog of London's streets, and when his breathing became most labored, the doctor was called, and a special ambulance came to take him away to a sanatorium on the coast. The family would be plunged into economic hardship, so visiting was out of the question. Then, about a month later, he would come home and do his best to pick up the reins of his business again—my father and his brother having kept things going as best they could, working after school. Granddad would get the family on an even keel once more until the next time, and the next. And my father was raised in a quiet house because my grandfather could not stand loud noises—they brought back unwanted memories of the fighting. Shell shock in World War I was often associated with sound and percussion injury, and my grandfather's wounding was no exception.

One day, when I was still a toddler and in my grandparents' care because my parents were at work, I was told I could leave the table and play with my toys—I'd been fidgeting since finishing my lunchtime egg sandwich. I remember everything that followed so very clearly—and though it might seem strange that a child so young has a clear memory of events, I believe an almost

fatal scalding accident when I was fifteen months old contributed to my extraordinarily long memory. I went to my toy box,
a wooden trunk my father had made for me, and pulled out
my favorite doll. Made of soft red wool, she had a face sculpted
of some durable material, with sweet painted eyes, a snub little
nose, and ruby-red lips, and I loved her.

I began running around the table, my energy effervescent,
and I was squealing. Around and around the table I ran, waving
my doll in the air. I can remember my grandmother telling me
to slow down, and I remember seeing my grandfather become
tense, his gray-blue eyes growing wider. Again, I ran around
toward him, but this time he grabbed the doll from my hands
and with his knife stabbed her time and again, a guttural cry
coming from the very core of his body—it was the same terrible scream that was trained into men for that rush from the
trench and over the parapet into battle, bayonets fixed. I just
stood and watched. I did not cry, but I know I felt deeply sorry
for him because I could see he was distressed in a way that I
had no words to describe because I was only a child. I believe
it was the first time I experienced compassion, though I would
not know or understand that word for a good few years. My
grandmother quickly put a bandage on the doll at the place
where a livid knife tear in her forehead was bleeding white,
fluffy filling. I was not wounded in the way that a child psychologist might imagine, but the scene remained with me, and
I know that when I wrote these words in *Birds of a Feather*, it was
my grandfather who inspired them: "That's the trouble with
war, it's never over when it's over, it lives on inside the liv-

ing." Indeed, the challenge of living with war's memories has been at the heart of bestselling fiction and nonfiction crafted by many writers.

Kate Atkinson, whose 2018 novel, *Transcription*, is set in World War II England, commented, "War is such a vast canvas to work on. There were so many real people whose lives were turned upside down by the experience. Violence and heroism, certainly, but also the less romantic side of plodding your way through something with no knowing what was at the end or when that end would come."

For his part, author, journalist, and historian Adam Hochschild has written about World War I, in *To End All Wars*, and explored the Spanish Civil War, in *Spain in Our Hearts*. I asked Hochschild what had drawn him to the subject of war in his research and writing. "I think any occasion where people have to risk their lives is inherently dramatic," said Hochschild. "It intensifies life, so to speak—and, sadly, does that even when the war involved is not worth risking your life for. And unfortunately, that is the case with most wars."

WITH EACH NEW NOVEL IN MY SERIES, AND ALSO WITH MY stand-alone non-mystery, *The Care and Management of Lies*, I have been asked whether I had planned the narrative to reflect current events. I know I'm not alone among writers who are asked this question. Given the deadlines writers work to, the research involved, and the time it takes to actually write, together with the fact that most published books go into production at least six months before the publication date, it is perhaps coincidence that the events of the day are reflected in the narrative. Personally, I think history is a bit like fashion—it comes around again but looks just a bit different. Sometimes, however, the look and feel of the present are reflective of the past and inspire a writer. "The political climate in our current world, the rise of white nationalism in so many countries, made me see the parallels with pre-war Germany," said Rhys Bowen, adding, "I felt compelled to tackle my theme."

I asked Adam Hochschild if his experience as an anti-Vietnam activist informed his interest in war as a theme for his research and writing. "I felt that the Vietnam War was senseless and that it was evil of politicians to send young men off to risk, and sometimes lose, their lives there," said Hochschild. "At one point, while working in the presidential campaign of the anti-war candidate George McGovern in 1972, I shared an office with several Vietnam vets also working in the campaign. One of them had lost his legs in Vietnam but came to work in the campaign every day in his wheelchair. If ever I had any doubts about whether it was worth putting twelve hours a day into this campaign, I just had to look across the room."

The heightened emotions that attend war are compelling for any writer. The themes of love and war were always of interest to me—love between sweethearts, love between men serving in a war zone, and the love of an officer for his men, all of which I have been able to explore in my work, both in the "action" of the moment and from the distance of time. Writing about any era, whether the past or the present, and with any theme demands research, and I have discovered that often the research will leave me in a very dark place. I have used the archive at London's Imperial War Museum on many occasions, sifting through letters and diaries to get to the essence of the human experience in a time of war. And sometimes there's that moment when I have to just sit back and close my eyes to assimilate what I have read because the depth of human experience revealed has taken my breath away—and sometimes that experience has been expressed in the most simple terms in a letter.

Author Jeff Shaara has written many books about war, both fiction and nonfiction, covering conflicts from the Revolutionary War to the American Civil War to Korea and World War II. I was curious about what might have shocked or surprised Shaara in terms of his research, and he drew attention to the way his research compelled him to create fully realized characters who could not simply be labeled good or evil. "I found that those characters easily labeled the *bad guys* were every bit as sympathetic as the *good guys*," said Shaara, adding,

> The impact of that process is that I learn to love every character I'm writing about. That's essential for me to get into their heads, since all of my stories are told through their eyes. If I don't feel a deep empathy for the character, it's impossible to feel comfortable putting words into their mouths, or to put myself into their thoughts. The powerful emotions I felt writing the death of the Red Baron caught me completely by surprise, as did the death of Rommel. I had a difficult and very emotional time writing those parts of the story, as difficult as it was writing the deaths of many of the American characters.

MOST WRITERS OF FICTION USE SOME ELEMENT OF PERSONAL story in their work. It might be a few words overheard while on a train or waiting in line at airport security. It could be an event witnessed and then reimagined as happening at a different place and time. I remember once, while on book tour, I went into the women's restroom at an airport to wash my hands when a young woman came in, clad in her army uniform, the camouflage indicating that she'd returned from service in the Middle East. She looked in the mirror, then reached into her kit bag. She brought out a plastic bag with her makeup and proceeded to apply mascara, some blush, and a quick swipe of pink lipstick. She brushed out her sun-kissed hair and tied it back in an elegant chignon before checking her appearance and reaching back into her kit bag to swap her canvas shoulder bag for a delicate Chanel-style purse. One more quick check, and she picked up her kit bag and left, her heavy black boots echoing in her wake, as if she had just put on a mask to meet our civilian world and her loved ones again. I haven't used that scene yet, but I will—it was too good to lose.

Other writers have had similar experiences, moments when some element of war was brought home to them in a moment they did not expect—and perhaps had all the more resonance due to their work. For Jeff Shaara, one of those moments came after he'd completed The Frozen Hours, telling the story of the US Marines and the Chinese at Chosin Reservoir in Korea. Says Shaara, "I was emotionally exhausted. I was fortunate to be able to interview survivors of that campaign, knowing how they turned out in the long run, which was almost always difficult—long-term awful effects of frostbite, for example—and, along the way, a number of those veterans who had offered me extraordinary material did not live long enough to see the book come out—that was tough. I had been given wonderful gifts from extremely generous men, and I never really had the opportunity to thank them or show them the respect I had given them by telling their story."

Adam Hochschild recounted the following experience:

I had just finished giving a talk about a new book—*Lessons from a Dark Time*. Afterwards, in the line of people to get their books signed was a guy who said he had read *Spain in Our Hearts*, and it meant a lot to him because an uncle—who he had never known—had been killed as a volunteer in Spain. The man who told me this—perhaps in his sixties—told me that he himself was an emergency-room physician who had gone to the demonstration at Charlottesville in 2017 to be on hand in case anyone needed help. Which, tragically, they did. Something about that continuity of people working for justice, in different ways, across the generations, always moves me deeply.

Perhaps there's something of that search for justice in our writing about war—and for me, personally, my respect has always been for those who go to war to write about war; the war correspondents who bring home stories not only of the nuts and bolts of military engagement but of the ordinary people whose lives will be changed forever by conflict. War correspondents are at the top of my list of people who write about war and who deserve our utmost respect—which is probably why the work of wartime journalists is a theme in my most recent novel, *The American Agent*. I can write about war only from hindsight, from research, and from personal engagement with others who have experienced war. I wrap my stories of war around a cast of characters so that they become both compelling and entertaining. I do not face guns every day. I am not risking death to tell my story. But sometimes the conflict a war correspondent encounters is on his or her own doorstep. In a December 2018 article in the London *Sunday Times*, veteran war correspondent Christina Lamb wrote about gang warfare on the home front resulting in young lives lost to knife crime. She recounted this experience: "As a war correspondent, I have always been interested in the people behind the lines, and last year I was giving a talk about mothers in Afghanistan, Iraq and Syria when a woman accosted me. 'You write about all these terrible things in far-off places, but what about your own city?' she demanded. 'There's a war going on here, against our sons.'"

Which brings us to the wars that we writers of mystery and crime are drawn to—the war within the individual, the community, and the wider world beyond that we explore in our storytelling. From the drawing-room whodunit to the searing thriller, almost every social ill or individual wound is encountered. Arguably, "mystery"—that broad-brush description used to describe so many very different books appealing to a diverse readership in the millions—is the literary genre with the power to go to the deepest parts of the human condition, encompassing everything from humor to grief, joy to despair, and love to hatred amid the madness of a world torn asunder, however small or expansive that world might be. It's why mystery has worked for me.

I have always seen mystery as that archetypal journey through chaos to resolution—or not, as the case may be. It's a journey, a pilgrimage that I push my characters to take through the fire of experience until they reach safety. And it's fair to say the foundation of my experience of writing about mystery and crime goes beyond reading books. I have many tales of crime tucked up my sleeve, and I am speaking not simply from having researched the subject but from what I look back upon as a certain innate understanding based upon family experience. That probably caught your attention—but no, I'm not related to the mob!

The postwar London my parents left to live in the country was one hallmarked by a flourishing black market—it was, after all, a time when the rationing of food became worse than during wartime, and rationing did not "officially" end until the latter part of 1954, with many foods in short supply for a good while thereafter. In southeast and east London, in particular, there was a dramatic rise in organized crime—it was something my parents still talked about even years later, I suppose because everyone knew someone who knew someone who was involved in a shady deal. Not many people would turn down a two-pound bag of sugar to keep quiet about something untoward they'd heard or seen while walking down the street. And later, to add to my worldly understanding of crime, there was my mother's job.

When I was in my midteens, she stepped onto the first rung of a new career ladder when she became a clerical assistant at a boys' detention center—a "correctional facility" for young offenders aged sixteen to twenty-one who were not on their first crime (that usually landed just a probation order). She began to work her way up, moving to a men's prison as assistant chief administrator and after that to a women's prison, by which time she was chief administrator of the facility. Then she was pegged to become the first woman chief administrator of one of Britain's most notorious high-security prisons, which was a few hundred miles away from home and pretty much in the middle of nowhere—*nowhere* is usually where you'll find a high-security prison. The Home Office (the government department overseeing prisons in the UK) paid for my parents to travel to the area for a week so they could get to know the region and look at houses and so my mother could visit the prison. They did the tour, viewed a few homes, and could imagine living at the edge of the nearest small town—but then came my mother's visit to the prison, and she turned down the job. "I felt the hair on my neck stand on end the minute I walked into the place and the gates slammed shut behind me," she said. This was a woman who had faced down a mob during a prison riot, so I knew it must have felt bad.

She returned to her job at the women's prison and was also involved in management training within prison administration in the UK, often traveling to prisons in other parts of the country to train new staff. Then one day she'd just had enough, and she resigned, having decided it was time to retire. But over those years from my teens until my early thirties, I heard many stories of crime, both run-of-the-mill and quite extraordinary, especially when she worked at the boys' detention center and later the women's prison. Her role was never disciplinary, but she had a lot of interaction with the prisoners and would talk to them because she was interested in their lives and what events had led them to commit a crime. Perhaps if she'd had the opportunity at a younger age, she would have made an excellent probation officer.

I remember one occasion when she arrived home from work, and after I'd made her a cup of tea, we sat down to talk. She seemed weary. I asked her why she thought most of those young lads in the detention center ended up with a prison record—one that would remain with them forever. She looked out the window, and it was as if a certain sorrow had enfolded her. She turned back to me and said, "Somewhere along the line, someone didn't care enough. So they end up with the wrong crowd or in the wrong place at the wrong time with no opportunity—and the next thing they know, they're inside, doing time. And that's when they really learn how to be criminals."

Perhaps that's why I've always been more interested in the events leading up to and the emotions behind a crime than in just sorting out who did it. To be honest, I have never really been too concerned if a reader guesses the "who" halfway through one of my novels—I usually guess before the denouement when I'm reading a mystery, but it doesn't spoil the story for me. The "why" is both the journey and the destination—that, to me, is the real mystery; the dynamics of our human condition revealed in story. And, as I realized while listening to all those "true crime" stories my mother told—because she had to get them off her chest, I suppose, and we certainly never repeated the stories beyond the house—the most baffling thing about character is often the life journey of a person and who they become as a result.

WE WHO WRITE ABOUT WAR, WHETHER IN OUR FICTION OR nonfiction, all have certain personal experiences to blend with our research, so what we're really writing about is that pilgrimage to the human heart—which remains a mystery no matter how many writers embark upon the journey. And if we write fiction, it's why we test our characters, as if we're daring them to endure a terrible time of upheaval. We want to see what they're made of. We want to know who sinks and who swims. War brings out the very worst and very best in people. Chris Hedges writes, "War exposes a side of human nature that is usually masked by the unacknowledged coercion and social constraints that glue us together. Our cultivated conventions and little lies of civility lull us into a refined and idealistic view of ourselves."

Ah, now we get to the nub of why war is so compelling a subject—it throws who we think we are into the air, and when our tightly held notions hit the ground, they fall apart. Such is the essence of story—especially, perhaps, the mystery. As writers, our curiosity and desire to make sense of madness through the creative act of storytelling prevail. But that madness we encounter in our research and writing can leave a mark on us. I know I have had some very dark days when deep in my research or in the bottomless well of the story, and sometimes it feels as if a veil has been lifted when I finish a manuscript and return to the world, so to speak. In 2018 I turned to writing a comedic short story to shake off the weight of wartime experience I had been delving into for years. As Jeff Shaara kindly shared with me, "I'm working now on a story about the Japanese assault on Pearl Harbor. But I just don't know how many more times I can do this. I keep thinking there might be other stories I could tackle . . . moving completely away from war. Time will tell."

Without doubt, that emotion has enveloped so many of us who write about war, yet we finish our manuscript and, having told our story, leave the territory of conflict, perhaps maintaining that we may never go there again. Yet we return for everything it offers us creatively—as writers we're always looking for that next vast canvas that Kate Atkinson talked about. Whether we like it or not, we submit to our fascination with war, and perhaps without realizing it, we're searching for that nugget, a tiny piece of historical fact connecting the personal to the universal in a way that inspires another story within us. And we go to work, digging in for another journey across war's landscape, ready to venture to the deepest horizon as we explore the darkness and light, the good and bad in humanity—and arguably, more than anything, reflecting where they meet.

WORKS CITED

Hedges, Chris. *War Is a Force That Gives Us Meaning*. Public Affairs, 2002.

Lamb, Christina. "Stabbings in London." *Sunday Times* (London), December 30, 2018.

Parsons, Martin. *War Child*. Tempus, 2008.

Wicks, Ben. *No Time to Wave Goodbye*. Bloomsbury Publishing, 1989.

CAN WE LIVE WITHOUT MYSTERY?

- Tasha Alexander -

PEOPLE FREQUENTLY ASK ME WHY SO MANY READERS ARE drawn to crime fiction. On the surface the answer is simple: few things provide more satisfaction than a well-solved mystery, whether in life or in fiction. Something in the human brain compels us to look for connections, solutions, and larger meaning. This comes as no shock. The emotional payoff is gratifying, and it's easy to accept that we long for explanations and order in a world that is often overwhelming. But is the answer what we crave? Thinking about my own relationship with mystery, I'd have to say no.

Ancient mythology gives us the tale of the Gordian knot. Sometime in the late eighth century BCE, the citizens of Phrygia, mired in civil war, learned from an oracle in Telmissus that their next king would enter the capital city driving an oxcart. Soon thereafter, a peasant called Gordius arrived in just such a vehicle. Why keep fighting when fate has solved your problem? The citizens hailed him as their new ruler, and Gordius tied up his cart, using a knot so intricate and complicated that everyone believed it impossible to untie.

Fortunately, another oracle stepped in to clear things up. The knot could be undone, but only by a man who would rule all of Asia.

Fast-forward to 333 BCE. Gordius's cart—knot still intact—has long been housed in the Temple of Jupiter in the city named Gordium, after the ancient king. The unstoppable young Macedonian, Alexander the Great, is making his way across the continent, conquering everything in sight. He seizes Gordium and heads for the temple, eager to get his hands on the knot. A student of Aristotle, Alexander has a well-trained mind and quickly realizes that he cannot figure out how to untie the rope. Undaunted, he pulls out his sword and hacks through it. Onward to the rest of Asia!

We see a similar scene play out in the film *Raiders of the Lost Ark*. Archaeologist Indiana Jones faces a scimitar-wielding swordsman on the streets of Cairo. Indy reaches for his whip, and the audience is ready for a drawn-out fight. Then, looking drained and exhausted, he instead pulls out a revolver and brings the challenge to a quick—and utterly satisfying—conclusion.

This satisfaction comes partly from our expectations being upended and partly from the wit lacing the story. Regardless of the punch of delight, neither Indy's gun nor Alexander's sword burrows into our minds and demands further thought.

As much as I appreciate irrefutable truth and elegant answers to questions, the search for them can be far more fulfilling than the end goal. Novelist Ken Kesey said, "The need for mystery is greater than the need for an answer," and I think he's right. If he weren't, why is it that sometimes, even when we learn the truth, we have difficulty accepting it? Is it because we object to the answer, maybe because it's not what we want to hear, or do we have a tendency to prefer a good story to a concrete fact?

We return again and again to mysteries that seem unsolvable. Will we ever *really* know who killed JFK? What is the government hiding about Area 51 in Roswell? Surely Princess Diana didn't die in a simple automobile accident? There is no denying the perennial appeal of conspiracy theories. We want solutions, but only when they satisfy our desire for justice and, perhaps more importantly, for meaning. Alongside that, we want a good story. I certainly do.

The staggering reaction to Princess Diana's death came as a shock to many, particularly the British royal family. In the months and years following the car crash that killed her, people began to speculate that it wasn't an accident at all. No one could deny the tension between her and her ex-in-laws. Few denied that the royal family had treated her shabbily, and many suspected that her popularity, even after her divorce from the Prince of Wales, could prove a threat to the monarchy. So wouldn't it be reasonable to suspect that the House of Windsor had ordered a hit on the inconvenient princess?

Not really. We're long past the days of medieval intrigue, and it isn't credible to believe Diana would ever have set up a rival court. Nonetheless, rumors flew that MI6 was behind the crash, that Prince Charles wouldn't be allowed to remarry unless Diana was dead, that the princess was pregnant (she wasn't). The results of the investigation into the accident proved that the cause of the tragedy was far more mundane: the car's driver was intoxicated.

An emotionally unsatisfying explanation. We want someone like Diana to have died for a bigger reason and yearn for a convoluted, serpentine explanation that gives us heroes and villains. Once again, fact is rejected in favor of an ongoing mystery.

Perhaps this need dates back to the days of early humans, when survival often meant fleeing when it felt like the right thing to do, even if everyone else stayed in camp because they didn't see or hear a predator. Sometimes paying heed to that prickling feeling on the back of your neck is a good decision.

This might explain primitive humans' reliance on their instinct, but I think it goes deeper than that for those of us who dwell in the modern world. The unknown can be daunting and scary, but it can also be endlessly diverting. We might not have to depend frequently on instinct to survive, but we get pleasure out of trusting innate impulse and giving precedence to intuition over fact.

A mystery gives us the opportunity to delve into delicious theories, to let our minds wander in all kinds of intriguing directions in search of answers, and to fill hours upon hours with discussion about the possibilities. It provides a reprieve from our mundane daily lives. Even when I know the solution to a mystery—whether it's in the form of a much-loved book or a historical event—I glean enormous pleasure from revisiting the story. I notice new clues, pick up on references previously missed, come to feel closer to the characters involved.

When I first started writing fiction, I did not set out to pen a mystery. My only goal was to draft a book that I would like to read. I figured that entertaining myself (and, perhaps, my mother, who would be more or less obligated to take a positive view of my work) was the only sure thing I could achieve in undertaking such a task. In the end, it turned out to be a mystery. I did, in fact, have a dead body in the book, but my agent and editor had numerous discussions about how it should be categorized. In the end, they went with *A Novel of Suspense*. Later, as I continued to write the series, they became *Lady Emily Mysteries*, and later still, each volume was *A Novel* until we circled back around to calling them mysteries. Nothing changed except the marketing strategy. Regardless of the label, each of the books included a mystery in the classic sense: a murder that my protagonist must solve. But I'd argue that nearly all fiction deals with mystery, just not always the sort that revolves around murders and crime. Those are not, after all, the only kinds that exist. The *Oxford English Dictionary* defines mystery as *a hidden or secret thing; something inexplicable or beyond human comprehension; a person or thing evoking awe or wonder but not well known or understood; an enigma.* (It is also, according to the eighteenth meaning of the noun in nontheological use, a kind of plum cake. Sadly, now obsolete and rare.)

Our fascination with mystery is closely tied to our natural curiosity: *The desire or inclination to know or learn about anything, especially what is novel or strange; a feeling of interest leading one to inquire about anything* (again, from the *Oxford English Dictionary*). We cannot resist learning about those hidden and secret things. Questions—which, in themselves, can be a form of mysteries—entice us, motivate us, and, when it comes to books, keep us reading.

In Jane Austen's *Pride and Prejudice*, we wonder whether the Bennets will be ruined by their Lydia's profligate behavior. Will Lizzie marry Darcy? Will her family ruin Jane's chances with Bingley? Perhaps the biggest question of all in the novel is how anyone could agree to marry a man as loathsome as Mr. Collins. Homer's *Iliad* makes us desperate to know whether Achilles will ever stop pouting and come out of his tent. And, regardless of one's interest—or lack thereof—in whaling, the reader of *Moby Dick* is consumed with a keen desire to see whether Ahab gets the better of that great white beast.

Even nonfiction appeals to our yearning for the mysterious. Facts can be presented in a way that draws us in as fiction does, weaving stories more fantastical than we might accept in a novel. The truth is explained, whether the author is illuminating historical events or uncovering answers to a long-unsolved crime. Consider the myriad volumes that attempt to figure out the identity of Jack the Ripper. We still don't have the answer, but there seems to be a collective insatiable desire to continue exploring the question.

Mystery requires a search for answers. When we're not dealing with fiction, there's a very real chance of finding out exactly what happened and the motivation behind it all. We can discover the truth. But that very search opens up endless possibilities—possibilities our imaginations are all too ready to fill with details.

One of the enduring mysteries of the twentieth century stems from the saga of the ill-fated last tsar of Russia, Nicholas

II, and his family. Facing riots and losing the support of the army, Nicholas abdicated his throne in March 1917, and he, along with his wife and five children, then spent over a year in custody at various locations. Their final prison was Ipatiev House—the House of Special Purpose—in Yekaterinburg, and here, in July 1918, a Bolshevik firing squad executed them.

That wasn't the end of the story. First, the Bolsheviks announced that Nicholas was dead but let the public believe the rest of the family was still in custody, very much alive. Rumors began to fly almost immediately, but the one that caught the collective imagination was that of a young woman who called herself Anna Anderson and claimed to be Nicholas's youngest daughter, the Grand Duchess Anastasia.

Naturally, controversy followed.

Surviving members of the Romanov family denied that she was Anastasia. A German girl identified her as her former roommate, Franziska Schanzkowska, a worker from Poland. But Anderson had many supporters as well, including Gleb Botkin, son of the tsar's personal physician. Botkin knew the family well and had played with the tsar's children. Although she was never legally recognized as Anastasia Romanov, Anderson clung to her claim until her death in 1984.

Her story fascinated the world. People wanted to believe she was Anastasia, that she had defied the odds and somehow managed to survive the bloodbath in Yekaterinburg. In 1991, the Russians exhumed a shallow grave that contained the remains of five members of the royal family, and more than a decade later, archaeologists found the two remaining bodies at a site nearby. There was every reason to believe the entire family had been located. But, still, many people refused to believe the evidence. Even exhaustive—and conclusive—DNA testing has not silenced those who are convinced that Anastasia escaped a grisly fate. Countless people continue to cling to the mystery in the face of incontrovertible facts.

Maybe, one could argue, when the Romanovs faced their firing squad, Anastasia wasn't killed by the first round of bullets because they ricocheted off the diamonds sewn into her corset (we know this to be a real possibility). Maybe no one noticed she was still breathing—ever so slightly—when they dragged the bodies out of the bloody room. In fact, the evidence for someone surviving is stronger than that. According to the executioners, not one but two of the girls were still alive after the massacre, moaning and finding it difficult to breathe. They reported that both of them were quickly dispatched, stabbed to death. But we know something else: that the men who wrote the report were drunk at the time of the executions. Evidently, they weren't eager to get on with their assigned task and decided intoxication would make it more bearable. Further, the grand duchesses were lovely, appealing girls.

Does the latter matter? Of course it does. Maria, two years older than Anastasia, had earlier become romantically involved with one of the family's guards, and he and some of his cohort considered helping the young ladies escape. Instead, their scheme was exposed, and new, less sympathetic men were sent to replace them.

But how do we know they were less sympathetic? Although the Bolsheviks would have liked everyone in Russia to despise the Romanovs, it's not so easy to eradicate the effect of centuries of tradition that had soaked into the people's bones, telling them the tsar was their *little father*. And even if Nicholas and his wife were reviled autocrats, were their young, beautiful daughters, who were never to have ruled the country, so awful?

Contemporary accounts tell us that those who interacted with the family in captivity found themselves surprised by the humanity of the Romanovs. They were no longer living in aristocratic luxury but more like ordinary people. Is it so difficult to imagine that even one of the executioners felt a tug of remorse when he noticed that two of the girls were still alive? In the midst of the gruesome scene, would it have been impossible for him to hide the condition of one of them, perhaps the girl he was charged with putting into a waiting truck? Couldn't he have pretended she was dead and placed her under the other bodies? And then, when they drove into the forest, what if he didn't throw her down the mine shaft that would become a makeshift grave?

Or maybe it's a better story if our conscience-stricken guard doesn't notice any sign of life until he's at the mine shaft, lifting what he thinks is a lifeless body out of the truck. What if Anastasia moves, just a bit, when he picks her up? And what if, in the confusion of the scene—we know it was several days before all the corpses were dealt with and that they weren't all to be buried in the same place—he manages to remove her, taking her somewhere safe, where he—or someone more qualified—can tend to her injuries and nurse her back to health?

Anna Anderson wound up in Germany, where she attempted suicide, explaining later that she had done so because she was afraid that her relatives wouldn't recognize her.

To be fair, she was right about the Romanovs. They didn't accept her. Her physical appearance would have changed in the years between that awful night in Yekaterinburg and the moment that the family first responded to her claims. Surely, they would have recognized something about her, even if she looked different. She would remember things that only Anastasia could. Or would she? The grievous injuries she had suffered might have caused memory loss, and the trauma of the experience had profound effects on her. Anderson could understand Russian but refused to speak it because it had been spoken by her would-be executioners. Regardless of what she did or didn't know, the family rejected her. Why?

Maybe, when they met her, it was obvious in an instant that she was not Anastasia. Even if you go years without seeing someone, you're likely to recognize the person when facing her. If her appearance has changed significantly, you might need to be reminded of her name, but once you hear it, you'll realize it's she. Something in your consciousness clicks, and that's that. However, if the person standing before you isn't who she claims, you'll know at once.

But do we really want to believe that's how the story of this poor woman—locked up in a mental institution (for that was where Anna Anderson first surfaced), scarred physically and emotionally (it can't be denied that her body was horribly scarred), with no family or friends—ends? We have to accept that the Romanovs refused to acknowledge her, but we can look for a more gratifying explanation for their actions.

Were they consumed with guilt for having done nothing to get Anastasia and her siblings out of Russia? Was it unbearable to learn about the horror they had left her to face? Or was her sudden appearance a threat to them inheriting the fortune that Nicholas II had placed in a bank in Germany, still waiting to be claimed by his heirs? Money motivates people to do all sorts of awful things.

Anna Anderson's story, if it were true, would be heartbreaking, but DNA tells us it isn't. At best, she suffered from severe mental illness, rejected her true identity, and believed she was Anastasia Romanov. At worst, she was a calculating psychopath, cunningly trying to exploit a grieving family. The DNA proves two things: first, that she wasn't related to the Romanovs and second, that she was related to the family of Franziska Schanzkowska. Remember that woman in Berlin who claimed Anderson was her roommate, Franziska Schanzkowska?

Even if one were inclined to reject the DNA evidence about the Romanovs—and there are plenty of people who do just that—isn't it a bit much to believe that by some coincidence, this German woman happened to come up with the name of a roommate whose family DNA does match Anderson's?

Of course not. Because if someone is ready to go down the road of denying DNA, there's no limit to where that might lead.

And it's complicated. Did the Russian government, after the fall of the Soviet Union, really want it to get out that the tsar's daughter had survived? And who trusts old DNA anyway? Doesn't it decay? Science is wrong (unfortunately, in our current climate, there are far too many people who believe this). Prince Philip, a maternal relative of the tsar's children, allowed a sample of his DNA to be used for comparison. Are we supposed to believe that he would allow it to be known that Anastasia had survived when the British royal family—his family—hadn't lifted a finger to save her? Furthermore, there's the matter of the Russian Orthodox Church, which canonized the Romanovs and named them martyrs. Saints' bodies are relics, and there are rules about how those bodies are handled. For example, they can't be buried in an ordinary funeral.

After the DNA testing, the bodies of Nicholas, Alexandra, and three of their children were interred in the Peter and Paul Cathedral in St. Petersburg. But now that they're saints, the church is in an awkward position. If it officially recognizes the bodies as the Romanovs, then it has allowed the remains to be handled in a wholly inappropriate fashion. So, instead, it has decided to only sort of accept the recognition and ordered new DNA tests, the results of which have not been made public.

Which means the controversy isn't over. And, you may have noticed, only three of the five children received burial. Per the DNA, Olga, Tatiana, and Anastasia (sorry, Anna Anderson), are at rest in the cathedral, but the spaces left for Alexei (Nicholas's only son) and Maria are empty, their bones still in storage.

Why? Remember that the guards in the woods after the execution didn't bury all the bodies together. Two were found separately. That's suspicious, isn't it? Especially when those two bodies weren't interred with the rest in the cathedral. Why is that? Is it because someone affiliated with the church knows that those remains aren't, in fact, those of Alexei and Maria? And do we now need to go back and rethink everything? Maybe Anna Anderson wasn't Anastasia, but what *really* happened to Maria? I mean, if you'd gone through the hell she had, would you come forward and claim your birthright? Or would you quietly recede, careful to make sure no one knew who you really were, not wanting to draw the attention of those who had butchered your family? Might you even go so far as to convince a mentally ill woman that she was your dead sister so that everyone was thinking about Anastasia, not you?

A little confusion, a few well-chosen facts, and a ready imagination are all it takes to develop a mystery that could well intrigue people for centuries. We might want answers—and sometimes we even accept them—but the quest is often far more gratifying than the conclusion. Mystery excites us, engages us, and irresistibly pulls us into its twists and turns, providing endless opportunities to find a more satisfactory ending to a story. It lets us cling to hope far longer than we might otherwise be able to, satisfies the primal part of our brains that trusts instinct, and, on occasion, guides us to truths that, unexplored, would remain hidden. But most of all, mystery is good fun. Who would want to live in a world without it?

GODFATHERS, NANCY DREW, AND CATS

– Carole Nelson Douglas –

By the time I was five, I'd faced certain death at the hands of others. When I was nine, I testified as a witness to a physical assault. During middle school, I was a conscientious pupil yet ran an undetected smuggling operation out of the stately redbrick school building. At twelve, I was suspected of a serious jewelry theft. All of this was kid's stuff compared to the people I have strangled, poisoned, and pushed to their deaths through most of my adult life. Not bloody, anonymous, "mean streets" stuff, merely everyday murderous domestic malice among friends and family and associates. No, I am not a "gone girl." Just a veteran fiction writer who has wondered from childhood how ordinary people let their lives spiral into unhappiness, even violence and disaster. So I explore my past as prologue.

MYSTERY MAN

Age: Toddler

Location: House near Seattle in Sunnyside, semirural Washington state

Me, tiny feet sinking into a sofa cushion, leaning over the 1940s gray, chartreuse, and maroon floral sofa-cover fabric (destined to soon become drapes in St. Paul, Minnesota). I gaze out the window to the driveway, saying over and over, "Why doesn't he come?"

My father, a Norwegian immigrant salmon fisherman, was often away, but I don't recall ever getting the answer to my plaintive litany. My only mental memory of my father is a shadowy silhouette of a man wearing a fedora and standing near a big black car, the iconic image of a vintage private eye. No wonder old 1940s *Boston Blackie* and PI movie reruns of 1950s TV will entrance me later. By then, the only lasting reminder of my father, besides meager snapshots, will be the exotic new word I had to learn to spell and print on grade school class forms: *Father: deceased.* (Years later, my mother asked for the Christmas gift of a notebook "so I can record everything about our family and your father," as I'd been encouraging her to do. She died of a brain tumor within three months. Her few notebook scribbles concentrated on how he had died on that fishing trawler during a run of salmon. It portrayed a man of duty, Arnold, who became the Nelson in my writing byline for decades. Like his salmon prey, he never flagged in leaping up against the water, the sea.

Twice he lay down with chest pains and arose. The third time he didn't, making my mother a forty-three-year-old grade school teacher, a widow with a small child, a farm-reared woman who didn't know how to drive a car in post–World War II America.) My origins on the Norwegian side remained a mystery, making me curious about other children and families and fathers.

Did I search out father figures? No, but I can now discern key events in my evolving life as a writer/mystery writer when a man of celebrity or authority acted on my behalf, an unofficial godfather creating turning points in my life. Facing the mystery of my father's sudden and forever absence so young, and being an only child left to find answers for herself, gave me a lifelong need to solve life's mysteries small and large. I wanted to see and understand the people and situations behind doors other than my own. I became a neighborhood kid detective, reporter and newsletter publisher, amateur psychoanalyst, snoop, actress, and playwright. My later adult occupations legitimized that need to know. I never again wanted to find myself in the dark, like that bewildered, forlorn child.

LOST FLOCK

Age: Two and a half

Location: Washington state

Wearing rubber boots in the damp, long grass, I watch my beloved bantam chickens pecking the ground. My mother and I are leaving Washington, and she has told me that the boy who lives next door, the son of a family friend, would care for them. This moment will come back to haunt me ten years later.

We retreated to St. Paul, Minnesota, to join her two sisters, so I grew up in the majestic shade of Nativity of Our Lord Catholic Church, looming like a Gothic ship's prow through the leafless winter elm trees. I was the youngest, smallest, and the only only child amid blocks of large, often disorganized Catholic families. Also, I was so myopic that it was a miracle I didn't get killed crossing the street before I got glasses at seven. No wonder my nose was always in a book.

Still, even in that cloistered neighborhood, I had childhood brushes with petty crime and punishment.

THE GREAT ESCAPE

Age: Five

Location: St. Paul, Minnesota

I'm in the backyard of a family with five older girls who have become my March sisters from *Little Women*. Older bully boys accuse me of blabbing about I-don't-remember-what and force me to climb wooden slats nailed into the trunk of a backyard elm tree towering far above the garage roof lines. "Your punishment," one says. "You have to jump down." Penned in, looking down, down, even half blind, I know that would kill me.

On that languid Minnesota summer evening, mothers were calling their kids home to dinner, including mine: *Car-ole. Car-ole!* The power of the parents prevailed; the boys let me climb down. Now I wonder if it's just coincidence that many murders in my mystery series set in Las Vegas are by falling rather than knife or gun. And that one protagonist is a bungee-jumping magician? Vegas teems with aerial shows, and deaths aren't bloody in traditional mysteries. But, subconsciously, am I revisiting that elm-tree ordeal?

THE BOOK SPY

Age: Six

Location: 1920s-vintage two-story family home

It's evening, and I'm supposed to be in bed. Instead, I'm peering down through the staircase overlooking the warm lights and sparkling stainless silver coffee urn at my mother's book-club meeting in the living room below. The women have left, but the books remain. (Years later, by daylight, I read and reread Kipling, George Eliot, James Fenimore Cooper, the Brontë sisters, Oscar Wilde, and my favorite, the complete works of Edgar Allan Poe, font of dark mystery.)

My mother's dark oak bookcase would soon house my own shelf of Sherlock Holmes stories and the ninety-nine-cent Nancy Drew hardcover mysteries begged from my mother every time she took me downtown to buy school supplies. "Please, Mother, please!" (Hearing children plead that at my later book signings is my greatest pleasure in authorhood.) Still, even in that cloistered, benign neighborhood, I glimpsed instances of violent death. One was the fatal fall of a girlfriend's mother down the basement steps—because of encephalitis, they said. The widower immediately married his much younger secretary, leaving his four children's lives in disarray and separation. I always wondered. . . . And then there was the wife and mother who showed up on her neighbor's doorstep so covered in blood that she was unrecognizable, asking for help. It was

St. Paul's most savage murder. She was the victim of a brutally executed murder-for-hire ordered by her womanizing but mild-looking and bespectacled attorney husband, T. Eugene Thompson. It shocked me, as if actor Wally Cox, in his 1950s TV role of the terminally timid *Mister Peepers*, had gone rogue. Could anyone like that live next door to *me*? I watched to make sure. I was a painfully shy child, but I had a secret bold streak.

NANCY DREW JR. (HORSE-CRAZY CUB REPORTER-SNOOP-ADVENTURER)

Age: Seven to thirteen

Location: Cruising quiet neighborhoods as far as my clunky Schwinn bike could take me

I've spotted a horse left alone while the owners work and feed Sidewinder (for the crooked white face blaze) carrot treats from a lunch bag. To reach him, I have to pedal across the mile-long tractor-semitrailer-truck-crowded Mendota Bridge over the Mississippi River flats far below.

It was unnerving. But that ride, plus climbing steep Mississippi river cliffs with a tomboy friend of Indian heritage and clambering behind the deserted, frozen Minnehaha Falls in winter would give me scenes of derring-do in future novels. I was primed. I held on for my life by fistfuls of whip-thin bush stalks and skidded over black ice, firing my cub-reporter interests. I lived in a boring grid of low bungalows and square two-stories, so I was fascinated by other people's houses. I discovered one with a castle-like turret and another on a bush-strangled double lot that had a curved driveway with matching lion statues. I often snooped those lion-house grounds like Nancy Drew and even produced a mimeographed *Neighborhood Newsletter* to flourish when I knocked on the door and asked the lady if I could see inside her house for a story. Uh, no. I'd heard the family name was Nightwine. Is it any mystery why a sinister character named Nightwine inhabits my mystery novels? In any case, I had developed a fierce code of justice from my Catholic education. If it was a school-based injustice, I believed that Sister could fix it. If not, Father from the rectory would. And if not he, then God surely would restore right and just order.

WITNESS FOR THE PROSECUTION

Age: Nine

Location: Fourth grade classroom at Nativity School

I am an incensed witness when the new kid, Arthur, beats up my friend Patty on the way to school. Called to testify, I fearlessly, passionately "finger" the new bully boy to his face. (Shades of "You dirty rat" from James Cagney gangster films on TV.) Patty sobs.

SOCIAL WORKER

Age: Eleven

Location: Large front bedroom of Patty's house

Patty sits amid a watching circle of older sisters, about to razor-etch a boy's initials onto her knee. I tell her I will never be her friend again if she does this. She does. I leave.

We never spoke again until a school reunion decades later. She and all her sisters had married controlling alcoholics, but she had been the only one to divorce hers. I told Patty she'd been the "Cool Hand Luke" figure on our block, like the jailed Paul Newman in the film, who was egged on to defy authority and pay the price, a scapegoat victim-hero for others. She called her four older sisters that evening: "Remember all those times Carole was over at our house? She wasn't just *there*. She was *observing*." It was true. I had been a victim, a witness, a prosecutor, and a "house" detective, and now I was a social worker, building characters, writing sketches of the girls around me, recording what we would later call dysfunctional ways. Patty didn't have a scar, but classmates later reported domestic verbal and physical abuse. Maybe I was better off with only shadowy memories of a father. And who knew all of this would find its way into my novels?

PROFESSIONAL CAT SMUGGLER

Age: Five to twelve

Location: Nativity Church's stately redbrick school

The school entrance is a set of huge, heavy, noisy double doors that buffer the severe winter climate. My father loved cats, as I do, but my mother won't have one in the house. (She allowed a parakeet, even finally a small dog.) I work a deal to bring a stray cat home for two meals and a night in the warm basement before I send it on its way. Strays abound near playgrounds, so I smuggle one into our ranked lines of students going in, I the last in line—like *The Wizard of Oz*'s Cowardly Lion marching into the witch's castle—and leave the cat in the between-door zone. Sometimes it is found and released. If not, I pick it up to take home, and my night shelter is in business.

Cat rescue would become a key element in my future writing career, but as a kid it taught me how to avoid suspicion, sneak around rules, and have a ready "story"—all those antisocial ploys of criminals that my mother wouldn't have encouraged. Our continual duel over cats gave me the relentless drive that it would later take to pursue work in rejection-based fields such as acting and writing. Some attempted rescues had heartbreaking, haunting outcomes. I learned that empathy is never enough in an often cruelly evil world.

DIAMOND THIEF

Age: Twelve

Location: Split-level home on Puget Sound

When I am twelve, my mother brings me by train to visit people from our brief life with Father in the Pacific Northwest. One couple, living on pricey Puget Sound, are our former modest rural neighbors. The son inherited my fluffy little chickens nine years before. Alone in the lower garage level, he torments his sister and me by tearing the wings and legs off bugs.

I realized that house was "split-level" in more ways than one, and the word psychopath was learned. (I still cringe wondering what that kid did to my flock.) But there was another revolting situation. I was accused of stealing the mother's diamond ring. Did I take it? No. "No" was not convincing enough, I saw as my heart sank. After we had returned home, a letter came. The ring had been found in the garbage disposal. Later, I would create and follow a doozy of a psychopath in more than two dozen books. I called her Kitty the Cutter, the graduate of a brutal Irish Magdalene Home for unwed mothers.

THREE LITERARY GODFATHERS ARE WE
Age: Eighteen to twenty-one
Location: University of St. Catherine, St. Paul

Writing is not my first love; acting is, and I thirst to find local role models who had made good in both "impractical" majors.

The sponsor of a Minneapolis-born actor's St. Paul Winter Carnival appearance wouldn't let me, a local college-paper reporter, interview him, so I *went full Nancy Drew* to finagle a meeting with my target, the late actor Robert Vaughn, a very intellectual and nice fellow Minnesotan and then-star of TV's hot *The Man from U.N.C.L.E.* series. I wouldn't hear about "fanfic" until long after, but I was writing and broadcasting a satirical *Eve Cain, The Girl from B.U.N.N.I.E.* serial on the campus radio station. "No" wouldn't have stopped Nancy Drew. And they didn't call it stalking then. I donned high heels and a smartly silly hat to look like a women's-club event coordinator and left a manila envelope addressed to the actor at the St. Paul Hotel front desk. When the bellman retrieved the envelope, I tailed him into the elevator and lurked in espionage mode to see the room number so I could call Mr. Vaughn personally, then cleverly (I thought) walked down four floors and summoned the elevator. The doors opened on Robert Vaughn standing alone in a velvet-collared Chesterfield coat, eating an orange. Speechless, and caught in the ridiculous outfit

I'd planned to dump in the cloakroom later, I got on the elevator and faced forward, then blurted that I'd sent the message: "Say U.N.C.L.E. and give a college reporter a break and an interview."

He not only escorted me to his welcome party but arranged to host a long interview lunch at his Minneapolis hotel when his gig was over. Why? Did he like my oddball combination of chutzpah and sincerity? A mystery . . . finally solved in his 2008 autobiography, *A Fortunate Life*. At twelve, he'd donned porkpie hat and sunglasses to get into a famous adults-only film, *Ecstasy*, featuring Hedy Lamarr. What was certain to me then: my writing the spy-caper radio series and a cheeky interview pitch had won over handsome Godfather I. My confidence tripled. It quadrupled when a later *The Girl from U.N.C.L.E.* spin-off featured Stefanie Powers as April Dancer (sounded like a racehorse name, I sniffed on behalf of Eve Cain, but I'd correctly anticipated a female spin-off). My writing and grasp of pop culture might actually sell. When I created my Las Vegas–set murder mystery series twenty-seven years later, my radio series inspired me to add an international IRA thriller subplot for added dimension, substance, and longevity. I call the result of my particular mix *cozy-noir*. A mystery . . .

IN VOGUE

Age: Twenty-one

Location: High-rise Manhattan penthouse
of publishing giant S. I. Newhouse

White-coated black waitstaff are swooping canapé trays past guests, raising my eyebrows. By now not so ridiculously dressed (hopefully), I am rubbing Midwestern shoulders in my sample-shop wardrobe with East Coast trust-fund babies wearing cashmere twinsets and real pearls.

I was one of twelve national finalists in the *Vogue* magazine annual Prix de Paris writing contest for women college seniors, won previously by Joan Didion and Jacqueline Bouvier (Kennedy Onassis). Thanks to Robert Vaughn, I had a hip, timely subject for the celebrity profile entry, one of nine assignments. (Not the one I dictated to a friend with a manual typewriter on her lap while driving to make the midnight posting date at the St. Paul Post Office. We were both wearing mittens.) I didn't win the year's job at *Vogue* but could have been an editorial assistant if I had learned shorthand and could have survived in Manhattan on a meager salary without parental underwriting. Unlike the rich girls, I was not going to live off my mother's modest teacher's income one minute after graduation.

OVERQUALIFIED

Age: Twenty-one

Location: Employment-agency office

They find my liberal arts ways fit only for teaching for the Famous Writers School. (*Sheer fraud!* I think, but maybe, in hindsight, it is an omen: author Jessica Mitford will "out" the school four years later.) In the *St. Paul Pioneer Press* classified ads, I find an interesting flunky job with little pay in the advertising department. But . . . Godfathers II and III are awaiting me. GII, the advertising manager, chooses "overqualified" me over eighteen others. An older woman coworker (Godmother I) urges me to take a theater review I've written for fun to editorial on the sacred fourth floor. GIII, the managing editor, is a hulking man who camps out on the paper's roof for charity every winter. Intimidated, I watch him skim my review and bark, "Five dollars." I'm hooked.

I was the only staff woman *ever* to accept a call for skit writers for the annual Gridiron Show and was invited to a gala dinner because the pro writers wanted to see this skit-writing "nobody" from advertising. I ended up next to Mr. Five Dollars and, when asked, said, "I'd like to be up where you are." GIII then catapulted me into the women's department as a reporter. I'd crashed the Newspaper Guild union without a journalism degree. The tickled ad manager, GII, showed me the "Overqualified. Should last a year" he'd written on my employment form. God bless 'em both. Male manager mentorship for women would not become a movement for years. Life was changing, but where was the mystery? At my fingertips, on the outdated mechanical typewriters we used. These women's departments, ignored by male management, were moving from society news, fashion, and food to women's equality issues and even protest bombing. Reporting is detective work. I learned to hear lies muttered over the phone. To track down a dodging source well before the Internet made it easy. I always called them at home on Sunday mornings so they'd know I was impolite and *implacable*. I met and learned from the homeless to the famous. My young artsy exploits gave me a chance to interview touring Golden Age (1930s through 1960s) actors and writers. My first "get" was the First Lady of the American Theater, Helen Hayes. I nearly swooned. The investigative articles and series that women's department reporters wrote changed and challenged society and won awards.

But . . . big surprise, male management didn't even *read* our section. Soon a national "news you can use" newspaper strategy had women's department reporters writing do-it-yourself articles on cleaning your gutters. Not what I had dreamed about. I *had* to escape the cage of a union-guaranteed wage "good for a woman" that clipped my wings. Time to finish my long-sidelined Gothic mystery and fiction-write my way out of this deteriorating job. That college-started novel would be the key, but it took another celebrated godfather to turn it.

SPLIT-LEVEL WRITING
Age: Twenty-four to the present
Location: Wherever I am

My tendency to use both humor and dark themes in my mystery novels perhaps can be explained by my "catholic" reading tastes as a college English and theater major choosing to read *The Red and the Black* and *Remembrance of Things Past*—and similar heavy-lifting sagas—but never deserting my childhood mystery genre loves, Sherlock Holmes and Nancy Drew. I binge on mysteries. Raymond Chandler for prose style, Ellery Queen, Josephine Tey, Dorothy Sayers (Dorothy Dunnett for historical suspense), and I love to escape into historical Gothic mystery paperbacks. To me, *Jane Eyre* provides a groundbreaking working woman heroine. (The earliest English novels, by men, were about working women as streetwalkers.) Daphne du Maurier's *Rebecca* is the most distinguished descendent of the genre. Yet the popular fictional governess heroines of my college days are terrified milksops getting locked into crypts from which wealthy and titled Englishmen condescend to rescue them. I want *women* who rescue, whether it is cats, people, or, if necessary, impossibly dreamy heroes. Where are they? In short supply.

So . . . I began to write. After three opening chapters, I had a protagonist, Amberleigh Dunne, a bankrupt suicide's disgraced daughter, an Ireland setting, and a title from an Irish protest song, *One Faithful Harp*. I listed the heroine's musts: she must be loyal to another woman, though it costs her dearly; she must have a man friend who is *not* a romantic interest; she must risk her life to save someone; and she must be recognized by Lord Whatsit as his equal. Or better, his superior. On a teenaged trip to Ireland, I had fallen in love with the lush, verdant land, the famous Irish charm that matched the haunting folk music. I recall sitting in a hotel parlor and watching a well-stuffed, *veddy* British couple as the woman intoned in her impeccable British accent, "Oh, this hotel. So dismal, and the staff"—a young Irish woman whisked by—"so slovenly." He replied, "So true, my dear." What? *Untrue!* Open anti-Irish bias still alive and well in long-postfamine Ireland? Shocking to a girl living in America's civil rights heyday. That dialogue fueled my vague urge to write a Gothic mystery novel with a mission and a theme: the indelible stain of ethnic hatred. My nineteenth-century heroine would be half Irish and half English, conflicted and endangered by ancient political divisions and plots. I was going mainstream. And I would not do it alone.

THE GODFATHER IV, ACT I

Age: Twenty-eight

Location: St. Paul department-store restaurant,
muted gray-and-gold elegance

Golden Age film and stage director and writer Garson Kanin is making an interview point by balancing a heavy restaurant-ware fork on his eloquent fingers. I adore his Old Hollywood stories of Kate Hepburn and Spencer Tracy.

A week later, I came into the office to hear the news: "You missed him. Garson Kanin called. Loved your story." Interview subjects had written but never *called!* (Five years later, I would call him on Martha's Vineyard to announce that my first novel had sold.)

ENTER GODFATHER V, FELINE EDITION

Age: Twenty-nine

Location: St. Paul Pioneer Press office

Journalists rejoice in finding a "hot story" in an unlikely place, a diamond in a hay bale. While perusing the pets category in the classified ads, I find an inordinately long, high-dollar ad seeking a home for a stray cat. It is big and black and has been flown two thousand miles as a "rescue" to Minnesota.

My feature on this savvy survivor illustrated all the hallmarks of a classic noir detective. He'd slunk around a fancy Palo Alto motel, cadging meals from room service trays and decimating the equally fancy $2,000-a-fish koi population in the pond when not ankling up to solo women guests at the outdoor snack machines and getting a bed inside on chilly nights. The guests called him Midnight Louie. Perfect. Although it wasn't done in journalism, I wrote the story from the cat's point of view. Sam Spade with claws.

THE GODFATHER IV, THE SEQUEL

Age: Thirty-three

Location: Minneapolis Cheshire Cheese Room restaurant

I am assigned to reinterview this enthusiastic subject, and Garson Kanin gleefully shows me my earlier article from the *Pioneer Press* sandwiched between his press-kit profiles in the *Los Angeles* and *New York Times*. I have never been one to leverage my job, but, overwhelmed, I mention my completed novel, hoping for an agent's name. He asks, "Is it good?" I chuck Midwestern modesty and say, "Yes." He volunteers to take the manuscript to New York! I surreptitiously check the level of his Bloody Mary (untouched) to ensure that I am not taking advantage of him. Then I drive back to the Minneapolis hotel that evening on an appropriately Gothic dark and stormy night to dash inside and leave *One Faithful Harp*, all 634 pages, at the front desk.

Kanin's Doubleday editor wrote that she would have bought it two years earlier (ouch!), but it was now "off-market." (You think?) "It's particularly well done," she said, recommending two other editors. The first bought it, and I was able to thank Sally Arteseros in person thirty-some years later. Liftoff. Whenever I feel kicked to the curb by life's inequities, I go to my final mentor's Wikipedia entry. He was a self-taught man, an "autodidact," of Renaissance creativity whose own mentor was triple Pulitzer Prize–winning novelist-playwright Thornton Wilder. Garson Kanin will forever be that charming, kind, unassuming writer-director fellow from Golden Age Hollywood and Broadway. Visit him online. You'll be amazed. And he keeps me hopeful and humble.

THE BOOK DETECTIVE

Age: Forty-two
Location: Sunny Texas

In *One Faithful Harp*, retitled *Amberleigh*, I learn I've written a chaste, nineteenth-century novel when bodice-rippers with rapist heroes were in florid flower. I skedaddle to high fantasy, offering imaginative adventure, but as sexually innocent as a hobbit.

My first two fantasy novels became "surprise" national best-sellers. The vice president of the publishing house told me the sales force was begging for my next book, and I soon would make the *New York Times* bestseller list. Surprise! Eventually, two publishers and three editors failed to capitalize on this gift from the publishing gods, and I became box-office poison in the fantasy genre after selling 400,000 books.

Time to visit Garson online. He had passed on, but his assistant said a book of mine had been permanently installed on his personal above-desk shelf. Still humbled. "We'll always have mystery," his ghost whispered to me, like Bogart to Bergman in *Casablanca*.

GODFATHER V, SHERLOCK HOLMES

Age: Forty-three

Location: My bookshelf

It is time to revisit my bookshelf of beloved reads. There are many male-written Holmes spin-off series featuring secondary male characters as detectives. Why not a woman? Woman author, woman character. Someone should do that. It is a mystery to me why no woman has.

So I reinvented Irene Adler, an American opera singer and the only woman to outwit Holmes. Latter-day books and films cast her as a sexy criminal or a villain's pawn. I envisioned her as a clever and bold independent woman of substance with personal and professional integrity, as Sir Arthur Conan Doyle had done. I might have been late to the historical Gothic mystery table, but now I became the first woman to create a spin-off series from the Sherlock Holmes canon and the first to take a woman character as a new detective protagonist. A decade after *One Faithful Harp* debuted as *Amberleigh*, my first Irene Adler novel won two mystery awards and was a *New York Times* Notable Book of the Year. A favorite writer, Sir Arthur, had gotten me to the *New York Times* again.

MIDNIGHT LOUIE RIDES AGAIN

Age: Forty-eight

Location: My North Texas office

In 1992, I promote my newspaper-article cat, Midnight Louie, to a feline PI and noir commentator on the sleuthing of two men, two women, two pro, and two amateur detectives. What is it about Louie, about any cat, that draws in readers? The cat's air of mystery compared to obviously emoting dogs? Maybe, but Louie's witty caustic comments are a wonderful vehicle for social issue explorations, being both homage to and critique of the great American noir male private eye tradition. In the Midnight Louie mysteries, I can invert classic mystery clichés such as the reluctant cop buddy who assists the despised PI . . . with both of them *women*.

Louie is no ordinary cat—his intermittent narrative voice dates from my gradeschool reading of two early-twentieth-century satirical and social-issue-oriented (like me) newspaper columnists. Don Marquis reported what a cockroach named archy (who couldn't reach the shift key) typed on his manual machine overnight, and Damon Runyon penned *Guys and Dolls* and other cynical-sentimental tales of down-and-outers on Prohibition- and Depression-era Broadway. Louie's Las Vegas setting parallels Broadway gamblers, showgirls, and mob bosses, and forty million annual visitors provide murders with such satire-rich characters as celebrity dance contests and Elvis-tribute artists.

Murder is where humor leaves off. Every death has a poignant history behind it . . . sins of envy, lust, greed, wrath, and simply, as in *Cool Hand Luke*, "a failure to communicate." A cozy-noir mystery series can have gravity as well as humor, mixing amateur and professional investigators: a single-mother homicide lieutenant with a devastating family secret, a newly laicized young Catholic ex-priest, a magician-agent with a tragic death in his wake. The One Ring to bind them all is *Miss Nancy*

Drew all grown up on spike heels, as Louie describes his roommate and partner, petite but strong-souled female amateur detective Temple Barr. Protective Louie calls himself her *muscle in Midnight black*. Like a Yorkie terrier who can dominate mastiffs, Temple is little but fierce, ready to root out vermin when murder strikes at events she reps for public relations. Louie is dogged by a tough unacknowledged daughter, Midnight Louise, who keeps his politically incorrect macho self in line. Again, the complex mysteries of the secret feline parallel universe intersect with the social and criminal realities of human lives and times. Definitions of "strong women" may vary, but this writing goal gives me multiple issues to play out in the plots and characters who provide the depth that I need in order to challenge them for, well, twenty-six years.

SOME GIRLISH GOALS ELUDED ME. THROUGHOUT MY LIFE OF crime in writing, I have never owned a horse or lived in Manhattan, but I have visited London, Paris, and Las Vegas for research, and I have contemplated naked, ruinous death and not fainted on tours of medical examiner facilities.

My childhood losses, creative drive, and struggles with right and wrong have clearly and unconsciously made a writer of me.

And yet I've also managed to be an actor all along in roles for which no director was needed to cast me: proper parson's daughter Nell Huxleigh, Irene Adler's "Watson," and Watson himself; savage Kitty and the earnest ex-priest, Matt; unwed mothers from two generations of American women. Sherlock Holmes and Sarah Bernhardt and Howard Hughes as a vampire.

And in creating my own version of the cast of *Cats*, including sassy Midnight Louise and tough Ma Barker, who is Midnight Louie's mother and the matriarch of the Las Vegas Cat Pack. And so the cozy-noir night goes on as the crime and mystery and T. S. Eliot and the cats go on.

And to the ghost of my one and only father, I can say that I have always been true, in life and fiction, to myself and my ideals and imagination and your beloved cats.

THE MYSTERY OF MY LOST VOICE

– Caroline Leavitt –

I'M AT THE TUCSON FESTIVAL OF BOOKS, PROMOTING MY tenth novel, *Is This Tomorrow*. Though I am a *New York Times* best-selling author, the turnout in this auditorium is small, and not only is that upsetting to me, but I'm on the verge of a cold. When I speak, my voice turns raspier than usual. I don't mind. I've had this voice since I was in junior high, when my voice inexplicably became so hoarse that my doctor was concerned it could be a sign of cancer. But I got a clean bill of health and, to my delight, a tonal shift that made me suddenly sound different than my mom or my sister, who kept pushing me to be more like them.

The panel ends, and I'm happy to leave the auditorium. Then the whole festival ends, and I feel better, less depressed because now I can go home and not think about any of this. That's what I tell myself, anyway, but I brood about it on the plane. I have the small turnout on replay, and I can hear the thunderous applause for a writer in another room—another writer who isn't me. I brood about it at home, too, not really taking good care of myself, and I promptly get bronchitis, and my voice grows even weaker. I know all about the mysterious mind-body connection because when I'm stressed, I can count on a cold the next day and for my voice to sound as if it has been rubbed with sandpaper.

But this time, after the bronchitis has been knocked out by antibiotics, after I've given myself a stern talking-to about calming down so I can get better, I still can't breathe, and my asthma meds aren't working. "You need to see a doctor," my husband, Jeff, tells me, so I go to a local clinic, and they give me a nebulizer treatment, which means breathing in a mist of albuterol, opening up my lungs. It does help, but only a little, and two days later, when I wake up, I can hardly breathe, and when I try to talk, my voice is reduced to a whisper. I'm panicking so much that Jeff calls my pulmonologist for me, who says to come in immediately, and I do. He runs breathing tests and then comes out and says, "I don't know what it is, but it isn't asthma. I want you to go see this ENT immediately."

So I do, and this doctor squirrels a tiny camera through one nostril down my throat while I grip the edge of my seat. It doesn't hurt, but it feels invasive and uncomfortable, and I still can't breathe. He finally takes it out and announces that I have laryngopharyngeal reflux (LPR), which happens when stomach acid gets into your lungs. I need to take proton-pump inhibitors, which reduce the production of that acid. "It could also be your heart," he says, "and I want you to see a cardiologist right away." I take the proton pumps for a week, and nothing changes, except my panic grows. I see a cardiologist, who tells me my heart is perfectly fine and I need to see a new ENT.

So I do, and this one tells me it's yeast in my throat, and he can clear it up in a day. "Yeast?" I whisper, and he dismisses me with "That's what I said" and then hands me a prescription. I get expensive antiyeast pills, and I don't get better. The pills make me dizzy, and they make everything taste like it has a fine layer of soot on it.

I next see an allergist, who says he thinks I have an infection in my vocal cords. It's the first time I've heard this, and he gives me small doses of Elavil, which I take as soon as I get home. They almost immediately make me worse. My voice vanishes. When I call him, gasping, he sounds annoyed. "I'm at the park with my kids," he says. He tells me to go into a steamy bathroom, which I do. It doesn't help.

I come out of the bathroom to find my teenaged son playing Scrabble with my husband. They both scrunch their faces with worry. "Are you okay?" my son asks, and I stand up straighter until the furrow in his brow uncreases. "I'm fine," I say, straining my voice so that I sound louder. I know it isn't true, but I want them to feel better. I'm determined to get to the bottom of this, plus I want my son to know that you don't have to take any expert's word for anything, that doctors are consultants, not gods. You can trust your own gut.

"I'm taking care of it," I tell him.

But Jeff, my husband, is more and more worried, and the two of us begin to research my symptoms nonstop. "I don't care if the right doctor is in Spain," he tells me. "Wherever there's hope, we're going." We stay up until two most nights, each on our own computer, calling across the hall when we find something. "Maybe it's a virus," Jeff says. "Wait," I call. "Here's a woman who had something like this, and it was an infection." But while there are lots of stories, lots of suggestions, there aren't any real cures. Worse, some of the articles I read insist that mysterious illnesses are usually all in your head, because if they weren't, medicine would cure them. The articles mention Morgellons disease, where colored fibers supposedly live in your skin (some people think they are signs of alien life. Joni Mitchell has this disorder, and she's hardly flaky). There are psychosomatic disorders, where people actually go blind even though their optic nerve is absolutely fine. But is this what I have? What is this mystery illness that is stealing my voice and making me question myself?

Someone tells me about a doctor in Manhattan who is famous—and famously expensive at $2,500 for just one appointment. Her office is a kind of mansion, with a living room with fine furniture, but what makes me anxious is that everyone in her waiting room has a tube coming out of their nose and taped to their face. Some of them smile at me. She's funny and raucous, and she has a video camera that shows us both what it looks like when she puts that tube down my own nose. "Oh, my God!" she says. "If I were grading you on having good vocal cords, I would give you a D! Maybe a D-minus."

She sits me down on her couch. She tells me I must have had Bell's palsy as a kid. "No, I never did," I start to say, but she raises her hand. "Yes, you must have," she says.

I tell her I have asthma, and she laughs. "No, you don't," she says. "Who told you that?" When I tell her my pulmonologist, she sighs. "He doesn't know anything," she says.

She writes out a special diet that she wants me on. She's convinced that food is the culprit, that what I have is acid coming up and eating away at my vocal cords. I look at the list of foods I can eat, and I want to hide under the couch. No cheese, no fruit, no pasta. No citrus. No anything. Only water. I tell myself my motto is *I will try anything.*

After two weeks, I lose twenty pounds, and I am skinny to begin with, but I try to be hopeful and show Jeff how I can slide my jeans right off my hips without even unsnapping them. But at night, I still can't breathe; I still feel terrible. I go back to this doctor, and this time she tells me that I need to buy a wedge for my bed so I can breathe better and that I need to stop my asthma meds because they are irritating my throat. "How will I breathe?" I ask, and she snaps, "Who's the doctor here?" She also wants me to have two tests, both of them painful.

"What will the tests show?" I ask.

She shakes her head, her voice as confident and strong as mine is shaky and unsure. "I won't know until I see the results!"

"But what will you do if you get bad results? More tests? Medicines?"

"Questions, all these questions," she says.

One of the tests is putting electricity into the muscles of my throat to see if there is nerve damage. A neurologist has to be present when she does it. Another is to swallow a tube into my stomach and keep it there for two days so it can measure whether or not I have acid reflux.

"But what if there is nerve damage?" I ask. "What if I do have acid reflux? What do I do for that?"

She rolls her eyes and then perks up. "I Googled you. You and me, we're both *New York Times* bestselling authors." She holds up a hand, leaves the room, and comes back with a huge stack of paper held together with a rubber band, which she settles on my lap. "This is my new baby," she says. "I want you to go home, read it, and e-mail me to tell me what you think. It's all about you, all about having a cough, and maybe Bell's palsy, too."

Stunned, I stumble out of her office and onto the street. I drag out my cell and call Jeff, and as soon as I hear his voice, I start to cry, and I tell him what happened. He is silent for only a moment. "Is there a trash can nearby?" he asks. I sob yes. "Okay, I want you to walk over to it and dump in the manuscript." He waits while asking, "Did you do it yet?" And then I do, and a weight flies off me. "You're never going back there," he tells me. "Come home."

Every night, I cannot breathe. It feels as if someone is strangling me. I wheeze and gasp for air. I'm afraid to call an ER because one of the doctors has told me that ERs don't know what to do with people like me. They'll give me a tracheotomy. Another doctor has told me that the best thing for me would be just to pass out from loss of air. "It'll be like a reboot."

I don't like the way that sounds.

I can't figure out what's happening, and I'm more and more scared. While I'm used to puzzling out plot problems, this is one I have no idea how to approach. I sit at my writing desk and don't put down a word. I go out in the world, and I feel unmoored. I see the best doctors in Manhattan, at NYU Medical Center, at Mt. Sinai, at Columbia Presbyterian. But why doesn't anyone seem to know what I have? Why do they all offer something different?

If traditional medicine can't help me, can the outliers?

I see an Ayurvedic healer, an Indian woman who drapes herself in fancy silks, hands me herbal pills, and, humming, takes my pulse. "I know exactly what this is," she says, nodding sympathetically. She tells me there is too much fire in me, and she gives me four bottles of expensive pills to take. She gives me yoga breathing exercises, which are mostly different ways of panting or holding my breath. I go home and take the pills and do the exercises, and I'm no better.

I see an acupuncturist for a year. She's a young woman who really helped my friend's mysterious back spasms, so I feel a little hopeful. She pricks me with needles and tells me something is off between my lungs and my stomach, and that makes me feel like it's a little bit of a diagnosis, so that makes me feel better, too. She has special Chinese herbs made up for me right in Chinatown, but all they do is make me vomit and suffer headaches so terrible that I feel as if my head is ripping apart.

"It takes time," she soothes me. I give it six months, and then another two, and I'm no better. One day, I walk into her office, sit on her table, and fall apart in tears. She has no idea what is wrong with me, and I become so hysterical, wailing that something is wrong with me and no one knows how to fix it, that she leads me to a private office to gather myself together. I use up all the tissues before I am able to leave, and, feeling ashamed, I never go back.

A psychic tells me it's my liver. "Forgive yourself, and you'll heal," she assures me.

"Forgive myself for what?"

"Only you can know that," she tells me.

I think about how I grew up in a household where it was safest for me to be quiet because silence didn't make you the target of rage. It didn't require you to fix someone else's problems. I think about how I left home at seventeen, how over time I changed myself to someone my mother and sister viewed skeptically: a woman strong enough to leave her husband when their marriages were unhappy, but they stayed because to do otherwise was too risky; a woman whose decisions mostly garnered disapproval. Did I really need them to forgive my life lived in a better way while theirs remained the same? Shouldn't they be the ones asking for forgiveness?

I don't know. And even so, knowing this doesn't help me feel physically better.

The next doctor I see is skilled in eye movement desensitization and reprocessing (EMDR) tapping. He says, "I know what it is!" And he sends me off for a thyroid biopsy, assuring me that I am lucky because that's the easiest problem to cure. My thyroid comes back healthy.

So I see a shaman, a young woman who tells me she cured herself of Crohn's disease. "How?" I want to know. "I worked hard at it," she says, and part of me feels that what she is really saying is that she worked harder than I am. She lays me on a table and runs her hands over me, but I feel nothing. "I think it's your kidneys," she says. When I ask her what I can do about this, she tells me, "You will know when you know." Then she takes a two-foot-long black crow feather and waves it wildly over me so I can feel the rush of air. "Ha!" she shouts. "You're going to be fine."

Except I'm not. And my voice is getting worse, more faint. Which makes me research even more. I spend a fortune on vitamins and special teas, but the only thing that happens is that our bank account slims down considerably, and I throw up two of the teas.

IT'S FOUR YEARS LATER WHEN I STUMBLE INTO A VOICE CENTER. Yep, there are such places, and there are more things that can go wrong with a voice than you can imagine. Nodules on your cords. Tumors. Inability to speak without trembling. I have to fill out a questionnaire before I see any of the doctors. But the questions seem geared to another person. Do I have trouble breathing when I walk? No. When I run? No. Have I tried to talk and then vomited? No.

I see the doctor, who frowns at my answers on the questionnaire. "Hmmm, you don't fit the protocol," he says. He scopes my throat and shakes his head. "Yep," he says. "There's something wrong with your vocal cords. Were you intubated recently?"

"No," I say.

"Did you have an infection?"

"Bronchitis," I say.

"That could be it."

The doctor shows me the video the scope took, how the membranes don't open or close properly, how when they smash together, it interferes with my breathing. He suggests

Botox injections. "They might work," he assures me. "Or we could do an operation and insert plastic, but that could make things worse." He tells me that no matter what I do, it may or may not improve my breathing. "But it will change your voice!" he says happily.

"But I love my voice!" I say. It's the thing that differentiates me from my mother and my sister, the thing that makes me stand out, that people notice and even approve of.

He shrugs. "Your choice," he says.

Finally, one day, in the middle of Times Square, I cannot breathe or even talk. I shake. I'm half sure that I am having a heart attack, and I see my life spinning down, as if I am being centrifuged into oblivion.

Lucky for me, I'm with a friend who is married to a psychiatrist. "You're having a panic attack," she tells me, and she digs out her cell and calls her husband. When she hangs up, she takes me by the arm. "Come on," she says. "I'm taking you to the ER." We're only a block away, and I am panting, my whole body clammy. When we get there, because she is a doctor's wife, someone sees me almost immediately (stranger things have never happened!). The doctor hands me a pill.

"What is this?"

"Very low dose of Klonopin," he says.

"Klonopin!" I think of Stevie Nicks, how addicted she was to Klonopin, how she hallucinated and had dry heaves, and how for her, getting off it, getting unaddicted, was like going cold turkey on smack. "I don't want that!" I argue.

"It's such a low dose, we don't even prescribe it," he insists, and because I feel myself hyperventilating, I take it.

I wait.

Oh, my God. He's right.

I don't feel high. I don't feel strange. Instead, I can breathe. And I'm calmer. "This worked!" I exclaim. "How did this work?"

"Anxiety," the ER doctor tells me. "It's all in your head."

I'm more than a little irritated because I've seen the video scope, and I know it's not just in my head, but I keep quiet because that Klonopin helped, and I desperately want more. The ER doctor gives me some just for short-term use because, after all, this is a benzo, right? And, unfortunately, he also needs me to go see a speech therapist and a cognitive therapist.

I sigh. Really? "What are they going to do for me?" I ask.

"Anxiety can make physical illness worse. There's a link," he tells me.

Because he gave me a prescription, and because I'll try anything, I go. To my surprise, I love both these therapists. The speech therapist is at Mt. Sinai, and when I tell her that I don't want anything woo-woo, she calmly hands me scientific papers that show the relationship between certain ways of breathing and mental health, that detail how vocal-cord problems can respond to, if not be cured by, certain breathing exercises. "I've seen it," she tells me. She shows me a totally new way of breathing, which feels awkward at first. You never breathe through your mouth unless you are panting. It's always through your nose. You sing through straws because it focuses your vocal cords. You blow bubbles into a glass. She has me try every exercise, and I feel like an idiot. I'm sure it's not working, but she's grinning at me. "Now speak," she says. I do, and there is my voice, clear and strong, and I gasp.

"See?" she says. "You sound better already."

I practice every day. I walk around trying out my new voice. I don't want to sound raspy anymore, and for the first time in years, I don't! I correct myself. I speak more loudly. People pay me more attention.

Best of all, the breathing problem that has been starting every day around four o'clock doesn't happen until ten, and then midnight. I go to the cognitive therapist, and instead of plumbing the depths of my past (do I really need to know how glad I was that my voice was different than my mother and sister's because they disapproved of me so much?), he gives me concrete things to do. He tells me to wait half an hour after I feel the need to take a Klonopin and see what happens. He tells me to be in the discomfort and see if I can control it. (I can! I do!) I spend one whole session desperate to convince him that I'm not an addict, that I take a tiny dose of the Klonopin, and honest, I swear, I am going to stop.

He nods, calm. "What if the problem doesn't go away?" he asks casually, the way you might ask someone how the pizza is at a certain restaurant.

I'm too stunned to say anything. And then I find my voice. "But I have to stop taking the drug," I say. "Don't I?"

"You're on a tiny dose," he says. "You don't abuse it. You could stay on this dose your whole life and be okay. Why do you have to put judgment on it at all?" Then he tells me not to future-think because there's no way for me to know what is going to happen. I tell him that right now, I need a quarter of a tiny dose. Maybe in a year I still will. "But maybe you won't," he says, and then he tells me, "You're a novelist; you deal in narrative, in the misbeliefs people have about themselves. Find the narrative here. Find your true voice."

I BEGIN NOT ONLY TO SPEAK MORE LOUDLY BUT TO SPEAK UP. My voice grows clearer. My relationships with my mother and my sister begin to change, because now, instead of not voicing my displeasure at their scolding in hopes of keeping the peace, I calmly say, "I'm happy to talk with you, but let's do it when you are not yelling at me." And to my surprise, it works. They apologize, or they call back, calmer.

And then, as my voice becomes stronger and, with it, my willingness to speak my mind, I start to remember, and those memories unfurl. Growing up, I was always told to be quiet, that my ideas didn't matter. If I spoke out, I was hit or yelled at, and this went on for so long that I finally gave up defending myself in my family altogether. My mother told me over and over that I was shy, that I would feel better if I stayed in the back of the room in my class. When we were outside, she told me that if I didn't say anything but just stuck close to her, I would be safer. I believed her. In the ninth grade, my voice began to rasp, to grow hoarse, and at the time I was happy about it because it was an effortless way to be unique. But truthfully, I loved my new voice because when I picked up the phone, for the first time ever, no one on the other end mistook me for my sister or my mom. They always knew immediately that it was me.

Of course, Jeff and I are still researching. When I find out that someone breathes better just by taking a half teaspoon of baking soda in water, I try it, too. Instantly things clear. Who knows why? Maybe I made my body more alkaline, which is optimum for health (and a fringe benefit is that it keeps me from getting colds). Maybe it's all in my head. It doesn't matter because I feel better, and I keep doing it. I feel more in control because not only is this something I can do, but I discovered it myself.

Now, with this new sense of myself, I begin experimenting. Telling people calmly what I want, what I think, and to my surprise, I feel stronger. My breathing is better.

And my writing voice begins to change, too. I stop comparing myself to other writers. I take a risk because a story matters to me more than the opinion of those who read it, especially the one person who actually tells me, after reading the fledgling start of a novel, that every writer has an idea they should burn, and this might be mine! "Who would want to read this?" she demands. La, la, la, I don't listen to her because I am busy listening to myself.

Instead, I take those pages, and I sell them as the basis of a novel. I have no idea what will happen next in the novel I'm writing—I usually outline extensively to prepare for every snag—but this time, it doesn't matter. This time, it's exciting to see the novel slowly spin out into what it needs to be.

Just as I am doing with and for myself.

HOW DO WE HEAL, AND WHY? WHY DO SOME PEOPLE GET better when others don't? Maybe it's a miracle. Maybe it's just me, retraining my vocal cords, retraining my thinking. Maybe my problem isn't with my vocal cords at all, or in my head, or even quantifiable. Maybe I have an energy blockage. Maybe whatever it is will vanish as quickly as it arrived. Disease can be thought of like this: dis ease. We've lost the ease of ourselves. Doctors can be thought of as consultants, not experts.

Maybe our bodies, our DNA, always know the right routes to the land of health, but first we have to learn the customs, the language, to broaden ourselves and be able to travel there.

Will I get better totally? Will I find my cure? I don't know, but I've stopped the future-thinking. All I know is, for now, I'm my own advocate for this illness. I speak for myself. I own my voice, and I'm responsible for it growing stronger. For me growing stronger.

Today, I remind myself that for me, sometimes the greatest pleasure of any mystery, whether it's a book, a play, or real life, is not knowing the answer, being immersed in all the delicious suspense, even as I somehow know that there will be a solution to it all. Instead, I focus on each and every moment of the story. I get more thoughtful about the here and now rather than the what will be. My voice, like my writing, like myself, is ever changing.

REMEMBERING THE PAST

− *Charles Todd* −

Both of the series of books that I write with my mother, Caroline Todd (Inspector Ian Rutledge and Bess Crawford), are set in Britain in the Great War, 1914–1918, and its aftermath. Our characters are living people to us, and their world has in many ways become our world. After over thirty books, we feel at home there. And we try to get our facts right. Careless research in a historical mystery does a disservice to those who tell us, "I didn't care much for history in school—but I love history with a story." For such readers, a fiction book is often the key to looking deeper and learning more. The cold, hard facts in a five-hundred-page work on the past aren't entertaining, *Downton Abbey* is. But aside from the history book vs. the historical mystery debate, there's something else to consider. What has living in that other world of our setting taught—or cost—or brought us over time?

We decided it was important to take a look at that question. And what we discovered has been a very personal journey as well as an insight into what touches our readers.

Research of course is the backbone of writing about the past, and we've used every resource we can find. Memoirs, newspaper accounts, firsthand histories of the war—all these give us a picture of what life was really like in this period. And when the written record is not enough, we go to England to do our research on the ground.

It's amazing what can be found in unexpected places. A postcard of a village street in 1910 or a watercolor of the churchyard in 1920 show the unpaved streets and the few motorcars, intermingled with carriages and hay wains and farmers' carts. The dark clothes of the people on the street are a reminder that the British government had to order the nation not to wear mourning—there were so many casualties that black was making that fact too obvious to everyone. It was, the government thought, bad for morale. Still, in a society not that far removed from Victorian behavior and a queen who had mourned her own husband for decades, it must have been difficult to lose a loved one at sea or in the trenches only to be told that one could grieve only in private.

When we are traveling, the stories that people tell us when we show an interest in the past are often heartbreaking. What is shocking is the number of men who suffered from shell shock and took their own lives, caught between what was seen as shameful cowardice and a lack of medical insight into their

condition. We're only just beginning to understand PTSD today, never mind back in 1916 or '17 or '18. There were stories about Uncle John, who was "odd," or a grandfather who
reacted wildly to sudden noises, or a cousin who spent the
rest of his life in a dark room, unable to join the family for a
meal or even a special event. And behind these, it's easy to see
the pain no one understood. It simply wasn't talked about to
anyone.

There are also stories of "Aunt Dora" or "my grandfather's
sister," who never married because the man she was in love
with or engaged to never came home from the war. Such
women, spinsters, were often called upon to nurse the elderly
or take care of the children or do the volunteer work of the
village. Sometimes they taught or found another respectable
occupation. One was postmistress, because the postmaster had
been killed or gassed or had his jaw shot away. Widows became
housekeepers to a rector, and those women with the confidence
to go out on their own might choose to work in a milliner's
shop or open a small tea shop if they had resources they could
call on. With a generation of men dead, many women were
condemned to a lonely old age, with no children or grandchildren to care for them. And this doesn't touch on the children
who grew up without a father. There are stories about how wild
this lad was, with no father to control him, and others about
that lad who had to leave school to make a living for his mother
and brothers and sisters.

Women earned the vote at war's end, not from marches and
being force-fed in prisons while on hunger strikes but because of
what they had done for the war effort. From growing vegetables

to feed an island population to nursing at the front, from driving omnibuses to setting fuses in artillery shells, women showed the government what they were capable of. But the question has long been: Would it have mattered, what they had shown the world, if enough men had returned to make them redundant, unnecessary in the postwar era?

And that's the problem. History books can tell us how many men died on this or that day, how many shells were fired, how many aircraft were shot down, how many tanks burned. What the books can't tell us are all the personal stories that were the lynchpin of those statistics. It is left to the author writing about that time to show the pain and grief and hardship firsthand. Twenty thousand British casualties on the first day of the Somme Offensive sound horrific enough, but it is the woman who lost two sons and a brother on July 1, 1916, who brings home the real cost of that bloody battle.

To get at the reality from our own point of view, we had to find out firsthand what trench life was like by walking one of the remaining ones and realizing how narrow—and how short—it was (what did a man of six feet do when the trench was barely up to his chin?) and how the mud and blood and bits of bodies underfoot caused the rather awful disease of trench foot for many soldiers. Wet shoes, wool socks, no chance to bathe—these conditions encouraged not only trench foot but lice as well, and fleas from the rats.

We had to clamber over tanks to get a feel for what it was like for four or five men to fight inside what was little more than an oven on treads. And go up in an airplane of the time to see what it was like to know there was only cloth and lightweight wood between you and the ground several thousand feet below. There was no parachute. To survive took skill, and many pilots never survived long enough to acquire it. Experiences such as these reveal more about the war than how many divisions were called up at Passchendaele or when the tank was introduced.

We learned to handle weapons, rifles and sidearms; to feel the weight of the pack a soldier carried on his back even as he raced across No Man's Land in heavy fire; to try on a gas mask and understand why soldiers at the front had to shave daily so that the mask fit properly when the gas came floating over on the morning wind. A World War I ambulance had no springs, and it must have been terribly painful for severely wounded men to be bounced over ruts and potholes on the way to the nearest base hospital. Sometimes the ambulances were strafed or harassed by enemy aircraft, and at night headlamps had to be kept off, making it even more difficult to find the flattest part of an already nonexistent road. Men died from the battering before they reached help. This is how the truth is told, not only in statistics.

There were real people out there on the seas, with a sub lurking in the storms. Or in a dogfight in the air. Or in the trenches. Real people at home hoping their loved ones would come back alive—and whole. Leave was not frequent, and some men didn't see their families at all unless they earned a blighty ticket—a wound that was severe enough to require sending a man back to England to be treated. That meant crossing the English Channel, then a hospital train to London, and finally dispersal by ambulance to the facility that was best able to treat the burns or the gas or the gangrenous limb, the stomach wound or shrapnel too close to the spine. If the patient was patched up and returned to the trenches, he often hadn't recovered fully enough to survive the next battle.

And adding to all that, there was the Spanish flu epidemic. Only the flu wasn't Spanish. It is said to have originated in a camp outside Topeka in Kansas. But wherever it began, it spread like wildfire in armies where men were crammed together and under stress, and in civilian populations where a man might leave for his job at eight in the morning and be dead by teatime. It was that fast in many cases, slower in others, but still deadly. There were no antibiotics, no real treatment as the lungs filled with fluids. The nurses and doctors did what they could and then they, themselves, dropped from overwork.

It wasn't only the flu. There were concussions from shell blasts; trench-foot amputations that made it impossible for a man to walk, much less charge; rat bites; gangrene; and infections from bits of dirty uniform being carried into a wound. There were a few antiseptics and fewer early X-ray machines to pinpoint where the bullet or bit of shell was lodged. The various forms of gas were particularly damaging to exposed skin and lungs. Some blistered, some were poisonous to breathe, some were blinding, and others seared the lungs. Early gas masks were rudimentary—the first protection, such as it was, was a handkerchief that a man urinated on and then held to his face. Masks had to have goggles to protect the eyes as well as the lungs. The warning that gas was coming meant literally dropping everything to get a mask in place. It often crept through the morning fog in a low cloud. And if the wind shifted, it could sweep back on the army that had launched it.

There were flamethrowers as well, useful for taking out a machine-gun nest or clearing a building. Another of the many ways man found to kill his fellow man, from the bayonet to the latest machinery devised by the various armies, led to a comment that we found telling: "The Great War was the price men paid for the Industrial Revolution." Rifles and artillery, submarines and battleships were improving, tanks were invented, and aircraft came into their own. In artillery alone, eliminating the recoil meant that a shell could be dropped relentlessly in the same spot as often as anyone wanted. Nobel's smokeless powder made it possible to see the battlefield clearly in spite of the number of weapons being fired at the same instant. The list goes on. When a trench was blown up through tunnels filled with explosives, the first shock wave could kill as many men as actual wounds.

There was a trend some decades ago to show that this war was not as horrible as it has been painted. The theme was that over time, embellishments made it appear worse. But when the stories of ordinary people flesh out the suffering, they contradict that historical perspective. By the time the Spanish flu adds its dead to the total, and an entire generation of men is wiped out, one hasn't even considered the refugee problem. The Armenians, the Russians, the massacres, and the horrors need a human face to make them real.

As one man said to us about serving in Iraq, "Once you're out of it, you don't talk about it. And you hope that by not talking about it, you'll finally forget what you've seen and done." Much of the story of the Great War—the *war to end all wars*—died with the men who survived it. They didn't want to bring their nightmares home to those they loved.

One of the saddest chapters of the war revolves around the missing. Records were kept of the wounded and the dead and men taken prisoner by the enemy. But there were the missing. They were sometimes presumed dead because fighting had been reported at the time, a sector was known to have been blown up, or someone had been seen to fall in the heat of battle, but the truly missing sometimes appear even now in Flanders Fields when a farmer plows up a boot with the remains of a foot in it. All that's left of someone's son or father or husband. DNA makes it possible to identify many of these now. But sometimes that, too, is damaged, and there is presently no chance to reconstruct it. Families had to learn to live with missing. Do you plan a memorial or go on hoping he'll be found one day? Not much hope at sea, but that farmer's plow has churned up the battlefield. Sadly, many family members themselves died not knowing. And a public memorial had to be raised to the missing, there were so many of them.

The Commonwealth War Graves Commission tried to find all the bodies hastily buried on the battlefield and remove them to more formal graves with markers. Too many are still listed on the crosses as Unknown, while others have been identified by name, rank, and regiment.

One good thing is the number of museums that have preserved the past. The National World War I Museum and Memorial in Kansas City. The Imperial War Museum in London. The In Flanders Fields Museum in Ypres. They keep the story alive, save artifacts and bits and pieces of personal gear such as the masks snipers contrived or the uniforms of the various regiments, to present the personal side. Many of the American commanders in World War II learned to fight in World War I. MacArthur and Patton and Bradley, just to name three.

The first time we were in Kansas City, we entered the displays over a clear glass flooring, like a drawbridge, and under our feet, down below, was a field of poppies, so many dead to each blossom. It brought home, before we saw a single exhibit, that this was also a memorial to the dead. Their war, the things familiar and important to them, the things that kept them alive—or caused their deaths. The aircraft are out near Dulles in the Smithsonian exhibits, and you can see how frail and small they were, housed with their descendants, the Flying Fortresses and fighter planes of World War II. How much courage—or desire to fly—it must have taken for a man to trust his life to some of those early craft.

It's hard, writing about the war, not to remember the dead. Stats in history books count the bodies, but they aren't just numbers when in every village in the UK there is a memorial to men who served their country and didn't come home. We read their names and realized that families often lost more than one member. And often in the same battle, because these men went to war together and served in the same company. They often died together as well. There were Pals units that made it possible for men to serve together rather than spreading them out over various regiments. It was moral support, of course, courage gathered from the courage of friends, but the consequences were often deadly. These Celtic crosses with names etched in the stone are well kept even today, often with pansies for remembrance and silk poppies for Remembrance Day—what we called Armistice Day until it was changed to Veterans Day.

It's different in northern France, rows upon rows of white crosses appearing just off a road you are traveling. Acres of them, it seems, and each one is a man. The grass around them is lush and green and well maintained even now. Once fertile farmland, some of it, and in the spring, you glimpse scarlet poppies among the roadside wildflowers. It's quiet in these cemeteries. Not many people come here; they aren't popular tourist destinations. Some of the people driving past might not know which war they represent.

There are more formal British graves all around the town of Ypres, with regimented but handsome stones behind low walls, and also monuments, often arches and gates, to mark the dead of soldiers of the Commonwealth who died for king and country. Many of them are from Imperial India, a whole gate of them in one place, with the names of those who died in a cold, wet climate far from home. Their ranks and their names are recorded for posterity, but standing under the arches of the gates, you realize how many there are, line upon line of officers and men.

Also near Ypres, in one of the smaller cemeteries, is the grave of the man who wrote the haunting poem "In Flanders Fields." John McCrae lies there now, where the poppies grow. Impossible to tell who the men around him are. Just names and ranks and regiments, not whether this man was a solicitor, that one a chaplain, the one over there from the slums of Liverpool or Glasgow. It doesn't matter; they are all here together, equal in death. You begin to see *people*, not just numbers of stones. *Individuals*. The writer in you wonders about them and is touched by them. Walk in these places, and you feel something, if only the cost of war. What makes a man willing to fight for his country—and die for it?

Outside Nice is a lovely and moving memorial to the heroes of Verdun, the battle that left physical and emotional scars on the French army and the French people. It is to them what the Somme is to the British, Gallipoli to Australians and New Zealanders. It is remembered with pride. As it should be.

There's an American memorial to our own dead in Washington, DC. Not very far from the elegant World War II memorial or the haunting Korean and Vietnam memorials is an out-of-the-way Grecian-style round temple. Not very large or impressive, in need of upkeep when last we saw it, and rather lonely. The war to end all wars has been more or less forgotten by those who come to visit the other memorial sites. There will be dozens walking and taking pictures around them, while here only the wind through the surrounding trees makes a sound.

There are German dead in France from World War I, their resting places marked by somber iron crosses, row upon row. Dark, sometimes foreboding, always rather sad. You wonder, standing there, if these men would rather have gone home, if only in coffins. But here they fought, and here they died. Perhaps it's fitting that they are also buried here.

Travel in Germany, and it's hard to find a memorial to the dead of the Great War. What happened to them? Were they obliterated in the next war? Or was Germany in such straits that feeding its people mattered more than monuments to those who couldn't come home to lie among their ancestors and, later, their descendants? Who knows? If there are separate cemeteries, they aren't pointed out to tourists.

But we found two of them. Memorials, actually.

In one town was a plinth with a World War I German helmet atop it, all in stone, with the dates of the conflict. It was in a small triangle of grass where two roads met, and the grass had grown nearly as tall as the top of the helmet, all but concealing it from view. It wasn't very tall to begin with. A far cry from the smallest obelisk in the tiniest English village churchyard, well-kept and often surrounded by flowers.

The other memorial was in a church in northern Germany—we'd rather not name it—where we accidentally strayed into a room below the tower. It was extraordinary, poignant, a place you find hard to get out of your mind. It could have stood in a castle, been a part of a palace, with its long plaques setting out the names of the dead. High on the wall are helmets, and there are spears flanking the tablets. An almost Gothic feel, as if it had been designed far in the past, not a hundred years ago. It honored the fallen in somber, shadowy beauty.

No matter that the Germans started the Great War by marching through Belgium to reach France, leaving death and devastation in their wake. No matter that they started the next war in 1939.

This wasn't a memorial to the kaiser or his generals; it was a remembrance of the ordinary man taken from his shop or farm or office and made into a soldier, sent off to kill. Nothing was said here about the posters and propaganda that had beat the drums of hatred. Those men fought as bravely as they could, they died far from home, and in the end their sacrifice was in vain, pushed out of sight. It was not the end of war, this conflict. The Germans had marched in 1870 and would march again.

We're not really sure why that memorial touched us so deeply—possibly because it was shut away where no one was supposed to see it. As if the past didn't exist. As if the dead didn't matter, the pain and grief and heartache didn't count any longer. Ghosts with nowhere to go now. At least the American memorial in Washington is still there for anyone to see, weathered and ignored as it is.

Our voices, although soft, echoed here, and our footsteps as we left. We felt like intruders. Did families ever come here? Had the memorial been shut away to avoid seeing it taken away? As lovers of history, we are never eager to see the past destroyed, however sad or wrong or best forgotten. Sweeping it away only serves to sweep its lessons with it. For it's knowing the past that makes us mindful of what we owe the future.

The fact that this was in Germany is beside the point. We'd learned a great deal about the average soldier in the Great War, from whichever army, whichever battlefield. Many were brave; some were cowards; others did what they had to do and wanted only to survive to go home. No one wanted to be there. They just were, because someone had decided their fate for them.

Whether we realize it at the time or later in our careers, what we've written about *has* changed us. The research, while enriching our story, also lingers in the memory, and the *personal* as opposed to the *general* somehow becomes a part of us. An experience that we've shared with people a century dead, but whose fate still has the power to touch us. Interacting with the past, through the people or the things left behind to tell their story, we've also learned from it. We see all too clearly how World War I changed our future, casting its shadow over much of the world today because of what happened there and in the treaty that was intended to end it. Instead, another war, a cold war, even problems today in Britain, Europe, Russia, the Middle East, Africa—the Far East, too—had their beginnings in the Great War. Without even realizing it, we have paid dearly for it and will go on paying. We've come to realize that history is made up of millions of people who aren't even a footnote in a book but whose lives shaped and informed that history. They became numbers, without names or faces or individuality, until their stories were lost. And with them, the reality of what they did and what they won or lost. Maybe it isn't formal history vs. historical mysteries after all. Maybe historical mysteries breathe life into the dust of time and revive the mistakes as well as the victories. For us, the journey has been eye-opening and humbling and very, very human. Who knows how someone else might see it?

As we left that German church, walking back into the sunshine of a spring day, we said something to our guide about finding the tower room, and he was more than a little embarrassed that we'd seen it.

Finally, he shrugged and said, "You did not treat the soldiers coming home from Vietnam any kinder. And it wasn't their war, either."

We didn't have an answer to that.

NUNS, MAGIC, AND STEPHEN KING

– Robert Dugoni –

IN THE SEVENTH GRADE, I WAS ASSIGNED TO WRITE A SPEECH from the perspective of a slave, a slave owner, or an abolitionist. I chose an abolitionist. I don't recall being particularly excited about the assignment, nor do I recall writing my speech. What I do recall, quite vividly, is the morning I stood at the front of my class, without even a lectern to separate me from my classmates, and delivered that speech. Soon after I began, their facial expressions changed from bored interest to fear and angst. Some picked up their speech and quickly read through it. Some frantically scribbled.

When I had finished, not one of my classmates clapped. They sat in silence, staring at me and looking uncomfortable. I looked to the back of the room, where my teacher, Sister Kathleen, stationed herself. She, too, looked perplexed. I wondered how I could have so completely blown the assignment. After a moment that felt like an eternity, Sister Kathleen seemed to recover. "Work on your speeches," she said to the class. Then she gave me the parochial-school finger—her index finger—bending it repeatedly, beckoning me to follow her outside. I did so reluctantly, certain she would be escorting me to the principal's office, a place where I had already spent a fair amount of time.

By the time I reached the breezeway, I was already contemplating excuses I would tell my mother. I never got that chance. Sister Kathleen stopped me outside the adjacent seventh grade classroom. "Wait here," she said without further explanation. A very long minute passed before she reopened the door and invited me inside. The students looked at me as if I had suddenly grown a second head. Sister Kathleen marched me to the front of the class, turned, and with a smile and touch of pride said simply, "Give your speech."

More than a little confused, I did as instructed, and I received the same reaction as in my own classroom. Sister Kathleen gave me a brief nod and escorted me to the door. As we left, I heard the teacher—I have long since forgotten her name—tell her students, "Work on your speeches."

What I had done and, more importantly, how I had done it would remain a mystery to me for many years despite many more writing assignments and newspaper articles. None would have the same emotional impact as that simple speech on slavery on my seventh grade class and teacher. It is the biggest mystery in writing—how to emotionally touch your reader with just your words.

By Christmas 2004, I had embarked on my writing career, though without much success. My goddaughter, Amanda, gave me Stephen King's book *On Writing*. Inside the cover, she wrote,

December 25, 2004

Dear Uncle Bob,

Hopefully you'll be a millionaire like Stephen King someday! Merry Christmas!

Always, Amanda

THAT WAS THE YEAR I'D HAD MY FIRST BOOK PUBLISHED—A true story of injustice called *The Cyanide Canary*. Sales did little to fulfill my goddaughter's hope for me. On the heels of that book, I wrote two novels, one of which, *The Jury Master*, reached high on the *New York Times* bestseller list. I signed another two-book contract and then a third. I produced five novels in a series based on an attorney protagonist named David Sloane, yet none of those novels elicited the emotional response that my speech on slavery had elicited from twelve-year-old boys and girls.

In July 2012, when the sales of my novels failed to satisfy my publisher, my contract was not renewed. I received the news while attending ThrillerFest at the Grand Central Hotel in New York City. I sat in my hotel room with two friends, discussing other possible careers. I felt like George Costanza in an episode of *Seinfeld*, throwing out the most ridiculous possibilities and trying to laugh at my failure. I came home from New York disillusioned and disappointed. I had two children in private school and a lot more tuition to pay to help them fulfill their dreams. I had no idea how I was going to accomplish that.

My books, I had been told, were good. My writing was solid. But that was sort of like the detached statements a mechanic would make when evaluating a car: "The engine is good. The tires are fine. It runs well."

I hadn't struck an emotional chord, and I was left to wonder, again, why my novels had not impacted my readers emotionally, as that speech on slavery had done so many years before.

With unexpected time on my hands, I finally sat down and read Stephen King's book, which had sat unopened on the writing shelf in my office. I had never felt compelled to read it. I had book contracts to validate me as a writer. But I needed something now. I needed to read about how the most prolific writer of my generation had failed miserably and often at both writing and life. I needed to understand that great mystery—how a writer sitting at a desk can touch readers deep within their soul, move them to tears and laughter, and make them relate their own lives to the triumphs and tragedies of a fictional character.

I needed to understand that the mystery of writing was being so totally honest with your reader that your words will transcend time and space, what Stephen King called *telepathy*.

When I read that word, *telepathy*, I put the book down. I became that twelve-year-old boy again, standing in front of my classmates, baring my soul openly and honestly with raw, unfiltered emotion. I didn't know a thing about the writing craft in the seventh grade, yet somehow I had been able to use words not only to describe the shame and humiliation and anger that a slave felt standing on an auction block but to transport my classmates to that auction block to see that slave, hear that auctioneer and those slave owners' voices, and breathe in all the odors. I had not touched their minds. I had touched their hearts.

Telepathy. That, I decided, was the answer to the mystery. The trick was learning how to do it.

King's book made me think of something that had happened to me at a conference in Surrey, British Columbia, years earlier, when I had just a few published novels to my name. I found myself on a panel with Diana Gabaldon, the ubersuccessful writer of the Outlander series. A member of the audience stood and asked Diana if she could explain "the magic." He said nothing more. It soon became apparent that this was a question Diana had answered before. Without any hesitation, she explained to the audience that she wrote at night after her husband went to read or watch television. She said she would go into her office and shut the door. Then she'd light a candle and sit at her keyboard, waiting until her characters felt comfortable enough to speak to her. When a character spoke to her, regardless of the words spoken, she would type. She told the audience that the writer's job was, in some respects, to transcribe the words of a story already told so that readers could experience the same story.

Magic.

Mystery.

Telepathy.

I closed King's book and ruminated on his words for several days. During my years studying the craft, I had learned the traditional story structure espoused by Joseph Campbell and popularized by Chris Vogler in his book *The Writer's Journey*. I had studied Sol Stein's book *Stein on Writing*. I had studied Donald

Maass's book *Writing the Breakout Novel*, as well as a dozen other craft books. Intellectually, I had learned and understood story structure and character development. And then it dawned on me. I thought again of that word, *telepathy*, and I realized that maybe the reason I had not been able to touch my readers' hearts was because I had not been writing with my own. I realized that I had been writing from my brain, not from my heart. My words, carefully crafted, had lacked raw emotion, and my characters had been guarded, rather than honest. My writing had not been real, and so my words had not become real to my readers.

I had to find that place I had stumbled upon so many years before, without any understanding of how or why. I had to find what Stephen King called the mystery of writing and what Diana Gabaldon called magic. I had to find stories already written and characters already alive and transcribe them raw and unfiltered so that readers could experience them.

I had to believe in my very core, in my soul, that the mystery of writing was telepathy—magic.

After my release by my publisher, I became intrigued with a character from one of my earlier novels—a most unexpected character, a female homicide detective named Tracy Crosswhite. I had no idea where Tracy had come from or why she had entered my novel *Murder One*. I had no idea why or how Tracy had become Seattle's first female homicide detective, or how or why before becoming a Seattle police officer, she had first been a chemistry teacher in the small, fictitious town of Cedar Grove in the North Cascade Mountains. Her father was a well-respected country doctor, her mother a PTA mom who gardened and cooked. I had no idea about her relationship to her sister, Sarah, or why they competed in Single Action Shooting competitions, of which I had never heard or read a word. Though she had appeared on the pages of a novel I had written, Tracy was a complete mystery to me. I did not grow up in a small town. My father was not a country doctor. My mother was never a PTA mom. And I can count on one hand the number of times I've fired a handgun. I do have a sister. In fact, I have four. I also have five brothers. So Tracy's life was not some subconscious manifestation of my life, and she was clearly not someone I had come to know.

And yet she was alive in my novel and apparently just waiting to tell me her story.

So I let her.

I didn't outline the novel because I didn't yet know the story. I didn't create biographies for the characters because I didn't know the characters. I didn't perform research because I didn't yet know what I didn't know. I needed Tracy Crosswhite to guide me to those revelations.

I went into my office, I turned on classical music, sat, and waited. I waited until Tracy Crosswhite felt comfortable telling me who she was and how she had come to be. Her story. Was it frightening? At times. The left side of my brain, the side that focuses on logic, science, and mathematics, would occasionally kick in and tell me this was a crazy way to write a novel . . . without an outline, without well-defined characters with biographies, without research. But I had something else going for me besides the hours I had spent studying and developing my writing craft.

I had time. I had no contractual deadline to meet. I could be patient and allow the magic to happen. The right side of my brain would kick back in and tell me that writing was a mystery. Writing was magic. Writing was telepathy.

And so, recalling Stephen King and Diana Gabaldon's words, I put my butt in my writing chair. *The story is out there*, I told myself. *Trust the process. Trust the magic. Tell the story already written.*

And so I did. Tracy Crosswhite told me she had suffered a tremendous loss and was struggling to find her way through life, like all of us. She told me she was confused and hurt and bitter and angry. I understood in my heart what she meant because I felt very much the same. She told me she wanted to know why a benevolent creator would allow so much evil to exist and why she had suffered so deeply. She wanted to believe there remained something good in the world, something meant for her, and that she would someday find it. But in the interim, she was just fighting to survive.

I wrote the first draft of *My Sister's Grave* in two months. I realized that at some point during the process of writing that novel I had stopped thinking about what was going to happen next, who was to come on stage and who was to exit, what the climax was going to be, and how the story would end. Instead, I trusted the magic. I trusted that the story existed, that the characters would come into and out of the scenes as needed and, more importantly, as real people.

When I finished, I felt in my heart that this novel was different from the others I had written. This novel and these characters were real to me. The settings were real places. The events that transpired were real events. Would I be able to achieve what Stephen King called telepathy and Diana Gabaldon called magic? Would readers experience my novel as I had experienced it, in their hearts? Would they be moved as my seventh grade classmates had once been moved?

The book was published, and the first reader reviews didn't critique the plot or the characters' motivations. They didn't question the research or the fact that I was a man writing about a female protagonist. They wanted to know what happened next for Tracy Crosswhite, and they were deeply concerned that she would be okay. One woman from back East wrote, "You told the story of my life."

Telepathy. Magic.

Had I solved the mystery that had plagued me for forty years? Did I finally understand what the truly great writers meant when they said, "Write from the heart"?

About the same time, I went back to another project I had started but never finished. Oh, I had written the novel to the end, but something about what I had written made the story feel incomplete. The story was of a young boy born with ocular albinism—red eyes. This young boy, like Harry Potter, could not hide his anomaly, no matter how much he was bullied and abused. He had to learn to live with it. He had to grow from it. I had no idea where this young boy with the extraordinary eyes had come from. I had never heard of ocular albinism until I created him. I had no idea what Sam Hell wanted or why it was important that I tell his story. It wasn't enough that Sam wanted to be normal, that he wanted to be like all the other kids in his school. It wasn't enough that he wanted to change the color of his eyes, something that was not going to happen in the 1960s or even the 1970s.

As with Tracy Crosswhite, I did not know where this young boy had come from. My youngest brother has Down syndrome, but Sam Hell is not my brother. Sam Hell also lived in Burlingame, California, but he is not me. He's an only child. I'm one of ten. He has ocular albinism, which subjects him to ridicule. I can't recall a single instance in which I was bullied. Sam was another mystery, and the book had sat dormant in a file on my computer for years. Every so often I'd open the file and read parts of the story, but the mystery of Sam Hell remained hidden from me. I worked on my other projects, all the while with Sam in the back of my mind.

After my Stephen King epiphany, I realized that I had made the same mistake with Sam Hell as with my other novels. I'd written Sam not from my heart but from my brain, and in so doing I had failed to trust the magic. I had fit Sam into a well-conceived outline. I had not, however, let him live. I had not allowed him to tell me his story. I'd failed to grasp what so many parents fail to grasp. Our children are not us. Their lives are not our lives. Sam Hell had his own life, his own trials and tribulations, his own achievements and failures. I needed to get out of the way and let Sam tell me his story. To solve the ten-year mystery of who Sam Hell truly was, I first needed to let the magic happen.

And then one day, Sam told me what he wanted, why he had come into my thoughts, and the story he wanted me to tell others on his behalf.

On a Saturday afternoon, I was driving to church, and I looked up and saw the cross on top of the steeple. And in that moment a clarity came to me unlike any I had experienced before, and I realized what Sam Hell wanted. He wanted what so many of us want. He wanted to believe. He wanted to believe there was a reason he was bullied. He wanted to believe there was a reason he suffered. He wanted to believe his mother when she told him, "God gave you extraordinary eyes because you're going to lead an extraordinary life." He wanted to believe that all of his mother's novenas to the Blessed Mother on his behalf had not been prayed in vain, that her desire of a good life for Sam would not go unfulfilled.

I made an illegal U-turn, drove home, opened the file, and let the magic happen. I let Sam Hell tell me his story:

My mother called it "God's will." At those moments in my life when things did not go as I had hoped or planned, and there were many, she would say, "It's God's will, Samuel." This was hardly comforting to a six-year-old boy, even one "blessed" with a healthier dose of perspective than most children at that age. For one, I never understood how my mother knew God's will. When I would ask her that very question, she would answer with another of her stock refrains—"Have faith, Samuel." I realize now that this was circular reasoning impregnable to debate. My mother might just as well have responded with that other impenetrable parental reply, "Because I said so."

Six months later, I'd finished Sam's story, and in the process, I'd let him live his life.

The e-mails I have received regarding that novel have been touching and often heartbreaking. People have shared their own maladies that made them the subject of others' ridicule and bullying. I received an e-mail from an Ohio State graduate who wrote, "Fuck you. A grown man is not supposed to be bawling his eyes out as he drives down the road." Sam Hell's life had touched his heart and brought him to tears. He empathized with Sam's pain and his humiliation, and he related them to his own childhood. He told me how, for years, he, too, had struggled to understand the reason for his suffering, and he had found that reason in Sam Hell. He told me that Sam Hell had made him believe that everyone has the ability to lead an extraordinary life.

Magic. Telepathy.

IT'S A SCARY PROPOSITION WHEN SOMEONE SAYS, "WRITE FROM the heart." It implies that you sit down at a computer terminal and simply type. Not so. The mystery of writing revealed itself to me only after years of studying the craft and failing. Perhaps this is what is meant when they talk of a writer suffering. I still have much to learn.

Writing from the heart also requires first that you have one and, most importantly, that you're not afraid to share it, knowing that it will be trampled and criticized. It's about not being afraid to be vulnerable. It's about understanding that the magic doesn't happen to everyone, and the telepathy will fly right past those not on the same wavelength. The mystery of writing is never losing faith in the magic or in the knowledge that you, and you alone, are uniquely able to transcribe the story being told to you, a story about people you've never met. The mystery of writing is in believing that the story you tell will touch the hearts of readers you will never meet and never know.

Stephen King called it telepathy.

Diana Gabaldon called it magic.

Telepathy. Magic. Whatever you want to call it. The mystery of writing is being brave enough to let it happen.

I WANT TO BE
A MAGICIAN

– Anne Perry –

I WANT TO BE A MAGICIAN! NOT THE SORT WHO MAKES things appear and disappear inexplicably but the one who cre ates worlds and peoples them, makes events occur, marvelous, terrible, funny, heartfelt, and I want them to last so they can be revisited anytime. And, of course, all kinds of characters, old, young, eccentric, brave. I want to be one of them. Put more plainly, I want to be a writer. I want to make squiggles on paper and bring dreams to life, and understandings of anything that my imagination dares grasp, and then share them.

Does that sound arrogant? It isn't. Not really. Other people have done that down the centuries and shared their visions of the wonderful, the terrible, the elusive and mysterious, their victories and losses, the beauty and laughter and pain. I have been with them as they sought the reasons for everything. I have seen the Great Flood with Gilgamesh and watched the heavens rain and the hidden waters of the great deep spew forth. I have praised the rising sun over Egypt with the rebel Pharaoh Akhenaten, who dared to say there was only one God. I have seen the fall of Troy and the eruption of Vesuvius that buried Herculaneum and Pompeii. I have searched for the source of the White Nile. I have traveled alien worlds that don't exist, except in the imagination, and been with fantastical creatures.

And more than that, I have had companionship in my loneliness, courage in my fear, and beauty in the midst of pain through the words of others. I want to put something back into that great tide of human sharing. Perhaps it is an attempt to be like those I most admire and ultimately to belong to that golden fellowship who fill my daydreams. Don't we all hunger to belong? And where better? As long as we remember them, they are immortal.

Like everyone else, I have only one life here. But through these words on a page I can share the lives of people without number—I become a citizen not only of the world but of time. I like that! A citizen of time! I take the wealth of the past and give to the treasures of the future.

Letters that form meaning, especially if written down, are a kind of magic. Past civilizations recognized that. They believed that your name, if written down, could carry some essence of your identity. And in many ways, they were right. What is more "you" than your feelings, your beliefs, your dreams, your hope, your pain, and your courage?

When I have had no light by which to read, I have called upon stored-up poetry in my mind to repeat to myself and defy the void to dare the darkness of the spirit with sublime courage.

Up through an empty house of stars,
Being what heart you are,
Up the inhuman steeps of space
As on a staircase go in grace,
Carrying the firelight on your face
Beyond the loneliest star.
"THE BALLAD OF THE WHITE HORSE,"
G. K. CHESTERTON

When I remember that, I am not alone! I have a radiant companionship of all those who have trodden the same path, a web of light around me. I long to be like that—carrying the firelight of courage and vision with me into an unknown darkness. It ceases to be a terror and becomes a challenge.

What if God were to ask me, as the Bible says he did Solomon, *What gift would you have me give you?* I played with all sorts of answers, but there was only one that seemed right to me, and that was the gift of communication, to be able to reach out and touch somebody else with the passion of my feelings, the complexity of my thoughts, the wonder, awe, joy of what I sense in any way. Everything is too important not to be shared. There is no limit to the wings of the imagination.

Words! Palaces in the air, the way to capture and hold anything, everything, and multiply it.

SINCE THE STONE AGE, WE HAVE SAT IN THE NIGHT AND looked at the stars and then asked in awe, *Who are we? Where have we come from? Where are we going? And above all, why?*

I need to believe there is a purpose. There is sense to it all. What have other people found? What did they believe, and why? When I have sat and thought deeply, the parts have fallen into place, and I have a new piece of understanding. And each new piece adds a little; I just have to find the right place where it fits.

Stories tell of who we were from our birth in the skies, who were our first fathers, their greatness and their folly, all that they have bequeathed us, for good and ill. And, of course, where we are going, who are our gods and who our devils. I need to know in order to face the adventures that will surely face me, and all of us.

My mother told me that when I was very small, she used to sing a lullaby to me, but I remember the words repeated later. *Do you want the moon to play with and the stars to run away with?* She said my answer was "They'll do to begin with!" Loosely, of course. But I get her meaning, and "Yes, please, I do!"

I want words to frame the glory of the stars, the fire and the energy, and to envision the endless, wonderful variety of it all. I marvel at how it all makes sense! The more you look at even the beginnings of science, the more it all fits together.

And in my mind, to see beyond the obvious, I must explore not only the stars but also the cold and lonely places between them, the world of the night and the utterly lost. That is where the ultimate adventure is to be found, the way no one else has been.

The entirely new, the thing from another state of mind? How to frame it?

"The Greeks have a word for it." We used to say that when we didn't know how to frame a new thought. A new idea is a wonderful gift, one you can play with, holding it like a colored light to add a new dimension to all sorts of things. That sounds theatrical, but it is real.

I remember a train journey from Madrid to Barcelona. At sunset we passed through a high, lunar-like landscape to the south. Giant standing rocks of apricot and indigo seemed to burn where they stood and to cast gigantic shadows that turned purple and melted into the sky. Real? Of course . . . rock real. But when I remember it in words, it becomes more than that, sounding tender, soft-edged, cool wind rippling across the sand as the light seeped out of the sky and we were running alone in the dark. On our earth? Or on some planet out of *Star Trek*?

Without the words to describe it, I might forget, and then I couldn't share it. It would have gone.

LIFE CAN BE TERRIBLE, LOSS TOO BIG TO HAVE A NAME. A PRImal howl releases the tension for a while. Then it comes back, fresh and just as strong. Ordinary words help, used anything but ordinarily.

I carry the music and the passion of them in my head to make the hard things bearable. They are other people's words, but when I repeat them to myself, I am not alone, and all wounds hurt less.

> If here today the cloud of thunder lours
> Tomorrow it will hie on far behests;
> The flesh will grieve on other bones than ours
> Soon, and the soul will mourn in other breasts.

The troubles of our proud and angry dust
Are from eternity and shall not fail,
Bear them we can, and if we can we must.
Shoulder the sky, my lad, and drink your ale.

A. E. HOUSMAN

I can't write poetry in the same human world as that. But I believe I can write stories, create characters, and make them say and think and do things that stir the deepest emotions. I can give them actions and emotions and make you feel something you did not feel before.

In doing so I will try to discover new and deeper meaning. I must place myself in each character, share and see their lives as they see them, and understand what they want, with their fears, and feel pity rather than condemnation. There are two places to look. The first is in their lives: what are they, and what did they want? What are they afraid of? What hurts them, and why do they get some things wrong?

I can see in myself too clearly why I identify with a character's temper or fear that they have sidestepped, instead of facing, the excuses made. What would it be like to be that person? Have I ever been as alone as they are? Have I been scared stiff, rigid with fear, sick with it? Have I loved anyone enough to give all that I have, even my life, to save them? And if not, why not? What am I missing? Am I wiser or only less brave . . . only half alive? The pieces fall into place, and I understand more than I did before.

In trying to make everyone real, I discover odd things about myself, not only the eccentric or endearing things. The other things might be more useful as a writer, if not always pleasant.

It's time to talk about courage and what I think I would do, whom I would stand up for, whom I would help. Love can choke back fear. But we are talking about real loss, not something on paper. Try it. Burn just a little bit of your skin, and it hurts like hell. Would I stand up and step forward for someone else? Once you've done it, you can't go back.

Excuses are reasonable. They flood the mind. Well, maybe next time! There is so much to treasure, so much to lose. The act of one second can change everything. Wait a moment! Think what you are doing! Are you sure it will work?

Too late! The chance is gone. But when it is real, the person you did not save is gone. You will never see him or her again.

Courage is real. Make heroism matter.

I HAVE TO WRITE, BUT WHY DO I WRITE MYSTERIES RATHER than anything else? Why not romances, Westerns, literary novels, adventures? Lots of reasons, starting with because I like them. I have always enjoyed mysteries. I like the intellectual puzzle and, more than that, the moral one. Far more than in the past, they deal with real social issues. Guilt is cloudier, questions of degree rather than black-and-white. There used to be heroes and villains—oh, and victims, seldom morally involved in their own fate. Now all the players are complex. Social issues can be explored, family relationships, individual guilt or collective; very little is obvious or simple.

I can say what I really mean, ask the questions.

I love it when I close a book I have just read and feel I have learned something about people, judgment, issues that matter. I have been made to think! How wonderful. My world has been made bigger and deeper, and subtler. There are more colors in it than I had seen before.

I don't even try to work out the plots of other people's books, but it doesn't spoil it for me if I see it. As long as I believe it could be true, I care, and I am happy. I don't want cardboard heroes or cardboard villains. I want the villains to be understandable, perhaps even to feel sympathy for them or at least *a* sympathy. Above all, I want to feel that the hero cares for something more than his or her job or the answer to a puzzle. I need heroes to have emotions, and a stake in what happens, and why, and to whom. If they do not learn anything, then the journey wasn't worth it.

WHAT IS GOOD ABOUT WRITING MYSTERIES? WHAT IS VALUable and fun? I wrote unsuccessfully for years. I think I know what was wrong. I was writing historical novels, lots of enthusiasm and lovely scenes but no structure. My hero was all over the place. He observed things happening; he didn't make them happen. He had no driving need for anything! Nothing was explained, taken apart, or understood. He made no inner journey. And therein lies the key. My involvement was skin-deep. It must be to the bone. I did not explain issues in real people here and now. The wounds are still deep, infected; the corruption, the greed, the spoiling of the land—I could go on.

Daylight penetrated my murk at last. I had a hero who solved a mystery and became involved with the people. More than that, I had a heroine whose ideals and illusions about her own family, even about herself, were stripped away. She had to reassess everything, just as in the past I have had to at times. Disillusion faces us all, and it is one of the most difficult things we deal with. The more radical it is, and the more our beliefs are bound up in these people, the more difficult it is to accept the truth.

But I had a story! Change. Growth. And romance! But that's incidental. And since the hero is a policeman in London, it will not be surprising if he solves other cases in the next book. It's his job, and London, circa 1881, is the place for it. (Jack the Ripper is 1888. You have to have heard of him. He is the ultimate horror.)

London? Paris? Any place will do. That's another good thing about mysteries. They can be wherever there are people or, I suppose, beings with a moral sensibility. Absolutely anywhere at all! You can have a country village, the heart of a big city, a rocket station on Mars—or an alien world if you can be bothered to create one. As long as we believe it matters!

And it can be anytime, past, present, or future. As long as it makes sense and does not have any noticeable internal contradictions, it's fine. Unfortunately, humans can take violence, physical or emotional, with them anywhere.

Stories can also be set against all sorts of specific backgrounds, interesting in themselves, as long as you know the background or research it well enough to be believable. For example, the court of Queen Elizabeth II of England. Lots of color and certainly lots of violence. Or the court of one of the more eccentric popes, again color and violence. Or a free-thinking artists' group in Paris at the turn of the twentieth century, so vivid and unique. A modern city bank on Wall Street, a fashion house, a farm, a factory, the Secret Service. You get the idea. The world can be yours. Cheapest and safest form of travel ever.

But you must have a crime, a victim, a motive, at least two possible suspects, emotion. Oh, and a solution that makes sense. A reason why it all matters intensely. And if you can make a good story without one of these, good for you! *Miss Pym Disposes* by Josephine Tey broke most of these rules, and it is one of the best mysteries I have ever read. But she was special! She had a touch of genius.

The detective is the modern knight errant. You know, the one on the white horse who rides in and rescues everybody. The point is, detectives find chaos (not difficult these days), fear, and injustice. They sort it out and leave you with justice, or at least an understanding. Finally, we feel as if we have some sort of control . . . most of the time. We are not as helpless as we thought. Somebody knows what is happening. Then they ride off. Or stay, and we become part of the next solution to a problem, knights errant as well.

WHAT HAVE I LEARNED IN WRITING? ALL KINDS OF THINGS. Of course a lot of medical and legal details, which have to be as correct as you can make them and are also genuinely interesting.

One marvelous book that I relied on a great deal is the memoir of Larrey, who was surgeon to Napoleon. He kept voluminous notes on medicine in general, but for my purpose, far better than that, specific notes on such things as the amputation of a gangrenous limb. Description of the injury, how it appeared, how the patient's health was affected, what the surgeon did, where and how he cut, how the patient responded. And another horrific case of tetanus, treated by searing and cauterizing with a hot iron. (He lived!) And much more. It makes it possible to write medical scenes as if you were there. And be sure you have it right! Horrific. But accurate. Thank God we didn't live then.

Home remedies are wonderful, too. And domestic details are excellent as a background for emotional scenes. Clothing, transport, lighting, communication. Fascinating. And they can trip you up in a heartbeat.

Having said that, most research is to avoid mistakes. I learned through massive editing that it's really all about people, what they feel, believe, what drives their passions, beliefs, and heartbreaks. And of course—crimes!

For each story there has to be a motive that we understand, bigger than greed, more passionate than ambition, more interesting than the predictable or purely selfish. No matter what time period or what place you choose, there are always social and ethical issues that we still face today. Some are specific to the period, but you can find their progenitors in the past. Medical ignorance and malpractice, usury and manipulation of money from the corner shop to international exploitation, forgery, embezzlement, domination of one person over another. We haven't got rid of any of them. Child labor, sexual violence, use and abuse of the weak or vulnerable, all still alive and well.

Through a really good story you can feel the pain, the anger, and then see the shadow of it now. And care—very much.

In just ordinary living, day to day, I had very little idea what it would be like to be deaf. To be really poor, wondering what I would eat tonight, if anything. Where I would sleep. Was it safe, even dry? To be afraid of violence, in my own home, must be appalling. I have felt the darkness of it, all of it, after reading a good book, closing it, and still caring.

That is how change happens. One person at a time. Charles Dickens and child labor. Harriet Beecher Stowe and slavery. A passionate mind is more powerful than all the legislation.

It has constantly made me look a little harder at people I don't understand before leaping to harsh conclusions. One life is not enough to learn all we need just to be tolerant, let alone wise. But if you read, you can begin.

And, of course, you can be at the beginning of a profound inward journey of self-discovery. A bit frightening. It should be. In the end, all you have is who you are.

I still have time ahead of me to do something about it, but not as much as I used to have. I will discover a few things I don't like so much. Certainly, I will find several areas where I have got stuck and must change. You have to forgive yourself before you can forgive others. That is necessary to wholeness and the last dishonesty. Lesson one: forget yourself for a while. Understanding is a chance to be wiser, gentler, braver, altogether more what you want to be. You are not supposed to be a bit player in your own story; you are supposed to be the hero, the one who makes the journey, not the one who watches.

Maybe you think you know what is good and what is bad. At least you know what you like—maybe.

When you pull apart your villains and heroes, what is the real difference? Good question. Here is another: Why do you like some people when there are others who don't really have visible faults, but you can't stand them?

The people who are not wicked, you just don't like them. They are always right! From their point of view, anyway.

They don't like animals or children. Too noisy, messy,
  troublesome.
They have no sense of humor; they don't delight in the absurd.
They really do think their group, nationality, race, gender,
  etc. is superior to all others.
They complain about lots of things, even when it doesn't
  help, which is usually.
They tend to be the victim . . . of anything.
They talk a lot but seldom listen. They know everything,
  anyway.
They never apologize. Why would they? They are never wrong.
They mock the slow, the handicapped. Why? Different.
  Vulnerable.

And the people you like? In spite of their faults. And they do
have them. . . .

They can praise others, even people they don't particularly like.
They laugh hard at other people's jokes.
They like animals, children, old people, the handicapped
  and listen to them.
They like people regardless of age, gender, social class,
  nationality.
They don't repeat things they shouldn't. They keep your secrets.
They are basically fair. They don't tell tales. They don't lie.
  Except white ones.
They admit when they are wrong and apologize.
They share.
They love beauty, laughter, music and are interested in
  learning.
They are not self-righteous and don't talk down to you.

That's just part of my list. But I know why I like them or I don't. And there are bits of me in all of them.

Real good or evil is another matter, far deeper. One I am still exploring. But for a strong story there must be tension, real conflict, decisions that are so evenly balanced that the decisions are desperately hard.

I am told that in deep space there is both light matter and light energy and also dark matter and dark energy, actually far more of it. Light has its shape, its form of stars and planets, and all that we know from the power of the dark, the weight and the energy of it. Without it we would be formless soup.

Perhaps it is also the same with good and evil. Without this duality we would have no being. We would have nothing to struggle against. We would have no form, no strength, no virtue, no pain. If there is no danger of loss, there can be no courage. No want. Then there needs to be no generosity to give the last you have to someone else. No loneliness in need, so no compassion; no vulnerability, so no tenderness . . . and so on. In seeking to explain to the reader what I mean, what I believe, I discover more and more what it really is. So many of my voyages of the mind into tangles of darkness have been to make sense of my own beliefs so that I can find the thread of beauty and reason and even glory that weaves together all chaos and pain, perhaps a stitch at a time.

To make nothing new, fight no dragons, fill no need, is not my idea of heaven. I think it is just ceasing to have purpose or joy. Another name for death without the balm of sleep.

Endless life is full of big ideas! High mountains to climb, new people to know, things to learn and to create.

ACKNOWLEDGMENTS

My thanks to Laura Mazer, executive editor at Seal Press/Hachette, for her encouragement to take this idea and run with it. Without her creative thought and generous spirit, this project would never have existed.

To my agent, Jill Marsal, of Marsal Lyon Literary Agency, I offer loving thanks for guiding me—with patience and keen intelligence—through every stage of this, our seventh anthology. When we began the journey in 2006 with *The Other Woman*, who knew?

So many people have worked with me to bring this book to fruition. A big thank-you to production editor Kelly Anne Lenkevich, for taking my hand and leading me through the labyrinth of edits, and copy editor Connie Oehring, for her deft eye and editing skills. Publicist Sharon Kunz made sure the world knew about our book, and a hats-off to Chin-Yee Lai, who designed our stunning cover.

Acknowledgments

When I'm asked what I love most about creating an anthology, my response is always the same: each book creates its own community of authors, a family of new friends. To the twenty writers who gave us a glimpse into their own personal mysteries and worked alongside me with kindness, infinite patience, and humor, I thank you.

ABOUT THE CONTRIBUTORS

Tasha Alexander studied English literature and medieval history at the University of Notre Dame. *And Only to Deceive* was her first novel and the start of the long-running Lady Emily series. She is also the author of the novel *Elizabeth: The Golden Age*. Tasha has lived in Indiana, Amsterdam, London, Wyoming, Vermont, Connecticut, and Tennessee. She and her husband, British novelist Andrew Grant, live on a ranch in Wyoming.

Cara Black is the *New York Times* and *USA Today* bestselling author of nineteen books in the Private Investigator Aimée Leduc series, which is set in Paris. Cara has received multiple nominations for the Anthony and Macavity Awards, a *Washington Post* Book World Book of the Year citation, the Médaille de la Ville de Paris—the Paris City Medal, which is awarded in recognition of contribution to international culture—and invitations to be the guest of honor at conferences such as the Paris Polar Crime Festival and

Left Coast Crime. With more than 400,000 books in print, the Aimée Leduc series has been translated into German, Norwegian, Japanese, French, Spanish, Italian, and Hebrew.

Rhys Bowen is the New York Times and number-one Kindle bestselling author of the Molly Murphy and Royal Spyness historical mystery series and three stand-alone historical novels, including the international bestseller The Tuscan Child, which has sold over half a million copies so far. She has won twenty awards, including four Agathas, and her work has been translated into twenty languages. Rhys is a transplanted Brit who divides her time between California and Arizona.

Lynn Cahoon is an award-winning New York Times and USA Today bestselling author of several cozy mystery series, including The Tourist Trap series of ten novels and six holiday novellas, the Cat Latimer series, and her Farm to Fork mystery series, set in her home state of Idaho. She lives in a small town, much like the ones she loves to write about, with her husband and three fur babies. Visit her at www.lynncahoon.com.

Steph Cha is the author of Your House Will Pay and the Juniper Song crime trilogy. She's an editor and critic whose work has appeared in the Los Angeles Times, USA Today, and the Los Angeles Review of Books. A native of the San Fernando Valley, she lives in Los Angeles with her husband and two basset hounds.

Jeffery Deaver is an international number-one bestselling author. His novels have appeared on bestseller lists worldwide, selling in 150 countries and translated into twenty-five languages. He is the author of forty novels, three collections of short stories, and a nonfiction law book, and the lyricist of a country-western album. *The Bodies Left Behind* was named Novel of the Year by the International Thriller Writers association; *The Broken Window* and a stand-alone, *Edge*, were also nominated. *The Garden of Beasts* won the Steel Dagger from the Crime Writers Association in England. He's been nominated for eight Edgar Awards and honored with the Lifetime Achievement Award by the Bouchercon World Mystery Convention, the Strand Magazine Lifetime Achievement Award, and the Raymond Chandler Lifetime Achievement Award in Italy. *A Maiden's Grave* was made into an HBO movie, and *The Bone Collector* was a feature release. NBC is filming a pilot of *Lincoln* based on Deaver's Lincoln Rhyme. He has served two terms as president of Mystery Writers of America

Carole Nelson Douglas never plays it predictable. The Theater-English major was accepted by Northwestern University graduate theater school, the cradle of acting glory. She could have hit Manhattan as a *Vogue* editorial assistant and penned a tell-all novel about the rag biz. Instead, she stayed in St. Paul to become an award-winning journalist covering women's issues. A Golden Age stage-and-screen legend interviewee took her first novel to his publisher. Sold! Douglas then reinvented Sherlock Holmes's frenemy Irene Adler in a *New York Times* Notable Book of the Year and turned a stray black cat into a feline-noir icon. Her Tolkienesque and urban-noir fantasy novels and forty-five historical and contemporary mysteries have won twenty-three writing awards and graced national bestseller lists, including that of *USA Today*. Blending strong women (men, too), genres, social issues, satire, and substance in twenty-eight alphabetically titled mysteries, Midnight Louie, feline PI, kicks off his new Café Noir series with *A*, as in *Absinthe Without Leave*.

About the Contributors

Robert Dugoni is the critically acclaimed *New York Times*, number-one *Wall Street Journal*, and number-one Amazon internationally bestselling author of the Tracy Crosswhite series, including *My Sister's Grave*; the David Sloane series; and the Charles Jenkins series, which includes *The Eighth Sister*, as well as the bestselling *The Extraordinary Life of Sam Hell*, *The 7th Canon*, and *The Cyanide Canary*. He is the recipient of the Nancy Pearl Award for Fiction and the Mystery Writer's Spotted Owl Award and a two-time finalist for the International Thriller Writers and the Harper Lee Awards, the Silver Falchion Award, and the Mystery Writers of America Edgar Award. Visit him at www.robertdugoni.com.

Hallie Ephron is the *New York Times* bestselling author of eleven mystery/suspense novels, including *Careful What You Wish For*. She writes page turners rooted in reality. The *Boston Globe* praised her *You'll Never Know, Dear* for the way it "deftly integrates the mystery genre with women's fiction; it's made compelling by the depth and resonance of the relationships." Her *Never Tell a Lie* was made into a Lifetime movie. She is a five-time finalist for the prestigious Mary Higgins Clark Award. Her *Writing and Selling Your Mystery Novel* (Writers Digest Books) was an Edgar Award finalist. For twelve years she wrote an award-winning crime-fiction book-review column for the *Boston Globe*. A popular speaker and writing teacher, Hallie lives near Boston with her husband.

Connie May Fowler is the author of six widely acclaimed novels: *How Clarissa Burden Learned to Fly*, *Sugar Cage*, *River of Hidden Dreams*, *The Problem with Murmur Lee*, *Remembering Blue* (recipient of the Chautauqua South Literary Award), and *Before Women Had Wings* (recipient of the 1996 Southern Book Critics Circle Award and the Francis Buck Award from the League of American Pen Women).

She is the author of the memoirs *A Million Fragile Bones* and *When Katie Wakes*. Connie adapted *Before Women Had Wings* for Oprah Winfrey; the result was an Emmy-winning film starring Winfrey and Ellen Barkin. Connie teaches at the Vermont College of Fine Arts (VCFA) low-residency writing MFA program and directs the annual VCFA Novel Retreat. She is founder and director of the Yucatan Writing Conference. She lives on Isla Cozumel in Mexico with her husband, Bill Hinson.

Sulari Gentill went to university to study astrophysics and came out a lawyer. Though not quite sure how that happened, she maintains that the law was an excellent apprenticeship for writing fiction. Sulari is the award-winning author of the Rowland Sinclair mysteries, which chronicle the life and adventures of a 1930s Australian gentleman artist, and the *Hero Trilogy*, based on the myths and epics of the ancient world. She lives on a small farm in the foothills of the Snowy Mountains of New South Wales in Australia, where she grows French black truffles and writes about murder and mayhem. Sulari's most recent US releases include *Crossing the Lines*, an unusual postmodern crime novel that won the 2018 Ned Kelly Award for Best Crime Fiction, and *Give the Devil His Due*, the seventh in the Rowland Sinclair series, which was short-listed for both the Davitt Awards and the Australian Book Industry Awards. Sulari remains in love with stories.

Rachel Howzell Hall, author of the recently published *They All Fall Down* (Forge), writes the acclaimed Lou Norton series, including *Land of Shadows*, *Skies of Ash*, *Trail of Echoes*, and *City of Saviors*. She is also the coauthor with James Patterson of *The Good Sister*, which was included in the *New York Times* bestseller *The Family*

Lawyer. She is on the board of directors for Mystery Writers of America and lives in Los Angeles.

Ausma Zehanat Khan is the author of the award-winning debut novel *The Unquiet Dead*, the first in the Khattak/Getty mystery series. Her subsequent novels include the critically acclaimed *The Language of Secrets*, *Among the Ruins*, and *A Dangerous Crossing*. Her latest mystery in the series is *A Deadly Divide*. Ausma is also the author of a fantasy series for HarperVoyager that includes *The Bloodprint*, *The Black Khan*, and *The Blue Eye*. Ausma holds a PhD in international human-rights law with a specialization in military intervention and war crimes in the Balkans. A British-born Canadian and former adjunct law professor with roots in many places, she now lives in Colorado with her husband.

William Kent Krueger was raised in the Cascade Mountains of Oregon and briefly attended Stanford University before being kicked out for radical activities. His Cork O'Connor mystery series is set in the north woods of Minnesota. His work has received a number of awards, including the Minnesota Book Award, the Loft-McKnight Fiction Award, the Anthony Award, the Barry Award, the Dilys Award, and the Friends of American Writers Prize. His previous nine novels were *New York Times* bestsellers. *Ordinary Grace*, his stand-alone novel, received the Edgar Award. Visit his website at www.williamkentkrueger.com.

Caroline Leavitt is the *New York Times* bestselling author of *Pictures of You* and *Is This Tomorrow* and the critically acclaimed author of ten other novels, including *Cruel Beautiful World*. Her new novel, *With or Without You*, will be published by Algonquin Books in August 2020. She is a book critic for the San Francisco *Chronicle*, the *Boston Globe*, and *People* magazine, and she teaches writing on-line for Stanford and the UCLA Extension Writers' Program. She also works with private clients. She is a New York Foundation of the Arts Fellow and was a finalist in the Sundance Screenwriting Lab. Her work has appeared in Modern Love in the *New York Times*, *New York Magazine*, *Real Simple* magazine, and more. She can be reached at www.carolineleavitt.com.

Kristen Lepionka is the Shamus and Goldie Award–winning author of the Roxane Weary mystery series. Her debut novel, *The Last Place You Look*, was also an Anthony and Macavity finalist. She grew up mostly in a public library and could often be found in the adult mystery section well before she was out of middle school. Her writing has been published by *Shotgun Honey*, *McSweeney's Internet Tendency*, *Crime Reads*, *Mystery Tribune*, *Salon.com*, the *Independent*, and the *Guardian*. Kristen is a cofounder of the feminist podcast *Unlikeable Female Characters* and lives in Columbus, Ohio, with her partner and two cats.

Martin Limón spent twenty years in the US Army, ten of them in South Korea. While on active duty he began writing, using a Smith Corona portable that he purchased at the base PX. Four years later he published the first of more than fifty short stories. His 1992 debut novel, *Jade Lady Burning*, featured Eighth Army Criminal Investigation Agents George Sueño and Ernie Bascom and was a *New York Times* Notable Book of the Year, with thirteen more to follow. He wrote *Nightmare Range*, a short-story collection, and *GI Confidential*, about a series of bank robberies and murders in which an intrepid female tabloid reporter entices the unsuspecting into her rabbit hole of sex and treason.

About the Contributors

Anne Perry launched her publishing career in 1979 with *The Cater Street Hangman*, the first of thirty-five novels featuring Victorian policeman Thomas Pitt. Her new series features Pitt's son, Daniel, beginning with *Twenty-One Days*, with the third book in the series coming out in 2020. In 1990, she began the pre-Victorian William Monk series, thirty-three novels featuring homicide inspector Monk and Crimean War nurse Hester Latterly. She now has a thriller series featuring a young photographer in pre–World War II England, the first of which is *Death in Focus*. Anne won the Edgar for her short story "Heroes," which inspired a five-book series set in World War I. Other eras, places, and situations are explored in her nearly ninety books and novellas and many short stories. Her nearly thirty million books have been printed in seventeen languages, with all titles still in print. The London *Times* selected her as one of its 100 Masters of Crime of the 20th Century.

Charles Todd (the mother-son writing team of Caroline and Charles) is the 2017 Mary Higgins Clark Award winner and author of the New York *Times* bestselling Inspector Ian Rutledge series (*The Black Ascot*, Morrow, February 2019) and the Bess Crawford series (*A Cruel Deception*, Morrow, September 2019) as well as two stand-alone titles and numerous short stories in many magazines and anthologies. They have been guests of honor at the Malice Domestic convention and have won Agatha, Macavity, and Barry awards. Charles and Caroline live on the East Coast. Visit www.CharlesTodd.com.

Jacqueline Winspear's first novel, *Maisie Dobbs*, was a national bestseller and received an array of accolades, including *New York Times* Notable Book of the Year in 2003, *Publishers Weekly* Top Ten Mystery, and Book Sense Top Ten Selection. *Maisie Dobbs* was nom-

ABOUT THE EDITOR

MELANIE ABRAMS

VICTORIA ZACKHEIM is the author of the novel *The Bone Weaver* and editor of seven anthologies. She adapted essays from her anthology *The Other Woman* to create a play that is frequently read as a fund-raiser for women's shelters. Her play *Entangled* is in development. Victoria wrote the screenplay *Maidstone* and the documentary *Where Birds Never Sang: The Story of Ravensbrück and Sachsenhausen Concentration Camps*, which aired nationwide on PBS. Victoria created Women's Voices and is a frequent speaker and instructor at writing conferences and for women's organizations in the United States, Mexico, Canada, and Europe. She teaches creative nonfiction (Personal Essay/Memoir) in the UCLA Extension Writers' Program. She is a freelance book editor of fiction and nonfiction and has contributed personal essays to many anthologies. Visit her at www.victoriazackheim.com.

inated for seven awards, including the Edgar for best novel and the Agatha, Alex, and Macavity Awards. Including *The American Agent* (2019), Jacqueline has now published fifteen national bestselling novels in the Maisie Dobbs series, including eleven *New York Times* bestsellers. Her stand-alone novel, *The Care and Management of Lies*, was also a *New York Times* and national bestseller and a finalist for the Dayton Literary Peace Prize. In 2019, Jacqueline published *What Would Maisie Do?*, a nonfiction book/journal featuring insights into the inspiration for readers' favorite passages from the series. Jacqueline is also an essayist/journalist focusing on women's history, work, and social issues.